Ending
Hunger

Ending Hunger

The Quest to Feed the World Without Destroying It

Anthony Warner

ONEWORLD

A Oneworld Book

First published in Great Britain, the Republic of Ireland and
North America by Oneworld Publications, 2021
This paperback edition published 2022

ISBN 978-0-86154-218-5
eISBN 978-178607-927-5

Typeset by Geethik Technologies
Printed and bound in Great Britain by Clays Ltd, Elcograf S.p.A.

Oneworld Publications
10 Bloomsbury Street, London, WC1B 3SR, England

Stay up to date with the latest books,
special offers, and exclusive content from
Oneworld with our newsletter

Sign up on our website
oneworld-publications.com

So long as you have food in your mouth, you have solved all questions for the time being.

– Franz Kafka

Contents

Prologue

If you ever come round to my house, I can guarantee one thing: you won't go hungry. It is no accident that I chose a career as a chef. I love food, but most of all I have a powerful and seemingly innate compulsion to keep people fed. You might not always get served a twelve-course plated banquet made from the finest ingredients, but I would be devastated if you spent the afternoon with me and felt the need to pick up a kebab on the way home. My insatiable desire to feed is a well-established joke within my family. I frequently err on the side of over-catering and nothing gives me more satisfaction than knowing that people's bellies are full.

On the flip side, little makes me more anxious than guests going hungry, which was a handy compulsion throughout my career in restaurants and hotels. I hated the thought of a table spending too long without food, and I relished the challenge of organising a fast-paced service to ensure that this never happened.

When I moved into the world of food manufacturing, I had already honed my instinct for what motivates people to buy food over long years of worrying about how to keep my restaurant customers fed and happy. Most of my food manufacturing career focused on developing products that make cooking family meals a bit easier, such as stock cubes, pasta sauces and gravy granules. I was proud to be helping other people do the thing that gives me the most pleasure: filling the plates and bellies of loved ones.

When this becomes difficult or impossible, it genuinely pains me. I occasionally wake in a cold sweat, traumatised by the time I served a near-raw beef rib after foolishly attempting to show off a new low-temperature cooking technique. I still get anxiety dreams where I am stuck in a disastrous restaurant service, despite it being fifteen years since I last worked in that sort of kitchen. Such food calamities were just blips in a career where I successfully fed many thousands of people, but they still pain me to this day. The beef eventually cooked; the restaurant cheques eventually cleared. Food always got to the tables somehow, and no one ever went hungry for long.

Hunger and Pain

A few years ago, my daughter suffered what can only be described as a mental health breakdown. We started to notice one or two problems not long after her sixteenth birthday, but thought little of it. There were signs she might be struggling at school, which was out of character, but we put it down to normal teenage stuff. She always had the potential to be a bit moody and difficult, but nothing out of the ordinary for someone in their mid-teens. Her problems were largely hidden and easy to dismiss. We had no idea of the turmoil developing inside.

When the breakdown happened, it seemed to come from nowhere, and for around twelve months it tore our family to pieces. Brutal daily panic attacks completely overwhelmed her, sending her into frenzies of screaming and delusion. She would be shot for hours afterwards, barely able to move, function or think. The fear and exhaustion would eventually subside, but that only meant the panic attacks would be due to start again soon. For almost a year, it was impossible to leave her alone.

Many people blithely dismiss conditions like anxiety, claiming sufferers just need to be more resilient or pull themselves together. I suspect that anyone saying this has never experienced the condition up close. Perhaps they know someone who has an anxious personality type, or are prone to a bit of worry themselves, and it doesn't seem so bad in the grand scheme of things. But despite the similarity of the name, an anxious personality is nothing like a full-blown anxiety disorder. A panic attack is a profound assault on the senses, a vicious feedback loop where a misfiring brain enters full fight or flight mode, attempting to run in terror from an attack that is coming from within. This creates an uncontrollable rising tide, with the sufferer often screaming and shaking for several minutes, utterly unable to function. Imagine the most afraid you have ever been, and multiply that by about fifty. Then imagine that you are completely unable to escape, or do anything to counter the threat. Panic attacks are terrifying, exhausting and utterly debilitating. For a considerable period of time, my daughter was having several of these attacks every day.

Although her disorder was complex and deep-rooted, at its surface was a fear of vomit, known as emetophobia. She was constantly afraid of being sick, and terrified of situations where someone else might be. As with any phobia, this fear defied all logic. Almost overnight, she became afraid of eating. The look, smell or thought of food would send her into an instant panic. Once the attack had subsided, the adrenaline remaining in her body left her with no appetite. When that adrenaline died down, her thoughts would once again turn to food, and the panic would start to rise. Days would pass when she ate virtually no food at all. Days turned into weeks. Weeks turned into months.

Occasionally, if she suggested she might be able to stomach it, I would make a twelve-mile round trip to the nearest McDonald's. If she ate a few fries and drank a quarter of a milkshake, I would consider the journey worthwhile. When shopping for food I would bring home vast arrays of the safest, blandest foods in the vain hope that she would be able to stomach something. Many days, a couple of spoons of ice cream were all she could manage.

Although we thought she did not have much weight to lose, it began to fall off her. The physical changes, significant loss of fat and muscle, protruding bones, emaciation around the face, sunken eyes and patchy skin are hard to bear in someone you care for. Equally devastating are the changes to mind and personality. Weakness, confusion, dissociation, a constant feeling of cold, fear of going outside, a pervasive desire to shut herself away. She was constantly and excruciatingly hungry. Every day she became a little weaker. Every day she became a little smaller. It felt as if she was shrinking away from us, and soon there would be nothing left.

After a panic attack, one trick we learnt from her psychotherapist was to run on the spot for twenty seconds in order to burn off some adrenaline. This was best done in contact with someone else, to help make a connection and provide some motivation to overcome extreme exhaustion. Immediately after a panic attack, even though she would resist, we would take hold of her hands, look her in the eye, and encourage her to run. At the very worst point, after a particularly intense attack, I tried to do this with her. I gently held her wrists, now weak and frail from months without proper nourishment, and felt a genuine fear that I might break them if I gripped too tight. I looked into her sunken, terrified eyes and desperately tried to bring her back from the awful place she had been, the little spot of hell into which she kept falling.

She was weak and broken from hunger, barely able to lift her body. All the brightness and potential of her sixteen-year-old self, who only months before had been fiery and brilliant, obnoxious and frustrating, was gone. Mental turmoil and lack of nourishment had broken her spirit. Despite me being able to provide her with any food she desired, I was completely incapable of keeping her fed. She was starving in front of my eyes. Not for the first time, she begged me to kill her, unable to cope with the torment that her life had become.

Hunger is not the same thing as being peckish. True hunger is deadly and insidious. It robs you of your energy, then your body, and then it starts to take away your personhood. I have seen what real hunger looks like, and I would not wish it on anyone.

Thankfully, this story has a happy ending. With a heroism that I struggle to comprehend, over several months she managed to find a chink of light between herself and the illness, prising herself away from its grip. Despite being weak, she lifted herself up and was eventually able to keep down small amounts of food. Combined with hard work and therapy, this nourishment started to transform her, both physically and mentally. Before long, she returned to eating complete meals. Eventually, the voracious appetite that befits someone of her age returned. Once again she found joy in food and could eat together with friends and family. Colour returned to her face, strength to her arms and bravery to her soul. When she was occasionally obnoxious, frustrating and rude like a typical teenager, we secretly rejoiced after she had stormed out the room.

Recovery from such conditions is slow, incremental and ongoing, often without a clear destination. But the fact that my daughter is no longer hungry makes my heart sing and means that her world is once again filled with possibility. Although I have always rejected the idea that food is medicine, there are certainly times when it can perform miracles.*

The Surprising Truth About Hungry People

Many are not so lucky. Dr Jim Stewart is the Clinical Lead for Adult Nutrition at the University Hospitals of Leicester and lead physician to the Leicestershire Regional Eating Disorders Service. His work brings him into contact with many people deeply affected by a severe lack of food and he has seen the effects that prolonged starvation has on patients many times. These effects can be devastating.

Dr Stewart explained to me that even though thirty percent of people who come into hospital are suffering from malnutrition, it is something that frequently gets overlooked. He told

* My daughter is now an adult and gave full consent for her story to be shared.

me that even with the best diagnosis and treatment in the world, if you cannot feed a patient, they'll die. When people cannot take on energy, their bodies quickly go into starvation mode, shutting down any non-essential functions. Fat stores start to get broken down, and after a day they enter a ketotic state, essentially the body's reserve parachute. Fairly soon, muscles start to get broken down into amino acids in order to create glucose. As the starvation gets more severe, eventually, enzymes stop working, cells structures break down and biochemical mechanisms start to fail.

But some of the most devastating changes are not the physical ones. Resonating with my daughter's experience, Dr Stewart told me that as a physician treating patients, he often sees the profound psychological impact of malnutrition, and this can be even more harrowing. He told me, 'If a patient is severely malnourished and living on ketones, they cannot think rationally. People who are starving will often make really bad choices. When you start to feed people, you see their personality change. People begin to rationalise and make better decisions.'

Clear and Present Danger

The prolonged hunger of a single child is a tragedy that can have lifelong effects. This makes the prospect of millions, or even billions of people going without enough food something that a civilised society should consider unthinkable. Yet it is becoming increasingly clear that without significant change, this terrifying prospect could become a reality within the next few decades.

Over the next thirty years, the population of the world will reach approximately 9.8 billion souls.[1] The world's food system must produce enough to feed all those people, and somehow make sure that food is distributed efficiently in order to keep everyone from going hungry. This challenge – feeding a growing and increasingly affluent population – is beyond huge. Between now and 2050 we will need to grow more food than has been produced in the history of humanity. If the food system remains as it is, this will be impossible to achieve. Significant change is urgently required.

At the same time, there is an ever-increasing need to limit the environmental impact of the food we produce, and more broadly, the way we live. Modern agricultural systems are having a devastating effect on the natural world, making an ever-larger contribution to ecosystem destruction and climate change. To make matters worse, climate change is impacting upon our ability to produce and distribute food efficiently, leading to an increasing number of people going without. In 2017, for the first time in a decade, the number of people going hungry in the world increased, in large part due to the extreme weather events caused by climate change.[2] In a nightmarish feedback loop, agriculture is driving climate change, which is in turn lowering the efficiency of food systems, requiring us to increase production, so leading to even more climate change.

This is not a vague and intangible question about our future. Although it is often out of sight in the Global North, climate change is happening right now, with droughts, rising temperatures and extreme weather killing thousands of people every year. Dramatic events, such as typhoons and hurricanes devastating vulnerable island states, floods washing away towns, polar vortexes freezing cities, and droughts causing crops to fail, are newsworthy, yet such incidents are frequently dismissed as random chance, engendering sympathy but not blame. Among other things, this book will bring these threats into sharp focus, calling not for planning and strategy, but immediate action. And it will also examine why change is so hard, and why we freely dismiss such a clear and present threat.

Why Are You Picking On Food?

Although many people attempt to keep it separate and minimise its importance, the food system is a hugely significant frontier in the fight against climate change. This is not to diminish the importance of energy, transport, construction and the many other contributing industries, some of which are even more culpable. Unless the oil and gas industry changes quickly and dramatically, any shifts in agriculture and food will be of little consequence. But on a worldwide scale, food is a hugely significant part of climate change. In this book I will present the evidence, and much of it is not pretty.

As for solutions, you will be glad to hear that I will not be prescribing a correct way to eat 'guilt-free', and I strongly believe that any 'sustainability diet plan' is likely to be as damaging, misguided and insidious as any of the diets I have debunked in the past. In fact, I shall be looking in detail at how the environment and climate change is being used as a dietary battleground, a shiny new way to make us feel guilty and inadequate about the way we eat. As regular readers of my blog, The Angry Chef, might expect, I shall be picking apart the claims, hypocrisy and false certainty of those trying to commoditise sustainable food, and we shall see that much of what is being sold to us is just as ridiculous and damaging as detox smoothies, alkaline diets or Paleo lifestyles. When it comes to sustainability, the rampant greenwashing* of food choices is hugely unhelpful and increasingly common, with offenders that include some of the biggest companies and brands in the world. If we want true progress, this really has to stop.

---

* Greenwashing is a term used to describe when companies make an unsubstantiated or misleading claim about the environmental benefits of a product. I recently discovered that the only biodegradable thing about the dog poo bags I had bought was the cardboard tube in the centre of the roll, despite the packaging shouting loudly about them being more environmentally friendly. This definitely counts as greenwashing.

The Need for Change

Only one thing is certain, and that is the need for change. It is inconceivable that in thirty years' time we will be eating the same way as we do now, and hopefully this book will give you some insight into what that future might look like. As I will discuss, our food system has been shaped and developed to do a particular job over the past sixty years, and was transformed dramatically within a very short time. It changed in response to an existential threat, and perhaps over the next sixty years it can do something similar. We all have a vital part to play in this shift, from the executives of giant corporations through to product developers, politicians, farmers, researchers, journalists, campaigners and consumers. As a chef, it will be my job to make sure that even as diets change dramatically, they continue to be a source of joy and togetherness. If you want me over the next few years, I'll be in the kitchen trying to make this happen.

Many people will fear and resist these changes. Some may long for a return to an imagined past, but although climate change is a relatively new threat, it is a huge mistake to assume that our agriculture has ever been sustainable or benign. We should certainly not ignore lessons from the past, and I will explore and discuss many of these throughout this book, but history holds few clues when it comes to the challenge of feeding ten billion people.

In designing a future for an ever-changing planet, I strongly believe that one consideration trumps all else. Although this book is about many things, at its heart is humanity's continuing battle against its most profound and ancient enemy. In the next fourteen chapters, this book will cover greenhouse gases, extreme weather events, land use change, the destruction of rainforests, biodiversity, water stress, nitrogen fixation, gene editing, flatulent cows, Nazis, food waste, lab-grown meat, more Nazis, communists, cannibalism, plastic straws, green revolutions, robot bees and lasers that vaporise weeds. But this is not really a book about any of those things. This book is about hunger, and the unceasing fight to keep it from our door.

1

Hunger

When in poverty, people use their skill to avoid hunger. They can't use it for progress.

– Hans Rosling

Fighting for Food

It is often said that we are just six meals away from rioting in the streets. There have been many food riots throughout history, but they don't happen in the way that we might predict. The countries where food riots occur are not those with the greatest numbers of hungry people, or the worst food shortages. Riots happen where food justice is threatened, perhaps when corrupt merchants unfairly raise prices, governments restrict supply as a form of control, or the rich hoard, leaving the poor majority to starve. The rioters themselves are rarely the hungriest people in a given country, driven to violence by desperation and months of shortage. Often the rioters are from the cities, where access to food is always far better than in rural areas. Rioters have enough calories to fuel their anger, battling for their brothers and sisters quietly dying elsewhere. When people starve during famines, on the other hand, it is the end of a long process. They will have sold their livestock, their possessions, their homes. They will have gone for weeks with barely enough to eat before supplies run completely dry. When the hunger really bites, they are already too weak to fight.[1]

In the course of writing this book I have spoken to many people who have experienced famine and seen the shadow of mass hunger fall over a land and its people. Perhaps the most surprising thing I have learnt is how that shadow seems to fall. Alex de Waal is Executive Director of the World Peace Foundation and has studied the effects of famine and food shortage across the world. He is considered one of the world's leading experts on humanitarian crisis and response, particularly in Sudan and the Horn of Africa. His book *Mass Starvation: The History and Future of Famine* examines the nature of and reasons for food crises around the world. On the experience of entering a region stricken by famine, he told me that the biggest surprise is how normal it feels in the towns. Despite what many of us might assume, when you arrive you can get a hotel, go out for a meal and visit markets stocked with food. He explained that the reason for this is that famines do not involve everyone going hungry. They affect the poorest people, which means they are easy to ignore. As he told me, 'When there is a famine, that doesn't mean that there is no food around. You can always get food if you have money.' He also explained that in his experience, hunger is not the only thing that devastates the lives of those affected by famine. He told me, 'There is a societal breakdown, with people abandoning land and selling all their assets in order to survive. Most of the deaths are not from hunger, but from disease.'

Corrie Sissons works for the famine relief charity Oxfam as Emergency Food Security and Vulnerable Livelihoods Coordinator. Her work recently took her into South Sudan in the midst of the 2017 famine. She told me, 'It is sometimes hard to talk about these things as a white middle-class person who has never experienced hunger. We say we are hungry when dinner is half an hour late. But there are people in the world who consistently go for months, even years, eating less than required.'

Corrie explained that whilst she was in South Sudan, she came across groups of people who had been surviving for weeks off the roots of lily plants. Others were eating wild berries that caused sickness and stomach pains, because that was the only food available to them. But even in these desperate conditions, death from starvation is actually quite rare. 'It is disease that kills people,' she told me. 'Most of the deaths in children under five are from diarrhoea, which leads to malnutrition as it stops them from absorbing food. Or they are from other infectious diseases that become more common as immune systems are compromised and water supplies become contaminated.'

Kate McMahon is Food Security Advisor at the global humanitarian aid charity Mercy Corps, working in some of the most food insecure regions of the world. On the issue of what causes famine, she is very clear. 'All famine is human made. There is enough food today to feed the world, the real issue is access. Famine is an issue of markets and governance. There is plenty of food today, it is just that some have it and some don't.'

The Right to Food

Providing every person with enough food to live is the most important role of a civilised society. If the world falls apart and we can do nothing else, we need to make every effort to keep people fed. Without food, nothing else is possible. If people are hungry, there can be no science, music, art, poetry or progress. Food fuels everything we do, and without it, it doesn't take long for our bodies and minds to shut down. Why else is it that culture, art, science and politics have traditionally been the preserve of the rich and privileged?

Until relatively recently, only the rich have been consistently free from hunger. It was only when most of us gained access to adequate food that we saw the rise of popular culture, leaders, artists, scientists and writers from working-class communities. Freedom from hunger began to enable people of different backgrounds to achieve status based on merit.

In *The Truth About Fat*, I asked why obesity in the UK and Europe had risen so sharply since the 1960s. Although there is much complexity surrounding these issues, the most compelling answer is depressingly simple. Before then, many people in society did not have enough food. Those that did, the rich and growing middle class, were obese in much the same proportions as the rest of the population are today. In the 1960s, although it is a truth we now struggle to accept, hunger still dominated the lives of many of the poorest people, even in the Global North. Worldwide, despite huge increases in population, we now produce fifty percent more food per capita than we did in 1962. Although a lot of people still go hungry today, a far greater proportion did back then. As we free more people from the chains of hunger, so we free them to make their own progress.

When hunger dominates, all is lost. If you are ever unlucky enough to go without food, it will not make you rise up and fight for justice. It will not be the mother of invention, forcing you to create new solutions to confounding problems. Hunger breaks the strong and cripples the weak. Hungry people sink away from life, shatter bonds with those around them, and lie beneath the storm in the hope that it will pass. Hunger rips away humanity and turns societies into dust. Hungry people die alone and lose hope long before their fate is sealed.

It is up to those whose bellies are full to fight for them. We must prevent hunger at all costs, and make sure that the right to proper food and water remains the central right of all humanity. Although our agriculture and food systems are in desperate need of change, at the heart of that change must be the prevention of hunger. The environment, the climate, soil erosion, water loss, biodiversity, rainforest depletion, mass extinctions, sea level rises and extreme weather events are all desperate challenges that we must face to ensure that we have a future on this planet. But in my mind, they are dwarfed by one hungry child crying out for food.

Of course, you could argue that this is foolhardy and short-termist. The planet has limits and climate change is surely a bigger threat than one child's tears. If you place foxes and chickens in a field, the foxes will gleefully eat and breed without thought for the future, eventually consuming every last chicken, then slowly starving from lack of food. Humans, many will claim, are just the same. High birth and low mortality rates mean that the world population is growing exponentially, requiring huge, costly increases in agricultural production to keep pace with rising demand. We are just like hungry, randy foxes, thoughtlessly breeding and gobbling up delicious chickens, ignoring doomsday until it is upon us. Agriculture, food systems, social care, birth control, energy management, sanitation and medicines are simply clever tricks to push the fence back a little further. All our technology and innovation does is to buy us a few more precious years before the inevitable collapse. The world, the argument goes, needs to feel some pain now to avoid a greater loss down the line.

But the question we must then ask is: who will feel the pain of this inevitable hunger? Perhaps when we picture mass starvation, it becomes a little too easy for us to think of it as a distant problem. Maybe instead we should imagine our own children emaciated and crying, with us alongside them, too weak and destitute to find food. If images of white-skinned, European or American children filled our screens whenever the threat of starvation was mentioned, I am quite sure many campaigners would take a different view of how much misery we should accept today. I know that I am not brave or strong enough to accept my own starvation, nor that of my children, however noble the cause. I cannot see how it is fair to expect anyone else to make that sacrifice.

This seems to leave us in a pretty hopeless situation, as the world's population continues to grow. We cannot jump over the fence into a new field, and the chickens are sure to run out eventually.

Or perhaps not. Humans are innovators, creators, scientists, agriculturalists, statisticians, systems analysts, engineers, politicians, medics, cooks and builders. Unlike foxes, we spend a lot of time thinking about the future. Place humans and chickens in a field and, eventually, there will be more humans and more chickens, and perhaps some cute little houses for the chickens to live in. And although there will always be selfish individuals who care only for themselves, the field will also be full of people thinking about how to make a better life for everyone.

In researching for this book and speaking to some of the smartest people working in this area, I have been shocked by how bleak things really are. The problems are very real and the stakes extraordinarily high. But I have also been left with a surprising amount of optimism. Humans are an extraordinary and unique species, and although we will always be bound by the limits of the natural world, there is a chance that we might just find a way through.

In this book I will attempt to show that there is hope of a future where no one has to go hungry, and that this can be achieved without allowing the world to burn. I will also try to show that even though there is a pressing need for change, the future need not be a joyless desert of meal replacement shakes, plastic techno-burgers and compulsory vitamin injections. Food needs to meet the physiological needs of the population, but it also needs to be culturally appropriate, tempting and delicious. It needs to bring meaning and joy, bind us together in shared love, and help us define our identity. Food is more than just fuel, and if we are to create a better future, we need to develop new systems with that in mind. Throughout this book, I will be taking some tentative steps towards setting out what that future might look like.

But first we need to deal with a problem, and it's a big one. As populations continue to grow around the world, just how many people can our planet sustain? What stops the population from expanding for ever? And if, as it seems, we are perilously near to the cliff edge, how on earth are we going to stop ourselves from falling off?

2

A Brief History of Hunger

The first essential component of social justice is adequate food for all mankind.

– Norman Borlaug

Birdageddon

I am writing this in early springtime in the UK, and a pair of blue tits are busy preparing a nest box just in view of the window that I occasionally stare out of for inspiration. At this time of year, they spend most of their day frantically searching for nesting materials, pulling up any useful pieces of moss, leaf matter, hair or feathers in preparation for the arrival of their new brood. Most of the time, they look as if they are under a lot of stress. They are busy, hardworking and seem to be in constant fear for their lives.

On average, birds similar to them will lay around eight eggs per year, and perhaps six of these will hatch into fledglings. Each blue tit will probably live for a maximum of around eight years, and if they spend six of those years successfully breeding, then they can expect to produce around thirty-six chicks in their life-time. That's eighteen each. No wonder they're stressed.

Let's just imagine what would happen if every one of those blue tits survived into adulthood and had six crops of fledglings for themselves. Within two generations, we would jump from the two blue tits visible from my window this afternoon, to 648 birds. A generation on from that, if all those birds continued to breed successfully, there would be 11,664 frantic little critters, no doubt putting a fair amount of stress on the availability of nesting materials in my garden. A few more years down the line, there would be 209,952. Then 3,779,136. A generation later there would be over 68 million, more than one for every human in the UK.

If things carried on, in only twelve generations, or just under a hundred years, the two birds in my garden would have spawned around 25 billion tonnes' worth of hungry blue tit progeny, all desperately hunting for nesting materials every spring. That's enough to vastly outweigh all humans on Earth, and all of the animals we produce for agriculture.[1] In the unlikely event that they worked out how to organise themselves into a terrifying bird army, they would be capable of taking over the world. My great-grandchildren would wonder what I was thinking providing a nest box for the nasty little blue fuckers. All of a sudden, I feel compelled to rush outside and stamp on them. Or perhaps just buy myself a cat.

It is not just blue tits that have this remarkable talent for exponential proliferation, as almost all species have the same potential for rapid population growth, including our own. So long as it is possible to breed at above the replacement rate during a lifetime, populations can expand at an extraordinary pace. That's in theory. In reality, the natural world has pretty strong checks that prevent things getting out of control.

The harsh reality for blue tits is that the vast majority of their babies are destined to die prematurely. Some will get sick; others will be eaten alive by predators. Domestic cats will playfully clear out their carefully constructed nests, gutting and beheading baby birds with surgical precision, then proudly offering up the blood-ied corpses as gifts for their owners (I've never been a cat person). Others will be torn apart by sparrow hawks in order to provide a meal for chicks of their own. Some will be murdered by their own family, with weaker chicks being selfishly pecked to death by hungry siblings not keen on sharing. Or perhaps they will fall from the nest and be crushed underfoot by my blundering Springer Spaniel carrying out one of his regular garden patrols. In lean years when the weather is not kind, many young birds will die from a lack of food, as desperate parents cannot forage enough to keep them alive.

If blue tit populations are to remain stable, in all their years of breeding, only about two chicks from a possible thirty-six are likely to survive to adulthood. Any more and the population would rapidly rise, allowing avian world domination. Any fewer, and soon blue tits would disappear from our gardens. It is a brutal yet essential balancing act that nature inflicts upon each species. Every creature spends most of its time hungry, afraid and desperately clinging to life. Every time we look out at the natural world, even though it might appear serene, this is the drama playing out. A desperate life or death struggle, where death is the winner most of the time.

Certainly there are good times. A given species might breed prolifically for a few generations if they find themselves in an environment with little competition, few predators and plentiful resources. But inevitably, because of the remarkable speed of growth when times are good, natural limits would soon be reached. Often, that limit is the point when hunger starts to bite.

Life Is Cruel

When Charles Darwin and Alfred Russel Wallace developed their theory of evolution by natural selection, it was one of the most profound and important intellectual feats of all time. Outside the bizarre world of modern creationism, the fact that evolution is the driving force of change and diversity in the natural world seems obvious now, but for a long time it was controversial and divisive. Darwin had a devoutly religious upbringing and education, so he was well aware of the potential for his theories to be incendiary for the Church. He delayed publication for several years until his hand was forced by a letter from Wallace, who had made the same intellectual leap whilst travelling through the Malay Archipelago.

Darwin's reticence was not just because evolution took away the need for a divine creator and undermined biblical scriptures. Anyone who accepted the validity of fossil records had to accept that the Bible's creation story – of talking snakes and a fully formed six-thousand-year-old Earth – could not be taken literally. Darwin's greater worry was that in framing evolution as a constant mortal struggle, it would reframe nature as overwhelmingly violent and brutal. The idea that a just, benevolent God would oversee such cruelty and inflict profound suffering upon humans for most of their history was perhaps most dangerous of all. If we evolved by natural selection, it meant that for a considerable period of time, humanity had existed within an animalistic life or death battle, undermining any belief that we were special or stood apart from the natural world. The implications shook Darwin to his core and cast doubt on his own religious faith.

You Don't Improve Anything by Hitting It with a Hammer

It might seem unfair, or even against God, but pushing creatures to the limit of survival has been the driving force of biological progress since life began. Evolution by natural selection depends upon an enormous mortality rate in order to select creatures with a tiny advantage in evolutionary terms. If a baby bird is even slightly quicker, stronger, smarter or meaner than its siblings, then it might be a tiny bit more likely to survive until breeding age and so pass on its useful genes.

The mutations in the genetic code that produce these changes are entirely random and extremely rare. In humans, who have a DNA sequence about three billion base pairs long, they happen at a rate of around 175 mutations per generation, and most of the time they will hand the newly formed mutant no advantage. In fact, huge sections of our genetic code are seemingly pointless repetitions. About eight percent is composed of bits of viruses that have inserted themselves over time. It is estimated that only about fifteen percent of our DNA has a defined biological function, so most changes to it will have very little effect.[2]

Very occasionally, a mutation will occur in a piece of the genetic code that is involved in producing a protein, but even when this happens, it is generally bad for the animal.[3] The most likely scenario is that it will generate a faulty protein, leading to impaired function. The unfit gene will swiftly be removed from the pool, perhaps by a hungry cat. So most of the time, it might be more accurate to call Darwin's theory the non-survival of the least fit.

Evolution is akin to designing a new car by randomly hitting the one you have with a very small hammer, then testing it after each strike to see if you have made a difference. Most of the time you will find that you have made no difference to the car's performance. Occasionally, you will break something fundamental and have to start over with a new car. But if you keep on hitting it in different places and in different ways, then once in a while you might slightly improve the aerodynamics, or marginally change the engine's efficiency.

I would not suggest trying this at home. It would be a terrible way to design a new car, and although it might eventually lead you to something slightly improved, this would happen at too slow a rate and in too small increments to be in any way useful (you would also have to constantly repair the damage you were doing if it made the car worse, just as nature wipes out faults using hungry cats, oblivious dogs or similar). But when it comes to the natural world, this is the process that has proven so successful, with endless rounds of tiny random mutations tested in brutal real-life situations. A high mortality rate is essential for discovering if any of these mutations have created an improvement, and also in removing negative mutations effectively. When most babies die early, only the strongest, fittest and most capable will pass on their genes. If you repeat this again and again over geological timescales, then life slowly evolves, with positive mutations selected for, negative ones weeded out and neutral ones sticking around for no good reason.

This process is extraordinarily sensitive. In mice, many mutations that evolution has selected for over thousands of years do not appear to make the slightest difference if the gene in question is turned off in a laboratory. Even the world's most sophisticated scientific equipment cannot measure exactly what the gene is doing, but in evolutionary terms it has proven sufficient to pass on an advantage that makes survival more likely. A gene might look useless in the lab, but maybe that's because it does something that only helps mice when they are out on the town.

As the legendary cell biologist Lewis Wolpert has noted, many genes are insignificant in one context, but important in another. Until you have looked at every situation, drawing conclusions about the importance of a gene you have turned off is dangerous. Wolpert memorably asks, 'Have you taken your mice to the opera? Can they still tell Wagner from Mozart? It turns out from simple population genetics that, in order to pick up a 1 percent selective advantage – which is evolutionarily very significant – you would have to look at something like 10,000 mice.'[4]

Over a long period of time, these tiny increments can lead to some astounding changes, creating eyes, wings, flippers, kidneys, flowers, seeds, trunks, teeth, complex brains, opposable thumbs, lactase persistence, the appreciation of classical music and the ability to make hummus. It is also incredibly innovative, so much so that modern designers often look to the natural world for inspiration. When Japanese engineer Eiji Nakatsu was struggling to reduce the sonic booms caused by violent air movements as the Shinkansen bullet train entered tunnels, he turned to the beak of the kingfisher for inspiration. Fascinated by how it managed to enter the water at high speed with hardly a splash, he designed the train's nose in similar proportions. This not only removed the sonic boom issue, but the resulting train travelled ten percent faster and used fifteen percent less energy. Over millions of years, tiny hammers can do extraordinary things.

A Brief History of Us

Evolution has been an extraordinary force for progress, and has handed our species some remarkable talents and capabilities. The big trade-off has been the constant battle for survival, and the fact that until very recently most of our children were destined to die before adulthood. When we emerged as a species, most likely around 300,000 years ago across the African continent, we were middle-tier hunter-gatherers, neither at the top nor the bottom of the food chain. Life was short and tough, and death a constant presence.[5]

Around 100,000 years ago, at a point when we seemed to be developing an increasing ability to organise and plan for the future, there were mass migrations away from the land of our birth, as a few homo sapiens moved out of Africa towards Europe and Asia. Despite our apparent cognitive advances, huge numbers of children still died early throughout this period. Estimates of childhood mortality are around fifty percent, and the maximum age that anyone reached was around thirty. These figures speak of an extraordinarily brutal existence governed by hunger, violence, cannibalism and high rates of infanticide, particularly during times of shortage. To counter this high mortality, early humans had a lot of children during their short lives. Birth rates were around eighty per thousand people, which is over four times the rate today. Much like the birds in my garden, early humans led brutal lives, had lots of babies, and expected that many of them would die before their time.[6]

Also, like the birds in my garden, hunter-gatherer populations expanded to reach the natural limit that local resources could accommodate, before hunger or predators held back growth. It didn't take many individuals to saturate a particular territory. It is thought that fifty thousand years ago, there were around two million humans on the planet, slightly more than the population of Latvia. The population throughout this period was extremely unstable, as it was a time of huge turbulence and climatic change. Genetic records show that at one point, the human population dipped as low as one thousand breeding pairs, the very edge of extinction.[7] Somehow, this tiny number clawed its way back from the brink, and our expansion continued.

Although no one is quite sure why, an important transition seemed to occur around thirty thousand years ago, as it became more common for people to live slightly longer lives. Although infant mortality was still high, if people made it through child-hood, most could expect to live to around fifty or sixty years old, almost twice as long as was common previously. As lives began to lengthen, it opened the door to considerable progress. Living beyond thirty was a key point for humans, as reaching that age meant that it was common for children to have living grandparents. It is perhaps no coincidence that there were rapid developments in art, skills, technology, society and culture at this time. Older people seem to have been vital when it came to passing on knowledge, building social networks, and planning for the future.[8]

It is a common misconception that these early human populations were reminiscent of existing hunter-gatherer groups today. Insights from tribes such as the Hadza in Tanzania, or the Nambikwara of the Amazonian rainforest, are often extrapolated in order to provide a picture of this time, with self-contained groups gathering wild produce and hunting for game. But it must be remembered that the Hadza and the Nambikwara are not archaeological curiosities, frozen in time as if from a 1950s lost world movie. They have lived in contact with merchants and traders for many thousands of years, with their behaviours and societies shaped by this contact.

The idolisation of small tribal lifestyles, and the perception of them as an Edenic state from which modern humans somehow emerged, has been consistently dismissed by archaeologists and anthropologists for many years. It is a tempting fallacy of a perfect, egalitarian, pre-agricultural society, rooted in the popular belief that our once perfect lives were forever contaminated by a bite from the forbidden fruit of modernity. The reality is that thirty thousand years ago, humans were already capable of organising themselves in large numbers. There is a great deal of evidence that they lived in large social structures with hierarchies, deities, temples and grand cooperative projects. Although much of the evidence for this comes from Europe, that is almost certainly because research in this area has traditionally been Eurocentric.

The truth is that, for humans, there has never been one way to live. Evidence points towards social structures shifting with great regularity, as people came together in large numbers in response to animal migrations or other seasonal bounties, then dispersed into smaller groups at other times of the year. This required further cognitive changes, and an ever-increasing ability to conceptualise and plan. These changes would set humans up perfectly for the even more dramatic transition to come.[9]

Humanity Takes Off

Around ten thousand years ago, another transformation occurred, probably driven by an unprecedented period of climate stability. In human terms, the driving force for this change was surely a vision of the future where life was not quite so tough.

For the entirety of human existence, around half of the children born had perished before adulthood, and every human had lived with the constant threat of hunger hanging over them. An older population, with increased large-scale cooperation, opened up the possibility of a better world. When the climate settled down, people started to farm, setting humans off on a quite extraordinary path.

Although it is often presented as a sudden change, it is likely that the birth of agriculture was more of a slow transition over a few thousand years. Hunter-gatherer communities were planting rye fields as long as thirteen thousand years ago in order to supplement their wild foods, but the shift towards settled populations living largely on cultivated crops and captive livestock happened between eleven thousand and seven thousand years ago.

Mark Thomas is a Professor of Evolutionary Genetics at University College London and a leading researcher in human demographic and evolutionary history. He told me that the factors driving the development of agriculture remain a mystery, but climate stability would have been a prerequisite – without that, we wouldn't have seen the development of property rights and the attendant transition to a new way of organising society. Supporting the argument that an increase in climate stability was key, this transition occurred simultaneously across several different regions of the Earth.[10]

Around the world, cultivation of crops such as wheat, barley, lentils, chickpeas, potatoes, maize and rice allowed food to be stored in large quantities to help ride out times of seasonal shortage. Domestication of livestock animals reduced the energy expenditure and danger involved in hunting large creatures. Dairy produce from sheep, cattle and goats meant that a rich, high-energy and nutritious food source could be conjured up from the grass. For the first time, humans controlled their own food supply. We had taken our first steps in the battle against hunger.

The result of this new abundance, perhaps surprisingly, was a sharp decline in health. This occurred worldwide, no matter what livestock or crops were being farmed. Records show that post-agriculture, people became shorter and had more long-term health issues, and there was a far greater incidence of nutritional deficiency. Advocates of Paleo dieting often frame this decline as evidence that humans are not suited to a diet based on wheat and maize,*

---

* Paleo dieters believe that they only eat the type of food that our pre-agricultural ancestors ate, and so are eating in tune with our genetics or some such nonsense. There is a chapter on this ridiculous fad in my first book, *The Angry Chef: Bad Science and the Truth About Healthy Eating*.

but the real reasons are almost certainly more complex than gluten intolerance.[11] As Mark Thomas told me, 'The classical explanation is dietary change, but there is also increased population density and living in close proximity to animals, leading to more pathogens and more disease. Both factors are important. The dietary argument has dominated for years, but I am not so sure. Milk is the only food that provides near-complete nutrition, and even in early agricultural populations with high dairy consumption, we still see low health status.'

Professor Thomas told me that an alternative explanation for the decline in health is, perhaps counter-intuitively, an increase in the predictability of the food supply. For hunter-gatherers, the availability of food was always extremely variable, rising and falling dramatically with seasonal and climate variations. When it dropped too low, even for a relatively short period of time, people died en masse, no doubt preceded by a period of brutality and cannibalism. Agriculture, and particularly the storage of food, served to iron out some of this variability, meaning that human populations could survive with a lower *average* amount of food available. Early agricultural populations could live for years with a level of food far lower than hunter-gatherers could have survived on, and this led to diminished long-term health. In short, if you starve someone quickly, they'll probably leave a good-looking skeleton. But if they can live on small amounts of food for many years, you'll see the effects in their bones. As Professor Thomas explains, 'Essentially, agricultural societies traded off morbidity against mortality.'

It seems likely that the development of agriculture was a compromise to avoid the constant threat of hunger and death that hung over hunter-gatherer populations. Perhaps dinner wasn't quite so varied as it used to be, but at least you could be relatively sure you wouldn't be clubbed to death before you reached the table, or have to eat your children during the next harsh winter. Agriculture meant that the lean years were not quite so lean, and so a few more children survived to adulthood.

As a result, even though birth rates were falling, the population began to grow.

Around ten thousand years ago, the world population was around five million. After eight thousand years of agriculture, up to the year 1 CE, it had grown to around 300 million, representing a growth rate of about 0.05% per year.[*][12] From 1 CE through to the seventeenth century, the rate of population increase stayed fairly low, and it was hampered by the Black Death, which probably killed between one and two hundred million people during the 1300s. By 1750, the population had reached nearly 800 million and the birth rate had declined to around 40 births per 1000. At this point, a number of changes in agricultural practices were taking place throughout Europe, particularly in Britain, resulting in hugely increased productivity. This included more considered crop rotation, selective breeding, increased farm size, better drainage and improved transport networks. These productivity increases meant that a smaller proportion of the population needed to be employed in agriculture, causing large-scale migration to the cities. It was really this shift that enabled the subsequent Industrial Revolution.[†][13]

The world population passed the one billion mark just before the year 1800. It had taken around 300,000 years to reach this milestone, but at this point things were really starting to accelerate. Just 120 years later, driven along by the Industrial Revolution, another billion people had been added to the total. Although birth rates had fallen even further, because of huge advances in nutrition and healthcare, the population was growing at an unprecedented rate of around one percent a year. By 1988, it had

[*] The birth rate during this time had dropped slightly to around 60 per 1000, but lower rates of mortality meant that fewer births were required.
[†] Colonial expansion also helped meet the increasing food demands of European cities, and feeding the growing population was a driving force behind much of European brutality. But the revolution in agriculture around this time was still transformative.

passed five billion. On 31 October 2011, it crossed the seven billion mark. By 2024, it is predicted to pass eight billion.[14]

In just ten millennia, a population of obscure hunter-gatherers has taken over the world. The event that precipitated this takeover was the development of agriculture. After centuries of struggle, we finally found a way to defeat hunger, breaking the shackles of death and hardship that had contained us for so long. Our children are now far more likely to survive than to perish. The ingenuity and planning developed on the plains of Africa many millennia ago finally found a way to conquer our greatest enemy. (At least for now.)

Bumps in the Road

The path of progress was not entirely smooth. In order to grow, plants must have access to air, water and sunlight, but they also need soil containing nitrogen, phosphorus and potassium.* In a closed ecosystem, plants will draw these substances from the soil as they grow, returning them in equal quantities when they die. Soil microbes break down dead plant matter into its constituent chemicals, allowing new plants to utilise them. If any animals come along and eat the plants, taking up nutrients, these will return to the soil as urine and faeces. But animals also need nitrogen, phosphorus and potassium to live, so they keep some on board. Anything retained in the animal's body to build its muscles, bones or vital organs will eventually be returned back to the soil when the animal dies, rotted down by bacteria and fungi in much the same way as plants are. Almost everything in the system is recycled, meaning that, in a state of nature, the nutrients in the soil will never run too low to support growth.†

---

* There are also some other important soil micronutrients, but these three are the most significant when it comes to determining agricultural yields.
† I admit that there are some subtleties when it comes to the nitrogen cycle, particularly the fixing of atmospheric nitrogen, and the microbial breakdown and

When it comes to agriculture, however, the picture is very different. Plants pull nitrogen, potassium and phosphorus up from the soil, but they are then harvested and taken away from the land. Crops are consumed by humans who, unlike other animals, are unlikely to return their waste to the soil it came from, especially in the modern age when much of it is flushed out to sea. And when humans die, our bodies are rarely returned to agricultural land; they are either burnt or buried far away from the fields. As a result, whenever land is used to grow crops, vital nutrients in the soil become depleted over time.

Farmers have understood this for many years, and have found various ways to replace these vital nutrients, even before they knew exactly what they were. Compost and animal manure were traditionally the most common methods, but these have limitations. Composted plants and livestock do not pluck nitrogen, phosphorus and potassium from the air, they simply obtain them from the soil. The nitrogen in cow manure is originally pulled up from the soil by the grass and forage the animals consume. Applying manure is a great method for recycling nutrients, but it does not overcome the fundamental problem of depletion from agricultural land. Wherever humans are breaking the cycle, the nutrients in the soil will eventually run out.

In early agricultural communities, this was not too much of a concern. In order to support a small population, as long as nutrients were recycled reasonably effectively, soils would remain productive and plants would continue to grow. But as populations started to increase dramatically during the nineteenth century, it began to become more of an issue. The sheer biomass of more than a billion people required an awful lot of nutrients to sustain them, and the soil was reaching the limits of what it could provide. Improved sanitation, although it was brilliant at reducing disease, also meant that an ever-larger proportion of human waste was

atmospheric release of nitrates, but on the other hand I am trying to fit the entire history of humanity into a handful of pages.

being channelled into rivers or out to sea, meaning that valuable nitrogen, potassium and phosphorus was being lost for ever.

As our knowledge of fertilisers and soil health started to grow, the principles of industrial production and scientific discovery were applied to farming methods. Phosphorus and potassium proved fairly simple to get hold of. There were large mineral reserves that could be mined, and using new techniques from chemistry, the resulting rocks were transformed into bioavailable fertilisers and added liberally to the soil.* That left us with the problem of obtaining a ready supply of nitrogen, and it was going to take all the ingenuity of the industrial age to solve it.

In 1898, scientist William Crookes gave a famous speech at the British Association for the Advancement of Science annual meeting, outlining the scale and gravity of this problem. In the preceding years, wheat harvests had been declining, and existing sources of nitrogen fertiliser were either inadequate for large-scale production, or limited in availability. Crookes warned that 'all civilised nations stand in peril of not having enough to eat.' A brilliant chemist and physicist, Crookes was a firm believer in the power of scientific advance, and his speech was no doom-laden prophecy. Instead, he called for the scientific community to act. He outlined that there was an obvious solution to this looming nitrogen problem waiting to be discovered. 'The fixation of nitrogen [obtaining it directly from the air]', he claimed, 'is vital to the progress of civilised humanity. It is the chemist who must come to the rescue . . . it is through the laboratory that starvation may ultimately be turned into plenty.'

Brot aus Luft

It is not that nitrogen is difficult to find. It is literally all around us, making up nearly eighty percent of the Earth's atmosphere.

---

* Bioavailability is the degree to which a substance is absorbed into a living system. It is quite possible for there to be lots of a substance in a mineral deposit, but not in a form that plants can easily use, meaning it is not very bioavailable.

The problem with nitrogen is that being an extremely stable and inert gas, it is exceptionally hard to convert it into a form that plants can use. Some bacteria have a remarkable ability to pluck it out of the sky, and these are generally found in the root nodules of legume crops, including soya beans, clover, lupins, peas and alfalfa. As a result, growing legumes such as peas and beans in rotation is an excellent way of fixing nitrogen back into the soil, and red clover is often grown solely as a cover crop,* then ploughed back into the land expressly for this purpose. But unfortunately, the amount of nitrogen that could be obtained in this way was nowhere near enough to sustain the sort of crop growth required to feed the rapidly growing population of the world at the turn of the twentieth century.

Humans need a lot of nitrogen to live, requiring over four times as much in our diet as we do potassium or phosphorus. Nitrogen is contained in every living cell, and all biological processes depend on it in some way. Although living things have an even greater requirement for carbon, plants do a good job of pulling that from the atmosphere using photosynthesis. Nitrogen is much harder to obtain, and almost every biological system is constrained by its availability. It is such a limiting factor in our ability to grow food that the German chemist Justus von Liebig characterised agriculture as a quest to produce enough nitrogen to feed people.

Throughout the nineteenth century, we tried out various approaches to the nitrogen problem. Mineral reserves in Chile were used for a while, but because of insatiable demand from Europe and the US, these quickly started to run low. Guano, the large deposits of droppings found on many Pacific Island bird colonies, were also an excellent source. Birds consuming seafood would bring valuable nutrients inland, depositing droppings in enormous quantities at their nesting sites. These droppings could be harvested, and proved extremely effective when applied to agricultural land in

---

* Cover crops are plants that are deliberately planted to cover the soil and are not intended to be harvested. They can help with managing soil erosion, weed control and improving soil quality.

Europe. It was so effective that guano soon became known as white gold, making many prospectors huge fortunes.

But again, there were issues. Birds can only shit so quickly, meaning that guano was a limited resource. With extraordinary demand from a growing European population, it was clear that reserves would soon run out. Trade disputes, land grabs and even wars ensued, as hundreds of valuable guano islands were rapidly mined down to nothing. Perhaps worse than that, the conditions of workers harvesting guano were nothing short of horrific. Chinese slave labourers were forced by European and American companies to toil in clouds of toxic dust, dying in huge numbers just to meet the insatiable European demand. At the time these deaths were considered acceptable, such was the need to keep the growing population of Europe fed and happy.

Fortunately for this exploited labour, it was becoming clear that any agricultural system that depended on shipping fertilisers halfway around the planet was highly vulnerable to attack. Whoever controlled the supply and distribution of nitrogen had an enormous amount of political power, and could potentially hold the world to ransom. Hunger has always been a powerful weapon of war, and as agriculture was becoming increasingly dependent upon foreign fertilisers, many felt that it would not be long before it was used as such. Nitrogen also had a more literal role as a weapon. The ammonia made from it was an important ingredient in the manufacture of explosives, and at the time, the only economically viable source was the Chilean mineral reserves from which fertilisers were being produced.

Germany in particular paid close attention to Crookes's speech, and it was there that it inspired a flurry of scientific activity. The German authorities realised that any country with superior naval power could cut off the supply of Chilean nitrate, both crippling explosive manufacture and causing agricultural yields to crash. As things stood, whoever controlled the nitrogen supply would win any future war, and so huge resources were ploughed into nitrogen fixation.

Small amounts of atmospheric nitrogen could already be converted into ammonia under high temperatures and pressures, using something known as Le Chatelier Principle, but this process had never produced high enough yields to be commercially viable. But Fritz Haber, a German chemist working for the chemical giant BASF, proved tenacious. He spent years testing different temperatures, pressures and catalysts in a search for a workable system.* Walther Nernst, a more senior colleague, poured scorn on Haber's early efforts, claiming that his results were 'strongly inaccurate' and the synthesis he was attempting was impossible. By the standards of early-twentieth-century German chemists this represented some serious shade, but it only spurred Haber on.

His tenacity paid off. In July 1909 at his laboratory in Karlsruhe, using an osmium catalyst at 500 °C under 100 atmospheres of pressure, Haber produced a constant stream of ammonia from his test apparatus. The BASF team were impressed and made the swift decision to commercialise the process, for which they enlisted the experienced engineer Carl Bosch. With stereotypical German efficiency, even though there were a number of logistical problems that needed to be overcome, not least creating industrial-scale vessels that could function at unprecedented pressures, the first commercial plant opened just thirteen months after Haber's initial demonstration. From then on, similar factories sprang up all around Germany, finally freeing them from dependence upon imported nitrogen. Bosch's contribution to scaling up and refining the process was recognised as vital, and most nitrogen captured today is still produced in what became known as the Haber–Bosch process.

There is a good argument that the Haber–Bosch process is one of the most significant scientific breakthroughs in history. It is certainly one of the most enduring, as a very similar process is

---

* Catalysts are substances that increase the rate of a chemical reaction without being used up in the process.

still used to make the vast majority of nitrogen fertilisers. Despite a century of technological advance in which we have split atoms, edited DNA and beamed pictures back from the surface of a speeding comet, a better method for pulling nitrogen from the air has yet to be found.

Although Haber and Bosch won a Nobel Prize for their work, Haber's legacy is tainted by his later involvement in developing the chemical weapons used by Germany during the First World War, work that he later defended as having reduced suffering. The chemicals that he worked on, including the infamous mustard gas, are estimated to have killed around 1.3 million people and injured many more. Haber never accepted that his were any different from other weapons, but given that chemical and nerve agents are now banned internationally for the unnecessary suffering they cause, history has ruled otherwise.

As the Nazis rose to power, even Haber's blind patriotism was not enough to make up for his Jewish ancestry, and he became increasingly fearful for his life, fleeing to Switzerland in 1933. He died in exile shortly afterwards, devastated that he had been betrayed by the country he loved, and deeply hurt by the way the scientific community had ostracised him for the weapons he developed.

But one thing is certain. Fritz Haber and Carl Bosch had a greater effect upon the world than almost anyone in history. Without their process, our agricultural systems would not have been able to support the rapid population growth that occurred throughout the twentieth century, enabling food supply to keep up with demand. Much of the nitrogen that makes up our bodies has been captured from the air using a process almost identical to the one Haber perfected in his laboratory back in 1909. The results of his breakthrough are literally part of our DNA.

It has been estimated that without the Haber–Bosch process, at least half of the world's population would not be alive today. It is a miracle of modern chemistry that has allowed us to inch a little further from the shackles of hunger. Without it, none of the advances that followed would have been possible. Haber–Bosch fuelled a century of art, science, technology, engineering and culture. A hungry world would never have created antibiotics, strived for equality, looked into the depths of space, brought music to the masses, developed microprocessors, wiped out smallpox or flown to the Moon. An osmium catalyst heated in a high-pressure steel chamber was the breakthrough that underpinned all of those things.[15]

'Brot aus Luft' as they called it in Germany. 'Bread from air'.

The Green Revolution

Despite being able to grow bread from the air, as the century progressed, food production still struggled to keep up with unprecedented population growth. As farming became increasingly mechanised and large-scale production the norm, it ran into some brand new problems. Throughout the 1920s, huge areas of the American and Canadian prairies were converted to large-scale wheat and corn production, with new generations of tractors and combine harvesters allowing the creation of agricultural land at a previously unimaginable speed and scale. Farmers ploughed deep into the prairie topsoil, ridding it of deep-rooted native grasses, and planting neat rows of shallow-rooted food crops as far as the eye could see. When rains fell, yields were high and the new farms hugely prosperous. But as drought hit at the beginning of the 1930s, the unprotected soil quickly turned to dust. Without the roots that had anchored it in place for millennia, dirt rose up into storms that blacked out the sky.

It quickly became impossible to grow anything, and the regular dust storms made it impossible to live. In the midst of a recession, tens of thousands of farmers lost their livelihoods in this new 'dust bowl' landscape. More than half a million people lost their homes, causing the largest mass migration in US history.

With little protection and an economy collapsing around them, there was hardship and food shortage on an enormous scale.

During this period, at around the same time Fritz Haber was languishing in Swiss exile, a young plant scientist called Norman Borlaug witnessed a violent food riot in Minneapolis. Hungry men and women attempted to loot milk lorries only to be beaten back by security guards with baseball bats. The young Borlaug was deeply affected by the carnage he witnessed, and vowed to dedicate his life to fighting the menace of hunger. It is unlikely that he realised at the time what a significant impact he would have upon the world.

Having grown up on a small family farm in Iowa, Borlaug had witnessed the effect that the purchase of a small tractor had on his family's livelihood. Mechanisation freed his parents from toil, transforming the yields and profitability of their small plot. He channelled his belief in the transformational power of science and technology into learning as much as he could about plant science, eventually taking up a position in Mexico in 1944 to help them improve the yields of their wheat crops.

At the time, Mexico was dependent upon US imports, and desperately struggling to feed its growing population. The work was slow, laborious and dispiriting. Local farmers were highly distrustful of the newly arrived American scientists, and Borlaug, who had left his young family behind in America, doubted many times that he had made the right decision. For ten years he toiled away in Mexican test fields, attempting to breed strains of wheat resistant to the dreaded stem rust that was regularly decimating local crops. It was gruelling work, often in extremely poor conditions, but Borlaug was motivated by a desire to alleviate some of the poverty and hunger that he saw all around him.

He made a number of bold decisions during his time in Mexico, and had to fight with authorities several times to keep his funding in place. His decision to plant the same grain varieties across two different growing sites several hundred miles apart went against some of the fundamental laws of agronomy (laws that subsequently proved false). This technique ended up yielding a number of highly adaptable new varieties, and allowed his work to progress at a much faster rate.

Borlaug always considered that the application of large amounts of nitrogen fertiliser was key to improving wheat yields, but this came with a problem. It tended to result in crops bolting upwards too quickly, producing thin stems that collapsed under their own weight. To counter this, Borlaug obtained a number of Japanese short-stemmed varieties, crossing them with local strains, then searching for any plants with short, thick stems and a strong resistance to stem rust.

Eventually, he found what he was looking for and started to work with local farmers to grow these new varieties. After years of struggle, Borlaug finally won round the locals, who were astounded by the hugely increased yields. Before long, most of Mexico was growing these remarkable new plants. By 1963, Mexican wheat yields were six times higher than when Borlaug had arrived in the country. Shortly afterwards, Mexico became not only self-sufficient in wheat, but a net exporter for the very first time.

The world started to take notice. India and Pakistan were struggling to feed their people at the time, and one third of all US wheat was being exported to India just to keep people alive. Both countries purchased large quantities of Borlaug's new seeds, and after a few missteps, they too saw unprecedented yields. By 1968, Pakistan was self-sufficient in wheat and starting to export. By 1974, India was self-sufficient in all cereals.

Inspired by Borlaug's work, projects to improve rice yields led to similar transformations in that crop, vastly increasing agricultural productivity in many rice-growing nations. Short-stemmed wheat varieties were adopted across South America, most of Asia and eventually Europe and North America. It was only in Africa that Borlaug's techniques failed to take hold. Unfortunately, environmental campaigners from the US and Europe strongly resisted the expansion of this work into the African continent, and successfully campaigned for funding to be withdrawn. When Borlaug did manage to work there, government corruption, a lack of irrigation infrastructure and poor transport networks made progress far more challenging. But despite this, Borlaug's 'Green Revolution', as it became known, changed the world. Whilst it was Haber and Bosch that took the vital ingredient from the air, it was Borlaug who perfected the recipe for bread.

It is hard to overstate the importance of this work. The techniques and ethos of the Green Revolution completely transformed world food production. Look at pictures of people standing in wheat fields pre-1960, and you will notice that the wheat is often nearly as tall as they are. Today, when we think of wheat, we imagine a crop only reaching up to the average person's waist (to be clear, the wheat is now smaller – people haven't doubled in size). Borlaug's dwarf varieties dominate wheat production around the world, and they have proved popular for good reason. The productivity increases created by his revolution have been utterly transformational.

Since 1960, average agricultural yields have risen by 193%. We are now producing 217% more calories, yet agricultural land use has only increased by ten percent. The World Bank's food price index shows that between 1961 and 2002, relative food prices fell by thirty-seven percent across the world. Food is more abundant and cheaper, and, as a result, a far smaller proportion of people go hungry. Undernourishment in men has dropped from 13.8% to 8.8% of the global population. In women it has fallen from 14.6% to 9.7%. Despite the population more than doubling, there is now fifty percent more food available per person than in 1961.[16]

There are other reasons for this productivity transformation, including improved transport networks, valuable work carried out on maize during the 1920s, and a number of innovative new livestock breeding techniques. And the Green Revolution was not just the work of a single man – many farmers, politicians and agricultural researchers across the world played a huge part.

Borlaug was a huge believer in cooperating with local workers in the countries he visited, and his burgeoning global celebrity meant that his support often enabled their work to become recognised and implemented.

But an extraordinary amount of credit must go to Borlaug himself, a genuine pioneer who developed a number of innovative techniques and inspired so much change. As a young man he saw the devastation that hunger can wreak and dedicated his life to fighting it. More than anything, he saw hope in parts of the world that many had written off, and held an unshakeable belief in the power of human ingenuity to overcome the seemingly impossible. He pushed back the edge of the field, and it is often claimed that his work saved a billion people from starvation.[17]

There is also an argument that massively increased agricultural yields allowed many economies around the world to be transformed. Much like the European agricultural revolution in the 1750s, more productive agriculture precipitated increased urbanisation, leading to economies that emphasised knowledge and education over labour, and an increased prosperity that few would have thought possible. In just a few decades, Asia in particular was transformed from a region beset by poverty, into an economic powerhouse.

The legacy of Norman Borlaug hangs over the rest of this book. He embodied the spirit of scientific progress in the world of food, with an insatiable, single-minded drive to overcome hunger at all costs. In later life he became a passionate campaigner, understanding more than anyone that feeding people adequately was the key to unlocking social, economic and technological progress. This missionary zeal placed him in direct conflict with many environmental campaigners, who viewed the population growth fuelled by Borlaug's work as a great evil. Even today, many consider the Green Revolution a huge mistake, simply building up a debt that we will one day have to pay back with interest. But Borlaug only saw hunger, maintaining the belief that 'food is the moral right of all who are born into this world.'

A conflict between these two camps has raged ever since. On one side, there are those who believe hunger is an enemy that must be fought today at all costs, and that we shall work out how to pay our debts tomorrow. On the other, there is a belief that growth must be curtailed, and constantly feeding the population monster means that when it eventually does turn round and bite us, the wound will be deeper and more damaging the larger we have allowed it to grow. Both sides aim to reduce human suffering, but arguments about the best way of achieving this rage on.

This is not going to be a balanced book in this regard, but hopefully it will be a contribution to balanced debates. History may prove me wrong, but I will always sit firmly on the side that refuses to accept hunger today. I cannot accept a world where we allow people to starve, even if doing so promises us a better future. If we have the ability to put food in hungry people's mouths, then it would surely take a monster not to do so, even if that means we are only buying time to solve new problems down the line. Surely we would all put our grocery shopping on a credit card if the alternative was seeing our children go hungry.

However, there is no doubting that in recent years a more complex picture of the Green Revolution has emerged. Although the dramatic increases in yields were a huge force for good, cracks are now starting to appear with implications for the future of our planet. Some claim that these cracks are destined to destroy everything that Borlaug fought for; others insist that we will use our ingenuity and resourcefulness to work out those problems, too.

We shall look closely at these cracks over the next few chapters, including a particularly big, dirty one closely related to Borlaug and Haber's work. But first we need to understand the origins of our fear of overpopulation – a fear that leads to some very dark places.

3

A Brief History of Doom

The superior power of population cannot be checked without producing misery or vice.

– Thomas Robert Malthus

On what principle is it that with nothing but improvement behind us, we are to expect nothing but deterioration before us?

– Thomas Babington Macaulay

The Doom Master

Born around the time that the world population was crossing the 800 million mark, Thomas Robert Malthus was an English cleric and scholar whose book *An Essay on the Principle of Population* was to influence several generations of thinkers and environmentalists. In it, he noted that if left unchecked, human population increases in a geometric ratio, but the means of food production only increases at a linear rate. This meant that if people had enough food to eat, the population would increase in an ever-steepening J-shaped curve, just like the imaginary blue tits in the last chapter. As the food supply could only ever increase in a straight line, eventually demand for food would outstrip supply, leading to mass shortage and enormous suffering.

In short, Malthus thought that although increases in food production led to short-term benefits for people's welfare, these improvements were only temporary. If you didn't have a few people starving today, you would have a lot more people starving tomorrow. This would become known as 'the Malthusian Catastrophe', framed as an inevitable consequence of increased food production. It was controversial at the time, because the prevailing view across Europe at the beginning of the nineteenth century was that industrial progress was a limitless force for good.

Malthus worried that the impending catastrophe would have the greatest effect on poor people, feeling that a 'tendency to a virtuous attachment' would lead to inevitable population growth, something that would eventually 'subject the lower classes of the society to distress and prevent any great permanent amelioration of their condition'.

In Malthus's eyes, the only solution was moral restraint, the postponement of marriage and anything else that might reduce the unsustainable amount of 'attachment' going on. Perhaps unsurprisingly for an eighteenth-century Anglican cleric, he considered the hopeless situation to be a test from God, designed to show people the value of better morals and impose punishment on populations who failed to resist. Religion could free us from the brutality of the natural world, but only if we were 'good' enough in the eyes of the Anglican Church.[1]

Malthus predicted that this divine judgement would come to pass around the middle of the nineteenth century. But as with many apocalyptic predictions, his catastrophe kept being postponed. People enjoyed virtuous attachment a bit too much and populations kept on rising in a pattern that appeared exponential. But somehow the food supply kept up. And it kept on keeping up. Innovations took us through the nineteenth and twentieth centuries without population collapse or mass famine. Billions upon billions of mouths continued to be fed. Famine consistently decreased across the world. New techniques came along to push back the crisis. Innovators like Haber and Borlaug changed the rules of the game.

The Darkness

Despite the failure of his predictions, the ideas of Malthus persisted long after his death in 1834. He had an influence on both Darwin and Wallace as they worked on evolutionary theory, but also on later and more questionable thinkers such as Francis Galton. A Victorian polymath, Galton embraced Malthus's ideas, calling for a programme of 'eugenics' (meaning 'good genes'), whereby populations would be thinned out by forcibly removing those with 'undesirable' characteristics.

It is curious that the popularity of the eugenics movement throughout the UK, the US, Canada and Europe has largely been erased from our consciousness. It existed across the political spectrum and was firmly entwined with rising fears of unchecked population growth. It was not just a theoretical argument, either – it resulted in programmes of forced sterilisation and marriage prohibition, particularly in the United States. Criminals, people with low IQs, the blind, the deaf, 'promiscuous women', homosexuals, 'deviants' and various minority groups were targeted, the idea being that they should be stopped from breeding to thin the population down.

Eugenics became strongly associated with genetic determinism, the growing belief that much of our character, morality and achievement are determined by heritable characteristics. Galton was an advocate of this principle, and claimed that 'the unfit could become enemies of the state if allowed to proliferate.' Tellingly, his cousin Charles Darwin strongly disagreed, understanding that the relationship between behaviour and inheritance was a good deal more complex than Galton was making out.

Genetic determinism has always been more popular with the ruling classes, implying as it does that they are inherently superior, which is easier than having to accept that their achievements and status are largely based on blind luck. Intelligence, leadership, creativity and even a potential for criminality all have genetic components, but environmental factors tend to have a huge influence. One of the most powerful environmental factors in any life is the experience (or lack) of hunger. People who are well fed throughout their lives are far more likely to fulfil their potential, and at the end of the nineteenth century the only people consistently getting enough to eat were the ruling classes.

Eugenics depended on the demonstrably false principle that our genes seal our fate before we are born. In a hungry population, that is even less true than at any other time. Eugenicists believed that poor people were that way because they did not have the inherent drive to succeed, rather than accepting they were ground down, hungry and marginalised. They believed that criminals were naturally inclined to be bad, rather than victims of circumstance trying to fill the bellies of their hungry children. They also quickly came to the abhorrent belief that supposedly undesirable traits were prevalent in different races because of inbuilt genetic differences. And they wrongly thought that any traits they didn't like could be weeded out of the population by programmes of selective breeding.

There are multiple ironies when it comes to those that supported eugenics,* not least that there was no empirical evidence as to whether or not the traits they were selecting for were beneficial. Will a population better at passing IQ tests actually make better decisions? Would a society devoid of certain medical conditions be improved? Isn't the idea of homosexuality being a largely inherited trait a little counter-intuitive? Should we select against autism, and

---

* The depressing list of people who publicly advocated for eugenics includes H. G. Wells, George Bernard Shaw, John Maynard Keynes, Winston Churchill, Alexander Graham Bell, Theodore Roosevelt, William Beveridge and Helen Keller. Yes, that Helen Keller.

so lose all the astounding societal contributions made by autistic people? Should we select against those with physical disability, and so lose them too? If this is the case, then a supposedly objective scientific community was advocating for a world that would be without the likes of Stephen Hawking and Alan Turing.

Even if eugenics ever had good intentions at its heart, something I profoundly doubt, the selection of desirable traits only ever depended upon the prevailing tastes of the ruling classes. Unsurprisingly, they decided that Nordic and Aryan races like them were superior to all others. When Hitler came to power, he frequently praised the US programmes of forced sterilisation. During this darkest time in recent history, the justification and inspiration for many of his and the Nazis' actions came from the prevailing views of genetic determinism and racial superiority. What had started with Malthus led to abstract ideas of 'improving' the population and ended with an appalling genocide.[2]

In recent times, the concept of neo-eugenics has started to emerge, a supposedly acceptable re-emergence of the eugenics movement. Neo-eugenics is based on modern understandings of molecular biology, a truer picture of the extent of genetic determinism, and a more liberal interpretation of which traits are considered desirable. Many influential thinkers have advocated that we should be able to select for different genetic traits or perform genetic manipulations.* They argue that things are different this time and that we should not reject valuable tools of progress simply because of their chequered history.

It is true that we now know more about how our genes interact with the world, but the central problem of eugenics still remains. There is no objective evidence regarding which traits are beneficial

---

* Francis Crick, the winner of the Nobel Prize for his involvement in the discovery of DNA, apparently advocated for people to 'start thinking about eugenics in a different way'. More recently, the influential biologist Richard Dawkins argued for a rethink on the matter of selectively breeding humans for particular abilities. Both were seemingly disappointed that Hitler had poisoned the well when it came to eugenics policies.

to society, or even to an individual's well-being. A good example of the complexity involved is the gene for thalassaemia: while two carriers of the gene risk having a child with a debilitating blood disease, the carriers themselves are protected from malaria, which confers a huge advantage in some parts of the world. There is of course an argument for using technology to tackle some very specific diseases, but genetics can't be reduced to a moral calculus.

The reality of modern genetics is that there is not a single gene for every trait and characteristics cannot be ordered from a menu. There are complex interactions and feedbacks, and we still have little understanding of the full implications of a particular change. Genetic diversity exists for good reason, honed across millions of years of evolution. It often gives populations resilience in ways that we do not fully understand until they are needed. Changes are permanent and heritable; fashions, prejudices and beliefs are thankfully not.

Population Bombs

Malthus and his ideas have consistently resurfaced over time. Although there was a period of hope and positivity shortly after the Second World War, pessimism about the future soon returned. In a 1968 essay entitled 'Tragedy of the Commons', the ecologist Garrett Hardin called for society to 'relinquish the freedom to breed through moral coercion'. A 1972 report entitled 'Limits to Growth' from the influential Club of Rome group used computer modelling to predict how soon it would be before the Earth's resources ran dry, claiming that ecological collapse would occur in the mid-twenty-first century. In the same year, a number of leading scientists published *A Blueprint for Survival*, calling for people to live in small decentralised groups in order to prevent 'the breakdown of society and the irreversible disruption of the life-support systems on the planet'.

Most influentially, in 1968 a US biologist called Paul Ehrlich published *The Population Bomb*, a fiery reimagining of Malthus for the technological age. There was a significant Malthusian movement in the 1950s and 1960s, but it was Ehrlich's book that popularised these ideas and brought them to wide attention, selling over two million copies around the world. He compared the human population to a cancer, claiming that in treating the symptoms of population growth by constantly providing food, we were building up even greater problems for the future. He demanded that we turn our attention to 'cutting out the cancer', something that 'will demand many apparently brutal and heartless decisions'. Ehrlich advocated compulsory birth control and forced sterilisations, and even suggested the addition of sterilising agents to water and food supplies. Perhaps most controversially, he said that food aid to 'hopeless' countries such as India should be withdrawn, as mass starvation was the only solution to their population problems. He even encouraged the financial support of separatist movements that embraced population control, so that they might rise up and overthrow supposedly irresponsible governments.

Remarkably, his book became a rallying cry for environmentalists, and was embraced by many as profound and important. It is hard not to see the argument as racist, writing off the lives of those in distant lands, seeing their starvation as equivalent to removing a cancer. At the time, India and Pakistan were largely seen as basket-case economies, with out-of-control populations that were heading for disaster. It is clear that many regarded their predicament as an inherent consequence of their race, rather than their circumstances. It is ironic that at the time Ehrlich's book was being published, the Indian and Pakistani governments were among the first in the world to embrace and implement Borlaug's innovations, and on the cusp of unexpectedly transforming their food supply.

Ehrlich confidently predicted that 'the battle to feed humanity is over,' claiming that widespread famine and death would occur in a worldwide Malthusian catastrophe sometime around the mid-1970s. As predicted, world population did continue to increase, but so did the amount of food. Every time we approached disaster, a series of innovations would get us out of trouble.

Pierre Desrochers is an Associate Professor of Geography at the University of Toronto, where he studies food policy and innovation. He has long been a vocal critic of Ehrlich, and of the many other Malthusian prophesiers of doom throughout the years. He sighs when I mention the possibility of an impending population catastrophe.

The way Dr Desrochers sees it, fears of the limits to growth have always been around, since long before Malthus. He told me that the same beliefs resurface every generation and there is something of a deliberate amnesia about it. 'It always comes from people who think they know better and think that they should be put in charge of other people's behaviour.'

He also explained that it is a basic mistake to assume that the human relationship with food is the same as other animals', because humans are never limited to what is 'naturally' available. He suggests that it is no coincidence that many of the key pessimists come from fields of study that involve simple biological creatures (Ehrlich studied the biology of insects and butterflies). 'Unfortunately, people who share Ehrlich's biology training and outlook will not even have the decency of comparing human beings to other organisms that produce their own food. To them, we are essentially locusts.'

Similarly, despite having studied famine and food shortage all across the world, Alex de Waal from the World Peace Foundation also has no time for Malthusian prophecies. When we spoke, he said that he'd spent many years trying to slay what he calls 'the Malthusian Zombie'.

'I call it that because it keeps coming back to haunt you,' he told me, going on to explain that no modern famines follow Malthusian logic, as none are caused by overpopulation. But even so, he believes that Malthusian thinking often dominates discussions about environmental issues, especially as climate change becomes ever more important. 'It is not helpful in debates about climate change to say if population continues to grow, that will inevitably cause famine. Should famine occur, the cause will be bad policy or armed conflict. For the next thirty years, even the most pessimistic predictions show that food security will continue to improve. Undernutrition in peace time is reducing. Famines as we knew them are all but abolished.'

The Bomb Defused?

Perhaps even more remarkably, in recent years there have been signs that the foundations of Malthus's argument might be built on sand. Although populations have long increased along the lines that Malthus predicted, post-industrial populations all appear to level off naturally. In Europe, the population has already peaked and is now slightly declining. Globally, rates of population growth have been steadily decreasing since the 1960s.[3] Increases in prosperity have led to enormous and unprecedented drops in birth rate, and many predictions show that over the next seventy years, the world population will stop growing altogether. Human population growth appears to be S shaped ('logistic') rather than the terrifying J-shaped ('exponential') curve that Malthus predicted.

By 2050, the world population will reach around 9.6 billion, with half of that increase happening within Africa. By 2100, it is thought that the population will reach around 11.2 billion. By then, the majority of the world will be having only 2.1 children per couple on average. In many areas, the rate looks set to fall well below this, leading to population decline. The best predictions available show the world population declining sometime after 2100, before stabilising at around nine billion in the middle of the next century.[4] This gives humanity a tantalising chink of light: if we can keep on making enough food until the population stops growing, there is a chance that Malthus might be finally consigned to history.

The exception to the current population slowdown is Sub-Saharan Africa, where the fertility rate is currently a little above five. Although this is set to fall to around 3.2 by 2050, population growth is likely to continue. This region is currently home to just under one billion people, and it is thought that the population will more than double by 2050, perhaps reaching over four billion by 2100. Worryingly, it is already home to around thirty percent of the world's chronically hungry.

John Wilmoth is the Director of the United Nations' Population Division at its Department of Economic and Social Affairs. He has authored over fifty papers on the dynamics of human population change and the reasons why mortality and fertility shift over time. His work strongly indicates that any slowdown in human population growth has nothing to do with limitations on supply of food. The real reason follows a clear generational logic: when the death rate is high, people have more children; when the death rate declines and it is easier to guarantee that your children will survive to have their own families, people start having fewer children. This generally happens as part of a broader transformation of the economy to reward work based on education. It is particularly true when women are in work, as they tend to have children later in life. As for the food supply, the picture is quite clear: 'Populations can maintain high levels of fertility even when food is in short supply. Thanks to our evolutionary biology, we continue reproducing even under fairly adverse conditions. Therefore, population trends are fairly resistant to chronic food shortages, and poor nutrition and poverty are often associated with relatively high levels of fertility.'

When it comes to the accuracy of the models used to predict population growth, although these are only ever estimates, recent advances in the way they are generated has hugely increased accuracy. Dr Wilmoth explains:

We have a basic model of demographic change, but there are also many unanswered questions. To calibrate the projection model used by the United Nations, we look at changes from the past and assume that future changes will take place at a similar pace, taking into account current levels of life expectancy and fertility. We estimate the model in a Bayesian statistical framework, which is useful for assessing the uncertainty of our projections. We simulate multiple population trajectories by varying the parameters – guided by the historical evidence – and in this way we derive ranges of plausible trends for different countries and regions of the world.

Dr Wilmoth also explained that in the past, the UN created low, medium and high scenarios based on different assumptions about future fertility trends, with the low and high differing by plus or minus half a child for each country. The problem with this approach is that it often produced a very wide range of predictions, suggesting that the world population at the end of the century might be anywhere between seven and sixteen billion people. The Bayesian probabilistic method produces a much more narrow range of predictions and far more reliable results.

There is also a phenomenon known as population momentum, which makes accurate predictions even more likely. Rapidly growing populations are by their nature young populations, meaning that there are lots of people of childbearing age. In this situation, even if you lower the birth rate down to replacement levels, the population will continue to grow. All this means that although they have been unreliable in the past, modern predictions of population growth are far more accurate and should be taken extremely seriously. As Dr Wilmoth told me: 'Population trends are slow to change and thus quite predictable. There is no other social or economic variable that you could project to the end of the century with the same degree of accuracy.'

An important truth to remember when considering population growth is that, throughout human history, there has never been the slightest correlation between a country's population density and levels of hunger. There is, however, a strong correlation between government corruption and the likelihood of starvation. When famine occurs in the modern era, it is almost always because of the actions of a few bad people, not the existence of too many.

The Unacceptable Cost

Even if we do consider population growth an unspeakable evil, there have been various attempts to curb growth artificially over the years and none has ended well. Introduced in 1979, and reputedly inspired by the publication of 'Limits to Growth' the notorious one-child policy in China was perhaps the most significant. Parents were coerced into having only one child in order to curtail China's fast-growing population. There were enormous fines for violations, and families who refused to comply would end up losing access to education and healthcare services.

It arguably achieved its purpose, reportedly preventing an estimated 400 million people from being born, although many other countries achieved similar declines in birth rate over the same period without the need for such draconian policies. But behind the success is much darkness, with women required to have intrauterine devices (IUDs) fitted after the first child, and then to be sterilised if they had a second. Abandonment and illegal abortions became commonplace, and infanticide was often reported. Pressure on families to have a male child has led to a male to female ratio of 117 to 100 in China today, far higher than the expected biological baseline of around 103 to 100. This speaks of a history of sex-selective abortions, often carried out late term when sex determination is easier. Or perhaps it even suggests the gruesome thought that many baby girls were killed immediately after birth, such was the cultural and financial pressure to have a boy.[5]

In India, the subject of so many doom-laden Malthusian predictions in the 1960s, many states reacted by implementing two-child policies. On the surface these control projects seemed a little more benign than their Chinese equivalents, but an estimated eight million forced sterilisations were carried out between 1975 and 1976, eventually leading to a scandal that collapsed Indira Gandhi's government. And much like China, figures show that there are 63 million fewer women and girls in India than there should be. Cultural pressure to have male children has always been intense, and although the figures may be skewed by families stopping once they have had a boy, there are many reports of sex-selective abortions, infanticide, abandonment and disproportionate nutrition or medical care being provided to male children.[6]

There were countless other examples of forced sterilisations or state-sponsored abuse in the name of population control. It happened in developing economies like Mexico, Bangladesh and Indonesia, but also in places like the US and Sweden. Many countries and organisations offered perverse incentives to insert IUDs into as many women as possible, often in poor and unsanitary conditions, without recipients fully understanding what was going on. Policies led to huge increases in illegal and dangerous abortions. Many were sterilised without proper consent. Corruption and coercion has dominated every attempt to control the rate of birth. An enormous amount of suffering has been inflicted, almost all of it upon women, and almost all because of policies designed by men. The great irony of this is that if all that effort making women's lives miserable had been channelled into improving their health, education and equality, they might have actually achieved the stated aim of levelling out the world's population.

The Monster Returns?

So what are we to make of the more recent prophecies of doom? There is no shortage, from Al Gore's influential book *Earth in the Balance* in 1992, his equally apocalyptic documentary *An Inconvenient Truth* in 2006, through to the 2017 *World Scientists' Warning to Humanity: A Second Notice*, which calls rapid population growth 'the primary driver behind many ecological and even societal threats'. Then there is David Wallace-Wells's utterly bleak *The Uninhabitable Earth* from 2019, and Mark Lynas's *Six Degrees* from 2007. Hundreds of respected scientists and campaigners around the world are calling for curbs on population as the only way of saving the planet from environmental catastrophe. Are these just resurfacings of the Malthusian Zombie, or is it different this time?

There is no doubt that climate change is real. Too many of the world's scientists agree on the predictions and models for it to be dismissed. It follows that we need to exercise some influence over the world's population in order to reduce our footprint, but I can't countenance forced sterilisations, nor standing by while others starve. The only way of reducing birth rates that has ever proven successful and humane is social and economic development, the education of women and removing the constant threat of hunger. If we can continue to spread these ideas across the world, then there is no reason why population growth cannot be tamed.

Too much of the rhetoric around climate change still seems tinged by racist attitudes towards Africa, and the tacit assumption that it would be terrible if 'we' were outnumbered by 'them'. There is an idea that 'they' can never be helped and breeding is just what 'they' do. This quickly jumps towards the sort of cultural biases that led people to accept Ehrlich's calls to starve India out of existence.

It also hides an inconvenient truth that the Global North often struggles to face. We might be smug about having a handle on our birth rates, but we fly our children around the world on holiday, drive them to school in air-conditioned cars, buy them pets, fret if their bedroom is a degree too cold, and fill their lives with all the trappings of consumerism. As things stand, the world's richest ten percent produce around fifty percent of global climate emissions. Conversely, the world's poorest fifty percent only produce around ten percent of the total.[7] An average child born in the US will be responsible for the release of nearly twenty metric tonnes of carbon dioxide each year. A child born in the Democratic Republic of the Congo will produce around 0.04 tonnes, nearly five hundred times less.[8] When it comes to climate change, we are the drivers and Africa is very much the victim, disproportionately affected by extreme weather patterns and increasing average temperatures.

The Global North has spent the last few hundred years building up debts that the Global South is now having to pay. If it's all about the climate and the environment, we should really be limiting the harm done by the children of Europe and North America, and focus on shrinking our wasteful, polluting economies down to nothing. But we are often blind to our own excess, and the more pressure that our wastefulness puts on the food systems of Africa, the less likely it is that population growth there will decrease.

4

How to Change the World

The way globalization is occurring could be much better,
but the worst thing is not being part of it.
– Hans Rosling

The First Greenhouse

Our planet came into existence a little over four billion years ago,
and once it had cooled enough to allow liquid water to form, it
did not take long for the first signs of life to appear. For most of
Earth's history this life was pretty simple, comprising only single-
celled organisms floating around in a homogenous microbial
soup. Even though the light from the young Sun was not as strong
as it is today, high levels of carbon dioxide, methane and water
vapour in the atmosphere meant that lots of the energy reflected
back from the surface of the planet became trapped rather than
escaping off into space, causing the Earth to warm in a dramatic
early version of the greenhouse effect.

Soon, a few of the little critters started to have an impact
outside their cell walls. Some formed structures called stromatolites, layers of silt held together with mucus-like secretions, rising
up a few centimetres from the surface of shallow seashore bays.
Fossilised examples of these strange towers of mucus and dirt

have been found dating back nearly 3.7 billion years, making them the oldest known physical evidence of life on Earth.* Stromatolites were the first sign that the replicating coils of DNA that we call life were capable of altering the surface of the planet. Over billions of years, the continuing ability of microorganisms to build structures from their snot would have an enormous impact upon the world.[1]

It is thought that most early stromatolites were formed by cyanobacteria, tiny organisms that used these snotty columns to rise up towards the sunlight, which they would then use for energy. If cyanobacteria could reach high enough towards the light on their tiny columns of snot-mud, they were capable of converting carbon dioxide and water into sugars using the power of the Sun. In doing so, they released large amounts of oxygen. At first, this oxygen was either absorbed by the oceans, or reacted with a number of different minerals, particularly iron, forming stable oxides that sank to the bottom of the sea. But once all the iron was mixed with oxygen, and the oceans were saturated and various land stores exhausted, the oxygen gas they were relentlessly spewing out started to stick around in the atmosphere.[2] †

In the atmosphere, the oxygen reacted with methane, converting it into carbon dioxide and water. Although both methane and carbon dioxide can act as greenhouse gases, carbon dioxide is considerably less potent, and could also be used by the cyanobacteria in photosynthesis, making yet more oxygen and creating a powerful environmental feedback loop. As oxygen levels grew, the methane was almost completely removed and carbon dioxide levels fell dramatically, in what became known as the Great Oxygenation Event.

---

* The exact timeline is disputed in the literature, but my analysis is that it was a really long time ago, so it's hard to tell for sure. To be honest most of us could trip over a three-billion-year-old stromatolite without having a clue what it was, so how anyone works out when it formed is beyond me.

† Again, the exact process and timeline for this are disputed, but the changes were significant.

Minerals and metals became oxidised, forming into sediments and rocks. Atmospheric oxygen poisoned most existing life forms, creating an unprecedented mass extinction, but in doing so stripped away many of the energy limitations holding evolutionary progress back. It was not long before oxygen-fuelled mitochondria became the powerhouses of cells, leading the way to multicellular organisms, then plants, animals, hummus, power stations, skateboards and mobile phones. It was the gaseous waste produced by tiny microorganisms that led to all of these things, changing the Earth's geology, forming a brand-new atmosphere, profoundly altering the climate and opening the door to new forms of complex life.

If you are ever looking for evidence that humans are neither special nor removed from nature, remember that our existence depends upon an invisible microbe's farts. And if you ever doubt that the Earth can be changed dramatically by the actions of living things, a quick look back through its deep history will tell you something very different.

The Second Greenhouse

In 1949, just a few billion years after microbes first started building towers of snot towards the Sun, humanity was reeling from the effects of its worst ever global conflict. Harry S. Truman had seen America through the end of the Second World War, but after a period of economic upheaval he was widely expected to lose the 1948 election to Republican Thomas Dewey. Despite the *Chicago Tribune* producing a famous headline declaring Dewey the winner shortly before the result was declared, Truman won through, securing 303 electoral votes to Dewey's 189.

Truman's second inauguration in January the following year was the first to be televised live, and contained an address from the new president that many considered surprising and dramatic. At the time, the world seemed increasingly unstable. The post-war rise of communism was considered an existential threat to the West, with the Soviets known to be developing their own nuclear weapons, and communist propaganda convincing many underdeveloped nations that democracy and free markets could never provide a good standard of living to most of the world. It was becoming increasingly clear that the world's distribution of wealth and resources was grossly unfair, largely driven by the shameful exploits of Western colonialism. Many felt that liberal democracy was hanging by a thread.

In his speech, Truman outlined a four-point plan to address these threats. Points one to three were fairly non-controversial, calling for continued support of the UN, various programmes to aid economic recovery, and the protection of democratic nations against aggressors. But the fourth point, a bold strategy of technological and trade support to promote economic growth and prosperity in less developed nations, surprised many people, including a number of leading environmentalists. Truman told the American people:

> We must embark on a bold new program for making the benefits of our scientific advances and industrial progress available for the improvement and growth of underdeveloped areas. More than half the people of the world are living in conditions approaching misery. Their food is inadequate. They are victims of disease. Their economic life is primitive and stagnant. Their poverty is a handicap and a threat both to them and to more prosperous areas. For the first time in history, humanity possesses the knowledge and skill to relieve the suffering of these people.

The nascent environmental movement considered that the economic development of so many nations would fuel further population growth, leading not only to a Malthusian catastrophe, but also the wholesale destruction of the natural world. Most notably, the prominent US campaigner William Vogt wrote an article damning Truman's Point Four plan, claiming that if it led to 'speeding up soil erosion, raiding forests and land fertility, destroying watershed, forcing down water tables . . . we shall be known not as beneficent collaborators, but as technological vandals.'*

Despite criticism in the US and from leaders across the developing world, Vogt campaigned vigorously against the Point Four plan, convinced it would be a force for great environmental harm. But for others, Truman's speech was bold and inspiring. It placed America at the head of a global community that would fight for the rights of all of its citizens and attempt to lift everyone out of poverty. Truman believed that the only road to progress and lasting peace was global prosperity, increased international trade, self-determination and freedom for all. He went on to say:

> The old imperialism – exploitation for foreign profit – has no place in our plans. What we envisage is a program of development based on the concepts of democratic fair-dealing. All countries, including our own, will greatly benefit from a constructive program for the better use of the world's human and natural resources . . . Our aim should be to help the free peoples of the world, through their own efforts, to produce more food, more clothing, more materials for housing and more mechanical power to lighten their burdens.

It was not just environmentalists that raised red flags about the content of Truman's speech. Many Americans felt that the large-scale opening of trade barriers would cause tremendous harm to domestic agriculture, with cheap imports threatening the viability of production. There was much opposition and the Senate only passed the Point Four Program by a single vote.

---

* Vogt would spend the rest of his life campaigning against agricultural development and technological advance across the world, and years later would push for Borlaug's funding to be withdrawn in Mexico long before the Green Revolution breakthroughs. The story of his life and battles against Borlaug's work are brilliantly detailed in Charles Mann's *The Wizard and the Prophet*.

But it did pass, and as a direct result many world trade agreements were signed to encourage agricultural productivity in developing countries and link them to international markets. This would eventually be crucial to the success of the Green Revolution, but it also left many developed nations with the problem its critics had feared. Once the technologies to grow foods cheaply and efficiently had been exported around the world, the lower costs of land, labour and production meant that farmers in Europe and the US were often unable to compete. Worldwide trade pushed down prices and left many farmers on the brink of financial ruin.

Of course, farmers could have simply abandoned certain staple crops, instead focusing on less easily traded commodities, but this would have left many countries in extremely vulnerable positions if there were a crop failure. If a country didn't have enough wheat, maize or rice to feed its people, it could easily be extorted for money in peacetime or conquered in war. In order to preserve food security and still operate within a market economy, developed nations had to embark on hugely expensive programmes of agricultural support. Farmers were paid to produce certain commodity crops so that in the event of conflict or global failure, people would not starve.

This system proved complex and divisive. Subsidies helped stabilise domestic prices and protect farmers from volatility, but because they were generally linked to farm outputs, subsidies also encouraged overproduction. When the surplus was dumped onto world markets, prices would collapse, often destroying the livelihoods of farmers in developing nations. Food security around the world became severely threatened as suddenly unviable farms in the developing world were abandoned. Vital investment in agriculture was discouraged by this price volatility, especially in Sub-Saharan Africa, which always seemed to be hit hardest. Food price subsidies undermined much of the progress that the opening of world trade routes had been designed to encourage, and a resulting lack of investment has left much of Africa vulnerable to this day.

To make matters worse, as subsidies focused on a small number of globally traded crops, the food system became increasingly limited. Wheat, rice and maize grew to dominate world production (these now represent over fifty percent of all calories consumed). The subsidies on production led to cycles of huge food abundance. More food led to cheaper food. Cheaper food led to more intensification. This led to the exhaustion of natural resources, causing productivity to fall. As a result, more land was required for agriculture. Forests were cleared, wetlands drained, grasslands cultivated. All around the world, countries focused on growing a small number of cash crops, converting more and more land in the process as the subsidy system quickly spiralled out of control.

By 1990, the European Union's Common Agricultural Policy was providing thirty-five percent of all local farm income. With subsidies so dependent upon productivity, the use of fertilisers increased. Between 1987 and 1989, European farmers were paid sixty percent more than the global price for wheat, so it made economic sense to spray as much fertiliser as possible. Throughout this period, EU rates of fertiliser application were twice those of the US, yet they only produced small increases in yields. Direct subsidies also encouraged the overuse of pesticides, the excess pumping of groundwater and an ever-increasing focus on a narrow range of crops.

Despite extensive reform in the early 1990s, in the European Union around twenty to thirty percent of farm income still comes from subsidies. In Canada and the US it is around five to ten percent, and in Russia ten to twenty percent. Some rice farms in Japan and South Korea are given subsidies totalling eighty percent of the value of production, meaning the vast majority of their profits come from the government. Between 2015 and 2017, in the fifty-one countries where data was available, $570 billion was spent on support for agriculture. The market for food is hugely distorted because of this, leading to problems on a global scale.

We now overproduce grains, fats and sugar, and at the same time, underproduce fruits, vegetables and plant protein. This narrowing might seem surprising to anyone my age or older when visiting the fresh produce aisle of a typical supermarket and comparing it to the diet of their childhood. From avocados to cavolo nero, we now have access to an astonishing array of exotic produce that I would never have dreamt of as a child, and almost certainly would never have eaten. These memories are not false. In almost every part of the world, the availability of food for individuals has vastly improved over the past fifty years, and the content and variety of our diets has been enhanced as a result.

But although it is true that at an individual level most of us have access to more variety than ever before, this obscures the fact that there are far fewer species being widely grown around the world. This loss of diversity is now becoming one of the greatest threats to food security, especially on a rapidly changing planet. A variety of crops is vital to food system resilience, but when the current subsidy systems to support global agriculture were designed, this was never taken into account, meaning that crop variety has declined around the world.[3]

On balance, the global expansion of trade and the spread of vital technologies after the Second World War were still forces for good. They lifted billions away from the most crushing effects of poverty and hunger, transforming economies and lives around the world. Even though subsidies and price volatility crippled agricultural investment in Africa, many parts of Asia, Europe and South and Central America underwent hugely positive transformations.* Although the rest of Truman's second term was turbulent and he was widely unpopular by the end of his presidency, his legacy has since been reassessed by many historians. His role

---

* Many countries, such as Japan, South Korea and Taiwan, invested in infrastructure to support agriculture long before subsidies caused this price volatility. Others, such as the Philippines, failed to do so, largely because of state corruption, and they still lag behind economically today.

in preserving democracy, spreading prosperity and fighting hunger is now seen as instrumental in shaping the modern world.

But there is no doubt that the opening up of international trade caused huge problems for global food systems, many of which persist to this day. We shall look at the harms in a bit more detail in the next chapter, but first it is worth considering the alternatives. Because although it is easy to criticise a deeply distorted market, especially one that is responsible for cata- strophic harm to the planet, it is possible that the alternatives might not have been that much better. In fact, if the prevention of hunger is the overriding aim that I consider it to be, many of the other games in town might actually have been far worse.

How Not to Change the World

One scientist who would have been horrified about the global decline in agricultural diversity was the legendary Russian agron- omist Nikolai Vavilov. He dedicated the early years of the twenti- eth century to travelling around the world, identifying and collecting heritage crops from different regions. His work focused on a small number of areas that he named the 'Centres of Origin', thought to be the places around the world where agriculture first developed.

Vavilov was among the first to realise that the resilience of agricultural systems depended upon preserving many different species and variants of crop plants, and identifying characteris- tics that were suited to different environments. Recognising that we would not always know what those characteristics were until we needed them (he understood that he had not taken his mice to the opera yet), he pioneered the creation of agricultural seed banks, storing huge numbers of obscure and forgotten variants of wheat, corn and cereals.

Even in our modern world, with sophisticated breeding tech- niques, genetic engineering and DNA sequencing, seed banks are now recognised as one of the most valuable resources in agriculture. Vavilov is widely thought of as being a pioneer and genius, whose breakthroughs and techniques changed food production around the world. But sadly, in his own country, it was to be a very different story.

Vavilov was a powerful and respected scientist in the early days of the Soviet Union. Much like Borlaug, he had experienced famine as a young man, and dedicated his life to battling against it. Yet his adoption of Western scientific thinking, particularly on genetics, inheritance and evolutionary theory, caused tensions between him and the new Stalinist leadership. Stalin was distrustful of Vavilov's Western education and quickly came to favour the work of another agricultural scientist, Trofim Lysenko.

Despite initially training with Vavilov, Lysenko had branched out into research of his own and had begun to adopt some very strange beliefs. He largely rejected the concept of genetic inheritance, claiming that environment alone shapes the characteristics of living things. Countless experiments had already shown genetic inheritance to be the primary way in which information was passed between generations, yet Soviet ideology decreed that this bourgeois science denied people and organisms the capacity to change.

Lysenko's views were largely based on flawed, lazy observations of the natural world. He believed that cuckoos were created when reed warblers fed their chicks hairy caterpillars, failing to observe that cuckoos lay their eggs in the nests of these birds and trick the warblers into raising the cuckoo chicks as their own. He developed a 'law of the species', believing that plants of the same type would never compete with one another, expecting that Soviet wheat would somehow conform to the tenets of Marxism. As a result, he recommended sowing crops far closer together than optimal, often causing them to fail. Despite the fact that this technique actually killed plants and decimated yields, he insisted it must be correct because of Marxism. The plants stubbornly disagreed.

Lysenko spent years grimly clinging on to a flawed belief system, hailing himself as a genius while displaying astounding ignorance about science. He conducted many bizarre experiments, and is thought to have faked many of his results just to please the Soviet leadership. Perhaps because his increasingly mad ideas complemented Marxist thinking so perfectly, and perhaps because if you cast him as a Russian villain in a movie you would be accused of stereotyping based on looks, Stalin embraced this plucky young scientist wholeheartedly. Lysenko rose to power, and Vavilov became increasingly marginalised.

At the same time as Lysenko was conducting his experiments, Soviet agriculture was undergoing huge structural change. Food production was moving even further under state control, with the forced collectivisation of many farms that had been owned by families for generations. A large proportion of the rural population were moved from their homes and sent to the cities to work towards rapid industrialisation. There was increased state management of grain procurement and of the food system generally, as part of the intense Stalinist drive towards complete central control of the economy.

These policies proved to be a disaster. Farmers stripped of ownership no longer had the incentive to work the punishing hours required to drive high yields. Rural labour and expertise was lost to the cities. Central control of such an enormous food supply proved too complex to measure and manage. When droughts hit much of the Soviet Union in the early 1930s, they should not have been serious enough to cause much hardship. But with the pressures already in place, they proved devastating. Between 1932 and 1933, the region experienced one of the worst famines in recorded history.

Given the secrecy of the regime, it is hard to know exactly how many people died. Most estimates converge on around ten million lives lost, largely in the grain-producing regions of Ukraine and Kazakhstan. Wherever grain could be produced, it was requisitioned and shipped off to the cities, leaving rural regions to starve. Many consider this famine a deliberate genocide, with Stalin using hunger as a weapon to quell the rising separatist movement in Ukraine. Soviet propaganda from the time led the industrial workers of the cities to believe that rural communities were conspiring to undermine the Soviet project, hiding food and living in luxury whilst the workers went without. But in reality they were being starved out of existence, either by design or incompetence, or perhaps more likely a combination of the two. What is definite is that the famine was almost entirely man-made, the product of failed policies and indifference to life.

Stalin never accepted that his programme of forced collectivisation contributed to the disaster, but the extent of food shortages throughout the period was impossible to ignore. He blamed Vavilov, still the country's most prominent agricultural scientist, who he claimed should have found a way to avert the crisis. Vavilov was swiftly demoted, and the golden boy Lysenko drafted in to replace him.

Lysenko's ideas quickly became the Soviet scientific consensus, and anyone maintaining a belief in the supposedly flawed science of genetics was suddenly in mortal danger. Thousands of dissenting scientists were imprisoned, tortured and killed at Lysenko's request. Vavilov, arguably the most important plant scientist in history, was arrested in 1941 and sentenced to death. Although his sentence was commuted to life imprisonment, he died of starvation in 1943 at the notorious Saratov prison.

Lysenko's ideas crippled Soviet farming, although his popular appeal and high-level influence meant that he managed to persuade many people to return to working in the fields. His flawed science is thought to have set Russian agriculture back fifty years, with only the country's huge land resources preventing further catastrophic famine. When Stalin died in 1953, Lysenko's power waned as the new regime became more open to mainstream science. By the 1960s, no doubt aware of Norman Borlaug's successes in Asia and Central America, the Soviet scientific community became openly critical of Lysenko's work.

Lysenko died in disgrace in 1976, just as the Green Revolution, based firmly upon the science of genetics that he had rejected, was transforming food production around the world.[4]

Even as Lysenko's work was being discredited, his ideas were taken up in China. Private ownership of land became forbidden, and millions were relocated from rural areas to join the new urban iron and steel workforce. This led to many of the same problems experienced in the Soviet Union during the 1930s, and, to make matters worse, the agricultural techniques pioneered by Lysenko appealed to the Chinese leadership of the time, and were widely implemented in the belief that they would improve productivity.

Crops were planted increasingly close together, based on Lysenko's 'law of the species', resulting in widespread failures. Deep ploughing, another of Lysenko's flawed ideas, became common, based on the false belief that the best soil was located a metre underground. As a result, rocks and infertile dirt were turned to the surface, causing yields to fall further still. Birds were killed en masse in the belief that they were eating grain from the fields, resulting in a proliferation of vermin that destroyed vital crop stores.

In 1959, years of poorly planned irrigation led to devastating floods in the Yellow River region, killing millions and destroying cropland. By 1960, there was severe drought, causing harvests to fall even further. But in the most fatal twist of all, reported yields kept on rising across the country. Local officials were terrified of the consequences of saying anything negative about the new agricultural techniques, so they simply lied. The Central Committee of the Party believed that they had more grain than ever, and felt confident that the ideas of Lysenko were bearing literal fruit. As a result of this remarkable surplus, they shifted production to cash crops such as cotton, sugar cane and beet. They diverted increasing amounts of rural labour to the steel industry. Even more food was allocated to feeding the growing cities.

When Chairman Mao visited agricultural sites across China, he was told that Lysenko's methods had produced miraculous results, with yields many times higher than previous years. But in reality, local officials were removing and transplanting shoots from other fields before inspections, shoots that would wither and die shortly after state visits. When Party officials travelled on trains, local workers were instructed to place fake crops in fields for miles along the route, giving an illusion of abundance. Huge industry and resources were devoted to fooling the political elite.

However, it is widely thought that everyone, right up to Mao himself, knew that a desperate famine was not far away. Yet they continued a merry dance, with local politicians pretending all was well, and state officials pretending to believe them. No one was willing to admit openly how bad things really were, right up until the stores were empty.

By 1960, harvests were down by seventy percent and people were starting to starve. As with the Soviet famine years before, exact numbers are hard to come by, but it is thought that as many as forty million had died by the end of 1961, making it by far the worst famine in human history. It has been reported that cannibalism occurred on a scale never seen before. There are countless reports of the most widespread and abject misery, placing this as one of the most appalling humanitarian disasters of all time. Unlike the rosy picture painted for sheltered Party officials, the reality on the ground was a vision of hell. Human flesh was openly sold in markets. People ate tree bark, bird shit and moss to survive. Children were offered for sale as food, just so people would not have to commit the additional sin of eating their own kin.[5]

Perhaps the greatest evil of all is that although China experienced both drought and flooding, the great famine was completely avoidable, even at its height. It was the result of human failure, muddled ideology, flawed scientific beliefs, draconian political control and fear. Grain was available to feed the starving people, and other countries could have made up any shortfalls. But the bloody-minded refusal of a planned economy to admit its failings meant that many of its people fell beyond desperation, down to a point where all humanity was lost. This famine, which occurred within living memory, is a stark reminder of how far we have come in the intervening years.

Who Exactly Is in Control?

The economist Paul Seabrook tells a story about the period shortly after the fall of the Berlin Wall, when many former communist bloc countries were attempting to move towards a free-market economy. Moving suddenly from a centrally planned economy to a free market was perhaps the most extraordinary economic upheaval in recent history, and as the communist leaders had been so isolated for so long, they had little idea of how free-market systems operated. As they started to visit the West on fact-finding missions, they marvelled at our ridiculous and colourful excesses, and perhaps recoiled in horror at the levels of crime and inequality. But one thing stood out for all who visited. Food. It was cheap, plentiful and easily accessed. Supermarket shelves were always stocked. There was huge variety, adorned with brightly coloured packaging and persuasive advertising. Queues were short and few ever went hungry. The rich never did.

During one of these fact-finding missions, Seabrook had a meeting with an official previously charged with controlling the production of bread in St Petersburg. The fascinated official asked Seabrook to divulge the secret to this food paradise: 'Who is in charge of the supply of bread to the population of London?' The answer – that no one is – is perhaps one of the most unheralded marvels of our time, and partially explains why most of the world has now abandoned central planning. As Seabrook notes, although the ability of bread to appear on our shelves without anyone being in control is quite extraordinary, 'Only in the industrialised West have we forgotten how strange it is.'

Almost all planned economies have struggled to provide basic resources for their people. Food queues and shortages were commonplace throughout the Soviet Bloc. When the best and brightest people in a society are wasting their time and efforts obtaining the essentials required to live, it is always going to stifle progress and lead to discontent. This is perhaps why most of the world's markets now operate using complex, emergent systems like the London bread supply, seemingly forged from nothing. A competitive system of manufacturing, distribution and retail has proven incredibly effective when it comes to keeping people fed. Supply and demand seem impossible to predict and plan to any useful extent, but leave the system to itself and the shelves somehow fill up with food. Even more remarkably, they stay filled consistently.

Despite their success, there is a widespread fear of these emergent systems. Because no single person is in control, they instinctively seem alien and uncontrollable. It might be comforting to think of countries and governments in familial terms, with parents making responsible decisions for everyone using the family budget, but this paternalistic approach simply doesn't work when you're trying to feed millions of people. To accept that no one is really in charge of the bread reaching our shelves is mildly terrifying, and every generation fights against it in some way. Yet in all of recorded history, capitalism has proved to be the best system when it comes to keeping people from hunger.

This brings us back to the problem that Truman faced in 1949. Capitalism was unfair and unjust in many respects, especially on a global scale, but it was also a better way of keeping people fed than central planning. His answer – to aggressively extol the benefits of a free-market economy around the world – brought better lives to millions of people. Many consider it to be our greatest achievement, and if we focus on food security alone, I am inclined to agree.

Yet it comes with a sting in the tail. Completely free trade would have damaged local food security in the richest countries, and so measures were taken to distort the market. As a result, the world came to concentrate on just a few crops, but also encouraged unnecessary use of fertiliser and pesticides, scorching the land, destroying natural habitats, poisoning waterways and changing the atmosphere forever.

As we shall discuss in the next chapter, the cost of progress has been immense. The damage has been massively compounded by a distortion of the market by wealthy countries, desperate to protect their ability to feed themselves. It was not greed or vice that caused this distortion, nor the dark forces of capitalism. A truly capitalist system would have let the market play out, perhaps resulting in the production of wheat and other grains concentrated in a few countries where the costs were low enough, leading to greater specialisation and more diverse, niche production closer to home. It was only the constant threat of war that prevented this from happening, so in reality, it is that part of our nature we should blame. Violence, not greed, ruined the food system.

But as you read the litany of destruction outlined, it is worth remembering that almost all of this cost has been incurred in the pursuit of worthy and sensible goals, with no humane alternatives on offer. The world was changed in order to lift people out of poverty, with the understanding that the transformation of a nation's food is the first step towards better lives for its people. Those that feed us, the farmers, distributors, manufacturers, restaurateurs and retailers, have only ever had the thoroughly sensible goal of keeping us fed. Although there may be greed, selfishness and short-termism within all those industries, in reality, most people involved in food strive for a sustainable, well-managed system that works for all. Food is not usually a place where people work solely for the financial rewards. Having worked in the industry for most of my life, I can attest that the rewards are a pittance compared to finance, fossil fuels, transport, pharmaceuticals or a number of other capitalist ventures. Almost everyone that grows, cooks or sells food does so through love, and the vast majority only want to bring the world some culinary joy.

5

What Have We Done?

We need things consumed, burned up, worn out, replaced, and discarded at an ever increasing pace. We need to have people eat, drink, dress, ride, live, with ever more complicated and, therefore, constantly more expensive consumption.

– US economist Victor Lebow in 1955

One of the biggest problems with agriculture is that it happens really slowly. Experiments to improve crop yields rarely produce the sort of miraculous returns Norman Borlaug made in Mexico, and even that achievement took fifteen years of extraordinarily hard work. Most changes are incremental and experiments take at least the length of a growing season to produce any data. Unless all the conditions are being carefully measured and controlled over a very long period of time, it is quite possible for significant change to occur so slowly that no one notices.

For this reason, agricultural land can sometimes degrade at such a gradual rate that it can be farmed for generations without anyone realising it is being destroyed. Throughout history, from Ancient Greece to the Roman Empire to the great Mayan cities on the other side of the world, civilisations have collapsed, largely because surrounding farmlands slowly stopped producing enough food. Often these great and progressive societies did not notice change was happening until it was too late – when they were surrounded by barren lands, completely unable to feed their people.[1]

If anyone can be said to have changed this, it is the relatively unknown British industrialist John Bennet Lawes. In the 1840s, he developed the first artificial fertiliser by treating phosphate rock with sulphuric acid to create something known as a superphosphate. Although this was an important breakthrough, it was the methods he used to study its effects that are his most lasting legacy.

The reason he knew that superphosphates had a beneficial effect on crop yields was through meticulous measurement. He planted fields of wheat on his experimental farm, treating different areas with specific applications, and then carefully measuring any improvements in yield over a number of seasons. Along with fellow researcher Joseph Henry Gilbert, he founded the Rothamsted Experimental Station, now Rothamsted Research, and developed principles that persist to this day. And one of those principles was that in order to know exactly what is going on with crop plants, field experiments need to last a really long time.

Rothamsted is famous for many things, and we shall be returning there a number of times throughout this book. Not only is it known for some of the longest-running experiments in history, but it is also considered to be the birthplace of modern statistics, as much mathematical innovation was required to analyse the vast swathes of data that the fields produced. It also marks an important transition in agriculture, because superphosphates are the first examples of synthetic chemistry being used in food production. Although welcomed and uncontroversial in Lawes's time, these sorts of chemicals would create a damaging split in agriculture that has lasted for generations, with Rothamsted at the heart of the debate.

The Best Things Come to Those Who Wait

There are long-term experiments, and there are Rothamsted long-term experiments. The most famous of all is the Broadbalk

Wheat study, started by Lawes and Gilbert in 1843, and due to the foresight of Lawes, who set up a trust to maintain it, continuing to this day. For 175 years, winter wheat has been sown on the Broadbalk ground in small adjacent strips, with different treatments, both organic and inorganic, applied to each. A control strip has had no fertiliser, manure or enrichment for 175 consecutive growing seasons. Not surprisingly, this piece of land has not done well. But other plots have shown that under the correct conditions and treatments, wheat yields can be maintained fairly easily over the long term.

Broadbalk has taught the world a great deal. Perhaps most significantly, it has demonstrated that as long as the soil is treated well, with plenty of organic fertiliser being regularly applied, wheat can be harvested for a very long time without significantly degrading the land, or noticeably damaging yields. We now know that as long as we do a few basic things well, the land will continue to produce food for many generations. Unlike the Greeks, Romans or Mayans, who unknowingly degraded their soil until it could no longer support them, we now have a pretty good idea of what those basic things are. Sadly, despite having more awareness than many ancient civilisations, we still seem to be hurtling towards a similar fate.

I don't want to get too Malthusian, but there are some big problems within our food system. Due to the sort of meticulous long-term studies conducted at places like Rothamsted, we now know what many of those problems are, and have a few potential strategies to mitigate them. Some problems are well known and obvious. Others are hidden from view and rarely discussed, but potentially just as serious. Put simply, agriculture is putting a strain upon the air, the land, the water, the soil and every creature on Earth. The production of food has more negative impacts upon the planet than any other human activity.

Producing food is also the one thing that we cannot stop doing. Shock figures about the negative impact of agriculture are commonplace, but if we were to return to hunter-gathering, almost all of us would die a slow, lingering death, with the end being marginally delayed if we had a few spare children to eat. Rather than abandoning the field, we need to find better ways of feeding the world. We know that the impact of our diet will never be zero. It has never been zero. Even at the dawn of humanity, we were changing the natural world to put food on the table (or cave floor, but you know what I mean). For nearly four billion years, life has been altering the planet. The only difference with us is that we are aware of that impact and capable of changing for the better.

Time for the Disaster Audit

Books about the environment have a rich history of presenting a mind-boggling array of terrifying statistics to make you feel thoroughly ashamed of your behaviour. This book is no exception, and over the next few pages I intend to outline just how bad things really are when it comes to the impact of food production on the natural world. Our battle to defeat hunger has resulted in a lot of collateral damage, especially over the past two hundred years. So here, for your catastrophe-porn entertainment, is a brief cut-out-and-keep guide to just how much we have fucked up the world.

It is unlikely that we will ever change the planet as significantly as cyanobacteria managed to, but over the past seventy years we have been giving it a pretty good go. As a direct result of human activity, atmospheric carbon dioxide levels have risen by thirty percent over the past 150 years, with over half of that increase occurring since 1989. There is now a universal scientific consensus that the increases in temperature, rises in sea level and greater frequency of extreme weather events are a direct result of these increases. We know how and why this is happening and we are regularly seeing people die because of it. We also know that if we fail to act, the consequences will be nothing short of apocalyptic. But instead of changing for the better, we have continued to make things worse.

It is very easy to dismiss the effect of agriculture on climate change, largely because the impact of coal, oil, transport and construction seems far more significant when compared to the manufacture of something as essential as food. But the food we eat is responsible for around thirty percent of all human-produced greenhouse gases, and it will be impossible to address global warming without significant change.

Between one and two percent of all global energy consumption is accounted for by the production of nitrogen fertiliser through the Haber–Bosch process (all that heating and pressure requires a lot of power). This is no doubt a lot, contributing significantly to greenhouse emissions, and organic campaigners often target this as a place where energy could be saved. But considering that the Haber–Bosch process underpins about half of all food production, and we probably couldn't support a population of more than about three billion people without it, this is perhaps not such a bad return.

Around twelve percent of food system emissions come from transportation, with a smaller amount coming from manufacturing and cooking, and roughly forty percent as a direct result of farming. The remaining forty percent is accounted for by another factor that is rarely considered, which we shall come to in the next section.

Farming produces a number of greenhouse gases. There is carbon dioxide associated with fossil fuel use, such as that produced by the operation of farm machinery. There is the carbon dioxide associated with the ploughing of soil, which lets in oxygen and causes organic carbon to be 'burnt' off. There is the nitrous oxide produced when excess nitrogen fertilisers are broken down by microbes in the soil. There is the nitrous oxide and methane produced in the faeces and urine of farm animals, especially when the two are mixed, as is common in intensive farming. There is methane produced when rice is grown in flooded paddy fields, when anaerobic bacteria digest carbon without oxygen present.

And then there are the notorious burps of cows and sheep, which contain methane because of the action of the intestinal micro-organisms present in the stomachs of ruminant animals (this also includes goats, buffalo, llamas, deer, camels and a few others).

Carbon dioxide is the primary driver of climate change because there is a lot more of it in the atmosphere, but methane and nitrous oxide are many times more potent. Methane has 34 times the heat absorption capacity of carbon dioxide. Nitrous oxide has an astonishing 298 times the effect. Fortunately, neither is as stable in the atmosphere. Methane breaks down after around twelve years, nitrous oxide in a little over one hundred years, whereas carbon dioxide can stick around for centuries.[2] It is worth noting that when methane breaks down it turns into carbon dioxide and water, so it still contributes to global warming. But before panicking about that too much, most of the methane coming from cow burps and rice paddies derives from carbon dioxide in the atmosphere, captured by plants in photosynthesis, then eaten by cattle or digested by microbes. This means that it is not fossil carbon such as that produced from burning coal or oil, so does not add to the net amount of carbon in the air. The problem is only for the twelve years when it is converted into methane and adds to the overall warming effect because of its increased potency.

To simplify matters, studies into greenhouse gases tend to use figures that take into account the increased effects of methane and nitrous oxide, and also their differing stability, to produce a carbon dioxide equivalent figure. This type of analysis is occasionally problematic, but most figures regarding the greenhouse impact of agriculture will use this sort of measure.

The Fat of the Land

Around forty percent of all emissions from the agriculture industry comes from something that rarely gets as much attention, perhaps because it is not quite as memorable as bovine flatulence, and that's the amount of land being converted from natural ecosystems into food production. The destruction of natural habitats not only releases massive amounts of carbon into the atmosphere, especially when forests are burnt, but it takes away valuable carbon-absorbing plants and massively disrupts the soil, a potentially catastrophic problem that we shall come to shortly. The carbon release is particularly bad when natural peatlands are converted, as peaty soil is defined by its high level of organic carbon.

Mark Twain once advised people to 'buy land, they're not making it anymore', and the joke is starting to ring hollow. A thousand years ago, only about one to two percent of the Earth's land was dedicated to growing food. By 1700 that had grown to about four percent. Today, over a third of the Earth's land is used for food production, with eleven percent taken up with crops and twenty-four percent being used for grazing land. When all the polar regions, mountains and deserts are accounted for, it actually represents around half of all potentially vegetated land. When you add the cities, settlements, mining land, degraded areas, lakes, reservoirs and managed ecosystems, less than a quarter of the Earth's surface is free from substantial human impact. Some types of ecosystem have been lost almost completely – eighty-seven percent of the world's wetlands have been converted to agriculture since 1700, with over half of that change happening within the past hundred years.

Norman Borlaug trained as a forester and strongly advocated for the world's forests to be protected from clearance, something he believed was only achievable by increasing agricultural yields. His work certainly contributed to the protection of forests, but although the total amount of land used for agriculture has not changed that much since the Green Revolution, in reality much farmland in Europe and Russia has been abandoned, and huge amounts of virgin forest in South America, Africa and Asia are now being plundered.

As the world population has grown and yield increases of staple crops have slowed to nearly nothing, the amount of land required to grow food has been increasing every year. Since 1980, half of that extra land has been created by clearing tropical forests, some of the most diverse and ecologically important ecosystems on Earth.[3] In Brazil alone, 2.7 million hectares of Amazonian rainforest is being destroyed every year to make way for crops and grazing land. In Indonesia, another 1.3 million hectares is lost annually. In the rich forests of the Democratic Republic of the Congo, home to some of the few remaining populations of gorillas and elephants, around half a million hectares are cleared each year.

Between 2000 and 2010, a total of thirteen million hectares of forest was cleared annually around the world to create new land for farming.* Wales was formerly used as a unit of measurement to demonstrate the shocking amounts of rainforest being destroyed, but at only two million hectares, the size of that country hardly seems adequate now. Thirteen million hectares is larger than England, so perhaps that should become the new unit of shame.

Whatever the measure, it is hard to overstate the seriousness of this problem. Much of the world's most biodiverse, species-rich and ecologically important land is being destroyed forever, releasing huge amounts of carbon into the atmosphere and compromising the planet's ability to capture carbon dioxide. The problem is only increasing. In the coming years, most land use change is forecast to happen in Central and South America, Sub-Saharan Africa and Asia, the areas with most land available for conversion, but tragically, also the most diverse and species-rich. But before we get too smug in the Global North, it is worth remembering that rates of conversion in Europe and the US are only low because we have already destroyed most of our natural ecosystems and are left with a sterile, barren landscape. In the UK, around seventy percent of our land is used for producing

---

* Net loss is far less, around 5.2 million, with a fair bit of reforestation occurring, especially in Russia and Europe. But much of this is planted, managed forest, which is currently seven percent of global forest area, and does not provide the same biodiversity.

food. Across Asia that figure is around twenty-five percent, and in Africa only ten percent. In expecting the rest of the world to stop plundering land, we are asking them to forgo the changes that brought us prosperity.

The total impact has been colossal. Annually, converting natural habitats to agriculture releases around 1.6 billion tonnes of carbon into the atmosphere every year, or around eighteen percent of total global emissions.[4] Since the beginning of the Industrial Revolution, the clearing of land has released an amount of carbon equivalent to everything produced by the burning of fossil fuels over the same period.* The vast majority of that change has been collateral damage in our war against hunger.

The carbon impact of land use change is an unspoken climate disaster, with many times more impact on global warming than bovine flatulence or nitrogen fertilisers. But incredibly, things get worse.[5]

Life on Earth

As if climate change wasn't depressing enough, there are three more problems that are probably just as serious, and depending on who you speak to, perhaps even more so. All three are related to land use change, at least to some extent. Considering that environmental campaigners have had such a laser focus on energy, transport and fossil fuels consumption over the past few years, many people might consider this surprising. But just because a problem has not had much publicity doesn't mean it won't end up killing us.

The destruction of natural habitats and their conversion to agriculture have had a devastating effect on the natural world,

---

* Land use change has released around 214 ± 67 gigatons (metric) of carbon. Fossil fuels have released 270 ± 30 gigatons of carbon. So in the worst-case scenario, land use change might actually be a bigger contributor, albeit with a higher degree of uncertainty.

most notably in the reduction of species diversity. Since the dawn of human civilisation, all wild animal species have declined by eighty-five percent, marine mammals by eighty percent, plant species by fifty percent, and fish species by fourteen percent.[6] Fish might seem to have got off lightly, but this is perhaps only because humans are yet to find a way of living in the sea, and have only relatively recently started sea fishing on an industrial scale.

As a direct result of human activity, species extinctions are currently a thousand times higher than the natural background rate. Humans have been more damaging to the natural world than the asteroid that wiped out the dinosaurs, or indeed any of the five known mass extinction events that have occurred over the past 500 million years. The planet is currently experiencing a loss of species diversity as widespread, swift and catastrophic as any in its history apart from the Great Oxygenation Event (those cyanobacteria left quite a legacy for us to live up to).

In recent years, this wholesale destruction of the natural world has really gathered pace. Between 1972 and 2012, wild terrestrial vertebrate populations fell by thirty-eight percent and freshwater vertebrates by eighty-one percent. A WWF report concluded that all wild animal populations have declined by sixty percent since 1970. One third of all freshwater fish species are currently under threat of extinction. One third of all marine fish stocks are currently being unsustainably fished. It is thought that one in four of all the animals and plants on Earth are currently under threat, an estimated one million species. Even if we some-how manage to lessen our impact over the coming decades, the world is unlikely to fully recover for tens of millions of years.

The Industry of Bees

A recent report on the impact of land use change concluded that the foundations of our food system are being seriously undermined. It might seem a little counter-intuitive that the creation of new agricultural land might be undermining the food system, but the reality of agriculture is more complex than just planting seeds and watching them grow. Natural ecosystems provide many valuable resources that work in harmony with agricultural crops. They provide pollinators, soil microbes and natural predators to control invasive pests. These 'ecosystem services' are vital for food security, but they are also complex and poorly understood. They are, however, thought to be of immense value, with insect pollination alone providing a service worth around $150 billion per year to farmers around the world.[7] A recent report from the United Nations body set up to assess the state of ecosystem services estimated that the loss of forest, grassland and wetland habitats each year costs the equivalent of ten percent of the world's annual gross product.[8]

One of the most concerning trends is the widely reported global decline of pollinator species. Ninety percent of wild flowering plants depend upon insects for pollination, and when it comes to commonly eaten crops, that figure is about seventy-five percent. This high proportion does not include many of the largest providers of calories to the human population; for instance it excludes wheat, corn, potatoes and many other staples which don't require the services of pollinators; but many other important species depend upon the action of insects for both yield and quality. Between five and eight percent of world food production is thought to be attributable to pollinators.

This figure might seem low given the catastrophic headlines predicting widespread global famine if insects are allowed to decline, but pollinator-dependent species are extremely important economically, underpinning the production of many cash crops such as coffee, cocoa, almonds, cashews, coconuts, oil seeds and grapes. Pollinators play a big part in the production of many fruits, vegetables, pulses and beans, which are important for nutrition. Insects also pollinate many clovers and cover crops, which are vital for both livestock and soil health.

There are around 81 million western honeybee hives kept around the world, and these also provide vital pollination services, with farmers often paying beekeepers to visit their fields with travelling hives. When it comes to pollination, however, honeybees are important but not sufficient. Pollination requires a diverse selection of species and the most vital tend to be wild bees, of which there are thought to be around twenty thousand different species globally. It is pollinator diversity that creates resilience, which is likely to be increasingly important in a rapidly changing world.

Almost all pollinator-dependent crops are visited by wild bees of some sort, and declines are a genuine concern. In Europe, figures show that around thirty-seven percent of wild bee species are currently in decline, with some global figures indicating that forty percent are under threat. Increases in honeybee hives, which generally focus on only one or two species, cannot compensate for this. When the weather and environment are unpredictable (hello climate change), diversity becomes even more vital. Encouraging beekeeping to address pollinator decline is akin to buying house cats to save Siberian tigers.

Around the world, most pollinator-dependent crops have not seen the dramatic yield increases that other crops have benefited from over the past fifty years. This may well be due to declines in the diversity and numbers of pollinating insects. Certainly, drops in yields of many important crops are known to correspond with falls in local pollinator diversity. Declines in insect numbers have been largely driven by land use change and habitat destruction, with more minor effects from pesticides (to be discussed in the next chapter), the introduction of invasive species, increased disease transmission and a rapidly changing climate.

In recent years, the prospect of an 'insectageddon' has entered the popular consciousness, with widespread, regular reports that there will be no insects left within a hundred years, or that declines are so rapid and devastating that the world is on the edge of catastrophe. Although it is true that several recent studies have shown some serious declines, often the reporting has paid little attention to the nuance and reservations of the authors, preferring instead to focus on the 'end of life as we know it' aspects. Most studies have looked at small areas of the world, yet findings have been extrapolated beyond all recognition.

Things came to a head with a particularly grim 2019 review paper that had little subtlety or nuance in its content or reporting. It claimed to have found enough evidence to state that 'insects as a whole will go down the path of extinction in a few decades.' The author of the study told the *Guardian* that the annual rate of loss would result in no insects remaining in just a hundred years' time, something that would go on to cause the wholesale death of almost all bird and mammal species, and the complete collapse of most of the world's natural ecosystems. Once the insects are gone, that's game over for the natural world. Humanity's destructive legacy would be complete.

But this particular study received a great deal of pushback in the usually reserved entomology community. The biggest criticism of all was that it was a paper review of other studies, and the authors had specifically searched for the term 'decline', thus skewing it to only include research into insect losses, ignoring any population gains. As many scientists in the field were quick to point out, insect populations are never very stable, and cyclic changes are commonplace in response to weather and food availability. If you Google the insect apocalypse, what you find is the insect apocalypse.[9]

Many recent studies apparently predicting the end of insect life as we know it have focused on a limited number of species, or a small selection of habitats, and are usually only conducted over a short time period. Genuinely long-term studies of the sort that might show up wider population trends are few and far between. In truth, although things are probably serious, there are still no definitive studies of insect population that show worldwide declines. Such studies are difficult, expensive and incredibly challenging to carry out, especially given the complex diversity of insect life on the planet and the lack of accurate data points in the past. Despite their importance to humans, there are not enough resources being ploughed into the study of insects, meaning that the data we have easily gets blown out of proportion.

One of the few genuinely long-term investigations, not surprisingly carried out by Rothamsted Research, showed significant declines in large flies and some other large insects over thirty years, but no significant trends for other species. Even this work showed that trends were highly localised, with completely different results across regions of the UK. Whenever anyone studies insect or pollinator numbers in fine detail, a complex noisy picture emerges, with global trends nearly impossible to find.

There have definitely been declines in some iconic species but shockingly there is no global red list of endangered insects, simply because there is not enough data. Although there is evidence for some worrying bee and butterfly losses, for the majority of insect types there is no available evidence on population change. In the Northern Hemisphere there is some data on a few species, in a small number of locations. As for the Southern Hemisphere, the picture is pretty much a complete unknown. Every entomologist you speak to will almost immediately tell you (with some bitterness) that all ecology funding goes to big charismatic animals like whales, pandas and polar bears, with little attention paid to bugs, flies, bees and beetles, despite the vital services they provide to humanity.* The public have an inherent prejudice against creepy-crawlies, and this seeps through into how academic money is spent.

It is arguably good that the insectageddon narrative has weevilled its way into public consciousness, as we need to raise awareness of the importance of insects. But if this is at the expense of public trust in science, it is almost certainly not a

---

* It is also fair to say that as well as being iconic, polar bears are considerably easier to count than bees, which might be another factor explaining the better quality data.

price worth paying. The threat of mass extinctions is real, but to face it, we really need a better picture of the enemy we are fighting.

Of course, many of us remember the presence of more insect life in meadows and grassland from our youth. Or perhaps we recall how we used to scrape off large amounts of insect matter from car windscreens and headlights after long journeys. It is easy to appeal to memory and imagine the world is heading for disaster, but we must not confuse our misty perception of the past with the complex reality of ecosystem change. The aerodynamics of cars have changed dramatically, perhaps causing more insects to be deflected out of the way, rather than splattered onto the glass. Maybe the meadows were always full of noisy, diverse insect life in my childhood, but it could also be that I just vividly remember a few days when cyclic populations were at their height, much as I misremember British winters as being dusted with snow, and summer holidays being endlessly hot.[10]

There is little doubt that damage to natural habitats has caused huge disruption to ecosystems, and this has almost certainly affected pollinator numbers. But instead of being terrified about unstoppable insect declines, perhaps we should be afraid of how little we really know about the most numerous and diverse class of creatures on Earth. The destruction of insect life is neither certain nor inevitable, but that does not mean it is not a serious issue worthy of our attention.

As for the rest of life on Earth, there have been many huge and well-studied declines and these seem set to continue at an ever-increasing pace, perhaps to the point of catastrophe. Our near-insatiable demand for food has ravaged the planet, destroying homes, taking lives and scorching the land, so that nothing else can live. From where I am writing this book, I am lucky enough to look out at vast swathes of agricultural land in the East of England. Although on this bright spring day, the rich pasture and dense crops seem serene and bucolic, I am actually looking at an ecological desert, stripped and plundered long ago, leaving little more than a hydroponic medium for the production of food. Land that once supported rich, diverse oak forests is now home to just a few food crops placed there by our hand. All other life is battled against, sprayed, hunted, trapped, burnt, chopped, mowed, tilled or buried. This is the fate of much of our planet, and it comes at a terrible cost. It has caused a change that will enter the fossil record as the worst ecological collapse in over a billion years.

Although the loss of life has been immense, and the release of carbon catastrophic, even these might not be the greatest cost of all. To discover a potentially more serious and imminent threat to the future of life on this planet, I would need to leave the converted spare room that I use as an office, and take a walk out into the fields to look below the crops and pasture. Because perhaps the greatest toll of our fight against hunger is being paid by the dirt beneath our feet.[11]

The Disappearance of Dirt

The existence of much of planet Earth's complex life is hugely dependent upon a thin, fragile layer of mud smeared across its rocky surface. Soil, the curious interface between geology and biology, supports almost every land creature in some way, providing the medium in which we grow almost all of our food. Without it, the Earth would be nothing but bare rock, sand and water. The soil seems utterly constant and immutable, as intrinsic to our planet as mountains, deserts and oceans. But in reality, soil is quite different from those grand planetary features. It is a living, dynamic and limited ecosystem that it is quite possible to destroy.

Soil forms as the rocky surface of the planet is weathered down into small particles and mixes with organic matter falling from above. A combination of physical and biological forces, from freezing and thawing, to microbes, fungi, lichen and the industry of worms, causes rocks to weather and break into smaller and smaller pieces. As these rocks become broken down, new stones rise up from the bedrock, mixing with more organic matter. At the surface, this forms the porous, nutrient-rich medium that we call soil. The soil type, depth and quality depends on the type of bedrock, the climate, the mix of things living on or under the surface and the type of organic matter that falls to the ground. Soil is complex and intensely local. Soil types might vary hugely within a small area. The type of soil defines what will grow above it, but is itself defined by the plants and animals it supports. It is a tiny, fragile, broken skin that we know precious little about, often disregarded as nothing but dirt. But without it, all terrestrial life would end.

As the interface between biology and geology, the creation of new soil is a bit quicker than the shifting of continents, but not quite as rapid as an unrestricted population of blue tits. On average it will take around twenty years to make less than one millimetre of new soil. Although soil formation is very slow, within natural ecosystems this is not much of a problem, as soil erosion also happens at a very low rate. Roots and other structures hold the soil in place, and plants and animals cover it with a layer of constantly replenished organic matter. As a result, over millions of years, the amount of soil around the world reached a stable equilibrium, forming a rich, diverse and fertile covering across most of the planet's land, capable of supporting a myriad of complex plant and animal life.

And then humans came along. Perhaps the worst moment in the history of soil was the invention of tilling – the clearing of land using sticks, hoes or mattocks to turn over the top layer. This aerates and loosens the ground, allowing more plant matter and manure to be incorporated, getting rid of weeds, increasing the availability of vital nutrients and making the planting of seeds easier, all at the same time. When oxen were first domesticated around eight thousand years ago, they were enlisted to pull along basic tools such as scratch ploughs, allowing vast amounts of land to be tilled very quickly. Eventually, this led to the introduction of the turn plough, which brought deeper soil to the surface, more effectively buried weeds, and allowed many less fertile lands to be cultivated.

Ploughing hugely increased yields and massively reduced labour. Over the short term it was highly beneficial for farmers, but in the long term it could be catastrophic for the soil. Clearing and regularly exposing the bare ground leads to extremely high rates of erosion. Although most early farming was on flat fertile soils around river beds, where this wasn't too much of a problem, population growth soon pushed farms out to the slopes, where the land did not fare so well. Rain would wash the soil away in huge quantities, not only devastating future yields, but choking rivers and estuaries with silt. In temperate regions, soil loss from hilly land is around ten to twenty tonnes of soil per hectare per year, compared to formation rates of 0.15 tonnes. In tropical areas with more intense rainfall, the erosion rate is far higher, with hill farms losing around fifty tonnes per hectare per year.

As a result, many hill farms that have been cleared and ploughed for the growing of crops rapidly lose their soil, often being stripped down to bare rock within a few generations. Once this has happened, recovery is nearly impossible. Land without soil cannot be left to rewild itself, because the slow rate of soil formation means that this would take many centuries. In human terms, that land may as well be lost for ever.

The results of this damage can be seen around the world, although often it is so ancient it seems as if it is part of the land-scape. It is easy to imagine that ancient societies had a stronger connection with soil than we do today, but often they were just as short-sighted as we are, sometimes even more so. Bare rocks across the hillsides of modern-day Greece are testament to the catastrophically unsustainable farming that led to the fall of the Ancient Greek civilisation. The rocky moonscape of central Iceland was largely carpeted with dense birch forest when the island was first colonised, before clearance and overgrazing exposed the soil to the elements. The Roman Empire felled hill-side forests all across the Alps, stripping back the soil so that in many areas, only lifeless rock now remains. When humans plough sloping land to grow crops, or overstock new pasture with grazing animals, they start to mine the soil. Once that happens, there is rarely a way back.

Today, although global understanding is marginally better, the scale of the soil problem is many times worse. With modern farm machinery, land can be ploughed at a previously unimaginable rate. In many parts of the world, it is often cheaper to move onto new ground than it is to care for the soil you currently farm. As demand for food increases, more and more arable land is carved onto slopes. Ploughing and sowing techniques suited to pancake-flat European flood plains are exported to the tropics, where heavy rain more than doubles erosion rates. A recent FAO report found that all conventional farming on hilly land is completely unsustainable and will result in total soil loss. Further reports have shown that although the picture on flatter land is greatly improved, it is still heading the same way. As the US dust bowls of the 1930s showed, even on the plains, once naturally protective vegetation is cleared away and the land regularly ploughed, it can leave the soil extremely vulnerable. It is a lesson that we are taught time and time again, yet consistently fail to learn.

Around the world, soil erosion from water, wind and ploughing permanently removes between 25 and 40 billion tonnes of soil every year. Almost all of this is as a direct result of agriculture, and represents around 100,000 times more than the expected background rate of erosion. Agricultural soil is being lost at an average of 0.9 millimetres per year, over twenty times higher than the speed of replacement. And unlike the ancient civilisations before us, we are now doing this on a global scale. If the dirt beneath our feet eventually runs out, we will not be able to move on to somewhere new. Even if our ingenuity somehow manages to halt global warming, without soil, we're all going to die anyway.

Around twelve million hectares of land are lost each year to degradation and soil loss – almost the size of England – with once fertile land becoming lifeless desert or rock. This loss places further pressure on new land, and the only parts of the Earth we have yet to exploit are tropical forests. Although forests look as if they must have rich and fertile ground to support their growth, in reality the soil is often in fine balance, maintained by large deposits of organic matter from leaves, animals and plants. Take away the natural plant cover and the soil often only maintains good yields for a few years, before ploughing or overgrazing leaves it barren. Before long, the land is worthless. Farmers move on, and the chainsaws start up again.

In some areas, pasture fares slightly better than constantly ploughed arable ground when it comes to soil erosion. The USDA estimates that grazed pasture only loses around 0.1 tonnes per hectare per year, possibly within sustainable limits, whereas the average US cropland loss is about twenty-five times greater. But in many parts of the world, particularly tropical regions where overgrazing is more common, livestock are just as devastating to the soil as arable crops, kicking up dust, stripping vegetation and leaving soil exposed to the brutally erosive forces of wind and rain.

To make matters worse, around four percent of all soil on agricultural land around the world has been further degraded by compaction, with increasingly large agricultural machinery squashing it beyond use in Europe and North America, and overgrazing of cattle doing the same throughout Asia and Africa. But even this devastating erosion and compaction are not the most urgent and serious problems when it comes to soil. Because over the past sixty years or so, the ground beneath our feet has started to die.

The Dying of Dirt

Despite its vital role in supporting life, there is probably a little bit too much romantic mysticism surrounding our relationship with soil. Some people feel it to be a living, breathing, conscious thing that they have an intense connection with, and these are definitely not the sort of people you want to get stuck in a conversation with at a party. But to give them credit, soil is teeming with life. Billions of invisible microbes give soil a complex, porous structure, producing mucus-like secretions very similar to the ones that cyanobacteria used to climb up towards the Sun on their muddy stromatolites. In soil, this structure performs many vital functions when it comes to plant growth, creating tiny, interconnected pores in which air, water, dirt and plant roots can mix. It holds on to moisture long enough for roots to drink. It keeps nutrients from running away, allowing plants access to the vital elements required for life. Four-billion-year-old microbial snot is the difference between soil and dust. It supports almost all the terrestrial life we see around us, including our own. It turns soil into the world's largest water filter and storage tank, providing the foundation of almost all of the world's food production.

Norman Borlaug once said that 'as far as plants are concerned, they can't tell whether that nitrate ion comes from artificial chemicals or from decomposed organic matter.' This is entirely true. Plants are fairly simple in their nutritional needs, requiring water, CO_2, sunlight and just a few nutrients from the soil. They do not really appreciate it if those nutrients are locked up in some sort of complex biological structures, which is the case with the organic matter that falls to the ground in forests, or when manure is used as fertiliser. Before inorganic fertilisers could provide nitrogen, phosphorus and potassium directly, plants' simple nutritional needs were entirely met by the action of soil microbes on complex organic matter. For millions of years it had been the job of these microbes to break down anything dead into the simple forms that plants can use, with plant roots producing carbon-rich 'extrudates' to feed the microorganisms in return. As a result, soil microbes, mostly combinations of bacteria, fungi and lichens, flourished and grew in synergy with plants.

As man-made inorganic fertilisers started to bypass the action of these microbes, the experiment that started with the work of John Bennet Lawes and hugely accelerated during the Green

Revolution, problems started to emerge. The nutrients that plants need are not the same as those that feed soil bacteria and so, as inorganic fertiliser use has increased, microbial soil activity has started to fall. Unlike plants, which capture carbon dioxide from the air, many soil microbes need alternative sources of carbon to flourish. In reality we don't really know that much about their exact nutritional needs. But what we do know is that most arable land has lost over seventy percent of its soil carbon in the past fifty years or so, which has suddenly made it a very inhospitable place for our microbe friends. We have cut out the middleman, and now he is dying.

Ploughing only exacerbates this problem. Allowing oxygen into the soil burns off carbon, reducing the amount available and releasing carbon dioxide into the atmosphere. It also breaks up the long mycelial structures produced by fungi, making it harder for them to colonise regularly ploughed soils and so altering the microbial population. As these fungi are thought to play a vital role in soil structure and fertility, this further degrades the soil.

With fewer microbes and less carbon, soil all around the world has started to lose its structure and fertility. Dirt is rapidly turning into dust, unable to hold on to water or nutrients. Valuable nutrients leach away, often devastating local environments. Because there is so much run-off, fertilisers need to be applied in ever-larger quantities, just so some can stick around long enough to reach the plants they are intended for. Too much fertiliser can also lead to acidification of the soil, causing even greater loss of fertility. The more we try to compensate for the dying of the soil, the worse the impact becomes. These cracks are becoming ever deeper, threatening to swallow up the yield gains of the Green Revolution.

In the past two hundred years, between seventy and ninety billion tonnes of carbon have been released into the atmosphere from the soil, a significant but rarely mentioned contributor to climate change. The worst culprits for this carbon release are wealthier countries, with their high-input, mechanised and

super-efficient arable farming systems, reliant on chemical fertilisers and rarely returning any organic matter to the land. But all
around the world, soil degradation is being driven by unsustainable management of crop and grazing lands. We are stuck in a
deadly race to the bottom, degrading soil so it loses its fertility
and structure, allowing unsustainable erosion to occur on an
enormous scale, seeing huge falls in productivity and allowing
the desert to encroach into farmland. All this leads to more land
being cleared and ever more soil being degraded. Eventually, if
we go on as we are, there will be nothing left.

Professor John Crawford is Science Director at Rothamsted
Research, studying how the integrated soil-plant-microbe system
affects the productivity and resilience of food production. He
told me, 'If you want to fix one thing, fix the soil. It is a risk hub.
If you want to address water security, food security, you need to
fix the soil, feed it better, introduce more mixed production.'
Every soil scientist I spoke to in researching this book agrees. If
there is one thing that world food production needs to address in
order to be sustainable into the future, it is the soil. Compared to
climate change and biodiversity, soil degradation is rarely spoken
of, but if we do not focus on it soon, the price we will end up
paying will be colossal.

Borlaug's project to transform agriculture was essential to stave
off the threat of mass starvation, but major cracks are now starting
to emerge. The biggest of these cracks is in the soil. In focusing
solely on the needs of plants, the microbes that support all growth
have slowly died. The soil that they held together for so long has
started to crumble, only to be blown or washed away for ever. For
thousands of years, invisible organisms that we never knew existed
have kept the soil alive and in place. It is ironic that not so long
after we discovered them, we have allowed them to die.

Many opponents of the Green Revolution will claim that this
sort of soil dieback was inevitable. But it was not the application
of inorganic fertilisers that stripped the soil of life. It was simply
that in focusing on the plants that feed us, we neglected the

microbes that keep those plants alive. If an efficient way can be found to feed them too, then the soil might be saved. The world badly needed a Green Revolution back in the 1960s, and scientists and innovators swiftly delivered one. Now, we might just need a Brown Revolution to save us once again.

There is hope. Experiments at Rothamsted have shown that even soil left bare and degraded for fifty years still has a diverse microbial presence. The microbes are just locked down into survival mode, and once the soil is fed with organic matter, structure is quick to return. But there is also much that we do not know. The nutritional needs of soil microbes are complex and poorly understood. The soil microbiome is proving to be as mysterious and unfathomable as the one within our gut, and there is even some evidence that it may have an influence on our own internal microbiome, perhaps suggesting that changes in the soil might have an impact on human health. There is also some tentative research showing that signalling between soil microbes and plant roots might affect plant growth and influence crop yields, opening up new avenues for increasing the efficiency of food production.

Improved land management can also increase the amount of carbon stored within the soil, which has the potential to pull huge amounts of greenhouse gases permanently out of the sky. Even after all the degradation and loss, there is still many times more carbon held in the soil than there is in the atmosphere, and many times more than in all terrestrial life, including plants. Soil's potential for carbon capture is immense and largely untapped, and using it in this way would almost certainly improve the health of its microbes at the same time.

Sadly, one of the most ironic and surprising effects of the Green Revolution was to alter the priorities of global food system research. The complacency caused by increased yields and improved food security meant that little funding went towards agricultural science in the 1970s, 1980s and 1990s, whilst resources were increasingly diverted towards studying the ecology of natural systems. Soil science centres disappeared from several major universities, whilst agricultural colleges concentrated on mechanisation, efficiency and pest control. In more recent times, focus has returned to the soil, particularly after droughts in 2007 and 2008 led to severe food insecurity in a number of politically unstable parts of the globe. We must hope that this increased focus yields swift results. If not, there is a chance that the dirt beneath our feet might be lost forever. But if it can be treated well, it might be turned into carbon capturing, water retaining, sustainably productive gold.[12]

Soil is uniquely vital to so many aspects of our existence, yet with our modern sanitised lives, most of us are now utterly disconnected from it. Unlike water, food or the air that we breathe, few of us come into daily contact with the dirt that sustains everything that we do. When it does cross our path, we battle against it, washing it obsessively off our hands and making every effort to keep it from our homes. Vast industries have grown dedicated to ridding our lives of dirt, with much of humanity now seeing it as a problem to be solved, not a solution to our woes.

Strangely, it seems that if we can learn to respect the dirt and feed it properly, it might just be the thing that helps save us from ourselves.

Spilling Over

One of the worst effects of soil degradation is the damage to its ability to hold water. Remove the fine, interconnected, porous structure held in place by microbial snot and water simply pours through, meaning that more and more has to be added so that plants can grow. A lack of soil structure also increases run-off, with not only water, but also nutrients and fertilisers being washed into water courses. This excess of nutrients is known as eutrophication, and it causes harmful blooms of algae that can devastate aquatic ecosystems. Nitrogen and phosphorus availability usually limits algal growth, so when simple, readily available forms are added directly to the water, it's party time for algae. Thick carpets of green slime rapidly coat the surface of rivers and lakes. This overgrowth blocks out light, causing aquatic plants to wither and die in the darkness below. When the algae eventually run out of nutrients, they start to decompose, stripping the water of oxygen and choking fish and other lifeforms.

When nutrients flow from rivers into the sea, the results can be equally devastating. Some species of marine algae can cause the infamous red tides when high levels of nitrogen and phosphorus reach them, devastating marine life. Red tide algae produce toxins that poison the food chain, killing everything from the smallest fish to apex predators. In 2018, marine life was devastated across Florida's Gulf Coast by a red tide, thought to be caused by run-off from highly subsidised sugar plantations. I was in Florida whilst the event was at its height and witnessed dead sea turtles, dolphins, manatees, goliath groupers and countless fish washed up on the shores every day. The wind blew in an acrid, burning stench that meant no one could stay on the beach for long. Despite poisoned fish piling up several feet deep, the local scavenging animals knew to keep a distance, with tonnes of toxic fish left to rot in the Florida sun.

Excess nitrogen in the sea is also thought to be the major contributor to an increasing number of 'dead zones' in the world's oceans. Since the 1950s, dead zones covering thousands of square kilometres have formed annually in the Gulf of Mexico, caused by nitrogen run-off from agricultural land in the American Midwest. There are now hundreds of these zones around the world, always situated near areas of high population density and intensive agricultural production, placing huge stress on marine ecosystems.[13]

It is thought that 95 million tonnes of nitrogen and up to seven million tonnes of phosphorus enter water systems every year, all running off from farmland. This is a waste of energy, resources and effort, but it is also causing huge damage to the natural world. Our food system has developed in a way that makes fertiliser essential and extremely cheap, which means that even when millions of tonnes run off into waterways, it still makes economic sense. The most wasteful and polluting farmers will often produce the highest yields and make the biggest profits, providing us with the cheap food that we crave and that subsidies incentivise. But the food they produce is only cheap because the natural world is picking up so much of the cost.

Running Dry

Whilst most of us think of water conservation as starting in the home, in reality only about twelve percent of all the fresh water used globally actually goes directly towards human consumption. Eighteen percent is used in industry, and the remaining seventy percent is used in agriculture. Increasingly, partly driven by degradation of the soil and partly by the increasing population, there has been enormous pressure on fresh water systems. In many parts of the world, these systems are already near breaking point.

Dr Richard Green studies the evolution of agricultural technology at Harper Adams University, one of the UK's most important agricultural colleges, set in a working farm in Shropshire. He told me:

> Agriculture is facing a number of challenges around the world, but the biggest of these is water. If you have water, energy and soil, you can pretty much grow crops anywhere, and in many parts of the world water is the limiting factor. Over the past thirty or forty years, increases in agricultural production have been driven by fossil water, irrigation based on pumping water out of the ground from aquifers. But this is depleting water faster than it is being replaced. By 2050, a lot of systems will run out of water, and this is being exacerbated by climate change.

As an increasing amount of water is being pumped out of underground aquifers, in many cases this is drawing seawater in to replace it, something that eventually renders these reserves useless. Combined with more and more land being converted to food production and an increased chance of drought caused by climate change, this means that water is perhaps the biggest immediate pressure on our ability to feed the world's people. By 2025, it is thought that all of South and Central America, all of Africa and the Middle East, and much of North America will be running out of fresh water. The biggest impact of these shortages will be on our ability to grow food.

It is thought that the planet can provide us with somewhere between 2,800 km^3 and 4,000 km^3 of fresh water every year. Although our consumption is still short of this upper limit, it is already around 2,000 km^3. With rising populations and a warming world, this figure is increasing all the time. Crucially, supplies of fresh water are not evenly distributed, meaning that many will feel the effects long before the upper limit is reached. Plenty of countries have more fresh water than they will ever use, but others are already dangerously short. In Sub-Saharan Africa, where European agricultural subsidies meant that crucial irrigation projects never happened, the situation is already dangerously close to crisis.

Only around sixteen percent of crops currently depend upon lakes, aquifers or rivers for water, the rest relying almost entirely on the rain. But if we are to continue to feed people in a globally changing climate, this figure is certain to rise, with rainfall increasingly unreliable. Where all the extra water will come from is currently anyone's guess. Like many of these issues, we are leaving things incredibly late before deciding how to address them.

What Now?

In summary, in our quest to fight hunger we have utterly ruined the planet, causing damage so significant that it will be etched onto the geological record until the Sun finally swallows us up in a supernova in seven billion years' time. Before then, when highly evolved ant palaeontologists (or perhaps crows, I genuinely think that crows are up to something) look back on the effect that humans had on the planet, they will see us as a violently destructive force, greedily gobbling up resources without a thought for the future. We have already been the most damaging single species in history, and there is a strong argument that we are only just getting started.

Whether we boil, drown, starve or die of thirst hardly matters any more. Our toxic disregard for the planet's natural resources has sealed our fate. Although I like to think of myself as an optimist regarding the future, it is hard to look at the destruction we have wreaked and not feel shame, or an urgent desire to put things right. At the very least, we should be worrying about these things a lot more than we currently do.

But this is the most curious thing of all about climate change, land use, ecosystem loss, soil erosion and the limits of water. However much we seem to know about it, and however loud campaigners shout, motivation is still incredibly hard to come by. I have spent the past few years looking at the grim details of our food system, and I only present the tiniest fraction of those details here. A few catastrophe highlights, presented in summary to set up the second half of the book. Yet even I feel disconnected from it, as if it is happening somewhere else. It is as if I somehow still believe that we will just hop across into the next field once this one is dead, despite knowing just how impossible that is.

For most of our history, especially the part when we have had enough food, humanity has convinced itself that it has a plan. A place in the world, a reason to exist, a motivation beyond just survival. Beyond religion and spirituality, this quest for progress has motivated human endeavour for thousands of years. We live safe in the knowledge that on our deathbeds, those that surround and succeed us will have more freedom, more opportunity, less hunger and less disease. Humanity is an enormous collective effort to ensure our children suffer a little bit less than we had to.

But the more our scientific advances have allowed us to glimpse the future, the more our grand project seems to be built on sand. The idea that we might be handing over a broken world, with knackered soil, toxic air, vanishing water and sterile seas is perhaps too much for us to take in. Predictions of increased famine, floods, drought and conflict do not fit with the story we tell ourselves, one of a supposedly selfless quest for something better. So most of us choose to ignore the future, flying around the world when we get the chance, turning the heating up when it's cold, and buying the fastest car we can afford.

Protests against climate change are met with a collective sigh. Passionate campaigners such as Greta Thunberg are derided and openly mocked in the media. Documentaries about habitat destruction are watched with interest whilst eating ice creams made from unsustainable palm oil. Protests against inaction on water stress or soil erosion are still virtually unheard of, despite the very real threat they pose. We are all sat on the deck of the good ship Ambivalence, gawping and staring at the deadly rocks up ahead. Changing course looks like such hard work, and it is still pretty nice sitting up here. No one wants to be the first person to get in a lifeboat – you'll look silly, sitting there on your own.

So we sit up on deck watching the danger edge ever closer, trying to enjoy the view. Surely the Captain will turn around soon. But the boat just keeps on the same course, and eventually we will have to accept that no one is really in control. None of us wants to admit that the unaffordable holiday we booked is going badly. So we hold on grimly, desperately hoping someone else will turn this stupid boat around. The problem is, a few of the rocks are already underneath us, scratching up against the hull. At some point, we know that these rocks are going to pierce through. Then we will all have to sit up and take notice, and presumably try to do something about it. In the next chapter we are going to look at just where and how this might happen.

6

The Outer Limits

> We have become, by the power of a glorious evolutionary accident called intelligence, the stewards of life's continuity on Earth. We did not ask for this role, but we cannot abjure it. We may not be suited to it, but here we are.
>
> – Stephen Jay Gould

Although we have mainly focused on population growth so far, there is potentially a far bigger problem when it comes to our ability to feed ourselves, which concerns a different kind of growth. The world economy just keeps on growing, meaning that even if the population were to reach a plateau tomorrow (which it definitely won't), we would still make more and more stuff every year. Although we only have one stomach each, this increase even applies to the food we eat. Perhaps unsurprisingly, the richer people become, the more food they consume, but they are also increasingly likely to choose more resource intensive diets. As we shall see in the next chapter, growing a kilogram of cereal crops has a lot less impact upon the planet than growing a kilogram of meat, and meat is the one thing that people tend to demand a lot more of as their affluence increases.

The global economy grows by about three to four percent annually, and this means that it will double every twenty years. Imagine all the pointless shit we make today – all the pollution, the excess, the dirty coal-fired power, the waste, the plastic – then double it, and that's what things are going to be like in 2040. We have already driven a million species to the edge of extinction. We have pumped so much carbon dioxide into the air that we have set humanity on the path to a climate catastrophe. We have degraded most of the soil, poisoned the seas, and are on the brink of running out of fresh water. Yet we are set to double the size of our impact over the next two decades. And in another twenty years, we'll double it again.

A 2060 economy four times as big as the one we have today seems impossible, and of course the likelihood is that much future growth will come from more sustainable technologies. Yet that does not stop many campaigners suggesting that humanity's quest for economic advancement is the greatest source of danger to the planet, and that immediately curtailing it is the only sensible way forward. For instance, the 2019 report into species extinction from the International Panel of Experts on Sustainable Food Systems called for governments to steer away from 'the limited paradigm of economic growth'.[1] The writer and environmental campaigner George Monbiot has frequently called for an end to growth, claiming, perhaps with some justification, that 'it is hard to see how it can ever be decoupled from the assault on the living planet.'[2]

As the economist Dieter Helm explains in his book *Natural Capital*, there are two problems with calls for a zero growth economy. The first is that it is not desirable. The second is that it is never going to happen. For a start, if the economy stops growing but the population continues to rise, that means that the majority of people in the world will end up being considerably less well off. For most people living in the Global North this would be an inconvenience. But an awful lot of people around the globe are still desperately poor, and a drop in income might pull them under completely. It is easy for rich campaigners to suggest that we could make do with less, but there are already over 800 million people who regularly don't have enough food to eat. And even for those who are not yet starving, it is neither fair nor realistic to expect the six billion people in the world that are considerably poorer than you not to want a life a bit more like yours. As Helm rightly notes, resisting growth reflects a lack of desire to engage with the world as it is, and is destined to achieve nothing. Many of us aren't even prepared to sacrifice our own foreign holidays, let alone see our children go hungry.

So given that we seem irreversibly set to grow in both number and wealth over the coming years, the challenge facing humanity is this. By 2050, we will need to produce over fifty percent more food than we do today, with some estimates suggesting that we will require as much as a hundred percent more.[3] Also by 2050, food production alone will be releasing around 15 billion tonnes of carbon dioxide annually, enough to exceed the entire Paris Agreement Targets.[*] So in the unlikely event that transport, energy, industry and construction reduce their emissions to zero over the next thirty years (spoiler alert – they definitely won't), just keeping us fed will cause two degrees of global warming all on its own.[4] Changing the way we eat might not be sufficient in the fight against global warming, but it is definitely essential.

Even if we can keep temperatures down to two degrees of warming, there are huge problems ahead. Just keeping up with the demand for food will require us to chop down all of the world's forests over the next thirty years, as this is the only realistic source of the 600 million hectares of new agricultural land required to keep people from going hungry.[†] By 2050 it is estimated that less than ten percent of land will be free from human impact, mostly just the uninhabitable and unproductive bits like deserts, mountains, tundra and the shrinking polar regions.[5] Every forest on Earth will be gone within most of our lifetimes. And even this horrific scenario depends upon agricultural yields

---

[*] The Paris Agreement was signed in 2016 by 196 countries and sets out targets with the goal of keeping global temperature increases below 2 °C.
[†] That's forty-six Englands. Or perhaps two Indias, as we are likely to have moved on to new units by then.

increasing at the same rate as they are today. It is widely predicted that due to land degradation and the effects of rising temperatures, global crop yields are set to decline by around ten percent. In many regions, particularly tropical areas where droughts and extreme temperatures will become more common, yields are set to drop by half.

As for water, demand is set to increase by more than fifty percent by 2050, despite the fact that much of the world is already close to capacity. Pesticide and fertiliser use, already causing devastating harm to waterways and biodiversity, is set to double. The capacity of the world's rangelands to support livestock is predicted to diminish significantly, with even greater swathes of land being lost forever to soil degradation. The worst effects are likely to be experienced by the world's poorest and most vulnerable people. Drylands, those most susceptible to desertification, are currently home to around 2.7 billion of the world's least affluent, and this population is set to grow to around 4 billion over the next thirty years. It is also predicted that extreme weather events, including droughts, flooding, hurricanes and storms, will increase significantly, with a potentially devastating effect on food security.

In a seemingly prescient warning of the disastrous road up ahead, in 2017, the Svalbard Global Seed Vault was flooded by meltwater caused by freakishly high summer temperatures. The facility, inspired by the work of Nikolai Vavilov, who we met earlier, holds hundreds of thousands of crop seed varieties, buried deep within a mountain on an island just above the Arctic Circle. It was designed to keep seeds frozen for a millennium, providing a lifeline for humanity in the event of an ecological collapse. Yet just nine years after construction, it was breached by weather so extreme the designers had failed to predict it.

There is absolutely no chance that our food system will continue to feed the world up until 2050 without significant, fundamental change. Perhaps a few nations in the Global North could attempt to pull up the drawbridge, protecting themselves and allowing everyone else to starve. Despite causing overall productivity to fall, climate change will probably lead to yield increases in some regions, particularly Northern Europe and Canada. But given how interconnected our food systems are, it seems unlikely that anyone will be able to isolate themselves from the devastation. Somehow, we need to find a way to change things, otherwise the Reverend Malthus might finally be proven right.

The Famine Today

Even today, the picture is far from rosy. We currently have quite staggering levels of food inequality: 821 million of the world's people are undernourished – around one person in every nine; in 2015, 155 million children aged under five had stunted growth caused by inadequate diets, while 52 million children were suffering from wasting due to acute starvation; and a quarter of people living in Sub-Saharan Africa suffered from chronic food deprivation in 2017.[6]

Even when people are getting enough calories to eat, often their diets are inadequate. Micronutrient deficiencies are the most common cause of non-communicable disease worldwide. They affect over 1.5 billion people, with women, children and adolescent girls at the greatest risk. Around one in three women of reproductive age are thought to be anaemic due to a lack of iron in their diet. Of all the women suffering from a food crisis around the world, twenty percent are likely to be pregnant.

The overall cost of malnutrition is thought to be around $3.5 trillion per year. Undernutrition accounts for forty-five percent of all deaths of children under five.[7] The slow creep of hunger strips away the human potential of billions of people, and is one of the biggest barriers to global progress. Those who should be using their minds and hands to improve the countries they live in are tied up in a constant battle to keep their families fed.

Climate change exacerbates all of these problems and is already impacting daily upon people's ability to feed themselves.

In 2017, extreme weather events, mostly droughts, caused food crises affecting 39 million people. In the same year, floods across South Asia devastated rice output, causing thousands to go without.

Gernot Laganda is Chief of Climate Disaster Risk at the World Food Programme. He told me:

> We respond to food emergencies, which is the prevailing business model of humanitarian organisations, but I see it hitting a wall very quickly. Achieving zero hunger by 2030 will soon be out of our reach if we do not take concrete actions to manage climate risk more effectively. People are falling back into poverty and the number of hungry people is not declining. Climate change is here, and it is playing out in real time. It is a humanitarian issue now, not just an environmental or development one. If you go to the Horn of Africa or the Sahel region, you will see hunger and people living in a world where risk is rising due to climate change.

When I asked him why the risks posed by climate change are often hidden from view and rarely translate into action, he said:

> Gradual risks are not widely reported on by the media – soil erosion, salinity in costal lands, melting glaciers, pest infestations. These things are often not visible to those involved in traditional humanitarian aid. $1 in risk reduction can save up to $3 of humanitarian aid down the line, but all too often there is still a choice we are forced into between saving a starving child and planting a tree. Risk management reduces humanitarian needs, but in a constrained financial environment the available budget will always need to be prioritised for humanitarian efforts.

The biggest change in food systems over the past sixty years has been globalisation and the linking of international trade. If we consider the current food system a truly global one, then perhaps what we are seeing now is the beginning of the first worldwide famine. Remember that famine is not everyone going hungry because of a bad crop. It is poor people going without food due to injustice, political incompetence, corruption and inequitable distribution of resources. Remember, too, that we should not expect starvation to be the biggest killer during a famine. The real horror of food shortage is disease. Insufficient diets leave billions with poorly functioning immune systems; 2.1 billion lack access to clean water, and 1.4 million die every year from waterborne pathogens.

Even if there is enough food today, poor people cannot access it, and many of them are dying as a result. In six of the eleven years up to 2018, we consumed more food than we produced, indicating that our food system is currently resting on a knife-edge.[8] There is little in the way of a buffer should we experience any problems, and with an increasingly unstable climate, frequent and ever-larger ones are inevitable. Maybe our food system is already starting to fail, and it is easy for many of us to ignore it because the failure is only killing the world's poorest people. Just like the Chinese government officials in the 1960s, we choose to believe the reports telling us that everything is just fine, and the world is getting richer. Instead of investing in technology that might stem this tide of death, we develop folding screens for our phones, find new methods of extracting fossil fuels, and fire sports cars into space. Maybe the damage caused by increasingly regular climate shocks will be the thing that finally tips us over the edge, forcing us to admit that the time of plenty is over.

Future Shocks

It seems increasingly likely that the upper limit on our ability to prevent hunger will be the land available, a limit we are likely to hit over the next few decades. But worryingly, there are a few other possible ends to the road.

As discussed already, plants need a selection of nutrients to grow, along with soil, water and sunlight. We will always have plenty of sunlight, and although the availability of fresh water is a serious issue that needs addressing, it is possible to produce it from the sea as long as we have plenty of energy.[9] There are many large-scale desalination plants around the world doing exactly this in places like California, Western Australia, Bahrain, Kuwait, Oman, Saudi Arabia and Israel, removing the salt from seawater to free it up for agricultural use. There are also an increasing number of smaller-scale desalination plants appearing around the African coastline, with the potential to provide sustainable fresh water from solar energy alone.[10]

But the water issue is still likely to be an immense and life-threatening problem in Sub-Saharan Africa over the next few years, due to a perfect storm of poor irrigation infrastructure, rocketing population, degraded soil and rising temperatures. Achim Dobermann was until recently the Chief Executive of Rothamsted Research, overseeing a wide range of projects to develop more sustainable agriculture, and working with the United Nations on the implementation of their Sustainable Development Goals. He sees water in Africa as one of the key challenges facing the world's food system. He explained to me that 'one thing that must happen in Africa is irrigation, but at the moment, investment in large-scale irrigation projects is a no-no. The problem is that finance is simply not available for huge infra-structure projects of this kind, and it often affects natural land-scapes. But I just cannot see how Africa can produce more crops without it.'

Water shock will almost certainly kill a lot of people over the next few years, especially in this region, but there are technical solutions, and these are becoming both cheaper and more envi-ronmentally attractive. The only real barriers are cost, political apathy and justified fears of a future where access to something widely seen as a human right suddenly becomes an expensive privilege. But we can be fairly confident that with the vastness of the world's oceans and an awful lot of fossil fuels left in the ground to exploit, water will not be the thing that places an upper limit on humanity's growth.

As already discussed, over the very long term, soil loss is probably many times harder to address. We are using it up far quicker than it can be replaced, and without it, complex life on land cannot survive. Although we could grow plants hydroponically, bypassing the need for soil completely, this is currently only feasible for a small number of high-value, low-volume crops. The question is, exactly how long do we have left?

In 2014, the UK periodical *Farmers Weekly* reported that there were a hundred harvests remaining in UK soils before yields collapsed, extrapolating the results of a Sheffield University study into allotment soils. In 2015, in a speech made at the UN's FAO, it was claimed that there were only sixty harvests left globally, although the original source of this figure is uncertain. In 2017, the UK environment secretary Michael Gove claimed that the UK was thirty to forty years away from the 'eradication of soil fertility', although again it is not clear where this number came from. In the years since, all these figures have been repeated numerous times in many different publications around the world.[11]

However much the media might demand apocalyptic headlines, predicting a date for the collapse of world harvests based on soil degradation or erosion is nearly impossible, and is not something any respectable soil scientist would attempt.* That does not mean that things are not serious. People are dying today because of desertification and soil loss. Rather than dying a sudden, dramatic death, in some places the soil will slowly, almost imperceptibly ebb away. Yet in others, it will probably remain productive for centuries.

Dr Anna Krzywoszynska is a Director at the Sheffield Institute for Sustainable Food and researches the social science of soil.

---

* Trust me, I have tried to persuade several of them for the purposes of this book.

She describes herself as a scholar of facts, not a producer of facts, although given that her work sheds some fascinating light on the complex interactions between soil science, politics, agriculture and history, I am not sure I agree with her understatement. Regarding the regular media forecasts of the number of harvests remaining in the soil, she told me that the spread of numbers can be very powerful, particularly the hundred harvest figure, which comes from a misunderstanding of a piece of research that keeps on being repeated: 'What it misses is that when it comes to soils, everything is local and everything is complicated. Erosion in the peat soils of the Fens is not going to happen in the same way as erosion in the clay soils around York. All around the world, soils are diverse and heterogeneous.'

When I asked her what is most frustrating about the way soil science is reported in the media, she told me that a lot of the discussion regarding soils misses almost everything, and that modern farming methods have evolved to remove soil from the equation completely. In the past, soil has been seen as a source of problems, and it is only quite recently that attempts have been made to try to reinsert soil into food production. But even now, she believes that we are often missing the mark:

> When we talk about soil quality, it is always in relation to a desired land use. We should instead be putting soils first, and talking about possible land uses in relation to the available soil. We need to start thinking about soils in a different way, and start to understand what it would mean to produce food in a way that supports the needs of soil, rather than making soil support the needs of agriculture. We need to think about what soil needs from farming, rather than what farming needs from soil.

The future probably doesn't lie in a single grand solution. It certainly doesn't lie in condemning farmers, who in my experience are more connected to the land than any of us. The future of improving soil health will probably be a thoroughly boring combination of hard work, clever insight and appropriate, locally based interventions. If we do solve the many problems of the soil, it is likely that this will happen so slowly and incrementally that it won't make the headlines anywhere in the world.

So what else might finish off humanity?

Thanks to Fritz Haber, we can now pull nitrogen out of the sky, and there is so much of it up there that we will never run out. Plants also need lots of carbon, but this comes from atmospheric carbon dioxide, and the main problem with that at the moment is that we have too much of it. Next on the list are potassium and phosphorus, and the availability of these essential elements is a source of much debate. But one thing is for sure. If we ever do run out, the consequences will be catastrophic.

In 2012, in a letter to the science periodical *Nature*, the financier Jeremy Grantham outlined the potential seriousness of this problem. In warnings reminiscent of William Crookes's 1898 speech, Grantham claimed that there were limited reserves of both potassium and phosphorus, and if we did not start to reduce usage of them drastically in chemical fertilisers over the next twenty to forty years, we would begin to starve.[12]

The problem he outlined is this. Humanity has been using plants to extract these minerals from the soil for a very long time, and only comparatively recently have we stopped returning them back there. Much of our potassium and phosphorus is now excreted in our urine and faeces, and ultimately flushed into waterways, before flowing out to sea. Once there, it cannot be retrieved, as it gets diluted away for ever. As a result, we have to obtain more potassium and phosphorus from mineral reserves and add these back into the soil in order for plants to grow.

Most of the world's potassium reserves, known as potash, are located in Canada and Eastern Europe. Almost all of the world's phosphorus reserves are located in Morocco. The reserves in these locations are limited and running out, with, according to

the letter, only around forty years' worth left. Grantham, someone who has made extraordinary amounts of money predicting
resource bubbles over the years, describes this as 'the most
important quasi-monopoly in history'.

If these predictions come to pass, it will make the rest of this
book somewhat irrelevant. Even climate change will be the least
of our worries if we flush all of the world's remaining phosphorus
down the toilet over the next thirty years. Crops would fail en
masse and almost all agriculture would cease. There would be
mass starvation on a scale far beyond anything we have seen. No
technological fix or clever last-minute replacement could provide
an alternative. Potassium and phosphorus are intrinsic to all life.
We cannot capture them from the sky, and reclaiming them from
the sea is probably impossible. The chemists will not be able to
save the world this time. Although, as it turns out, the geologists
just might.

Although many people share Grantham's fears, and calls for
recycling of human waste onto agricultural land are probably
wise, others have been critical of his Malthusian pessimism.
Most notably, the highly respected energy, resource and environmental researcher Vaclav Smil accused Grantham of making a
number of mistakes in his assessment of the phosphorus and
potassium issues, and the environmental writer Tim Worstall
described Grantham as making 'schoolboy errors' in his calculations. The confusion lies in the difference between reserves and
resources. Or to put it more simply, the difference between dirt
and ore.[13]

The difference between these two things is perhaps surprisingly an economic rather than a natural one. Dirt and rocks
around the world contain a variety of substances in differing
quantities. Pick up a handful from your back garden, and the
likelihood is that it contains all manner of valuable minerals and
metals, just in quantities so small it would be impossible to make
money extracting them. Ore is just profitable dirt, particularly
when geologists apply for it to be classified as such. The known

reserves of potassium and phosphorus might indeed run out over the next forty years or so, but way before then it will become financially prudent to search for the same substances elsewhere. Geologists will look at dirt around the world for particularly rich sources, and if they calculate that money can be made extracting minerals from it, it will magically transform into ore.*

It is highly likely that there are many rich reserves of phosphorus and potassium; it is just that as there are currently several years' worth of the good stuff left, it does not make economic sense to look elsewhere yet. In fact, most minerals only have enough proven reserves to last thirty to forty years, simply because it costs a lot of money to discover new ones and prove their viability to the satisfaction of mining regulators. When reserves run low enough, prospectors will magically turn dirt into ore, probably in quantities just large enough to last for a generation or so. To spend money prospecting for more would make no sense.

The most conservative estimates of phosphorus and potassium reserves indicate that we actually have a few hundred years' worth left, more than most other minerals. Estimates of total resources are harder to obtain and inherently much more speculative, but they tend to push this figure way higher, perhaps into the thousands of years. And the total amount of potassium and phosphorus present in the Earth's crust would suggest there is enough of each element to last millions of years, just so long as new ways of extraction can be discovered. If we are still around by then, we may even have worked out how to filter those elements out of the sea.

This indicates that phosphorus and potassium will perhaps not be the things that place a limit on humanity's growth, or at least not whilst we have the energy and technologies to discover and extract them. As an investor such as Grantham should

---

* Geologists don't just wander around randomly, but use their knowledge and experience to narrow the search. Most of us never paid much attention in Geography at school, but given that it would have equipped us to transform dirt into money, perhaps we should have.

presumably know, if resources are likely to become severely limited in the future, the price tends to increase now rather than later, especially if those substances underpin all of the world's food production. All indications seem to show that the price of these valuable agricultural minerals is not increasing. If Morocco really did have a monopoly on a factor that could limit all agriculture, it would probably be the economy to watch over the next few years. The reality, although a concern, seems to be very different.

It is vitally important, however, that this good news does not distract us from the need to act. NPK fertilisers, containing nitrogen, phosphorus and potassium, have underpinned increases in agricultural yields since the 1960s, and it is a huge positive that they are not likely to run out any time soon. But their use comes at a cost to the world in terms of both energy and pollution. We should make every attempt to limit how much gets sprayed, prevent run-off, maintain soil, recycle waste, and maximise how efficiently nutrients are incorporated into our food.

The idea that the end of potassium or phosphorus is nigh is a powerful call to action, a subtle mistruth that might prompt action. In his letter to *Nature*, Grantham, a passionate environmental campaigner, calls for scientists to engage in 'overstatement' and 'be arrested if necessary'. Perhaps this is justifiable, given the dire situation that we are in. But maybe, as Smil counters, science should really exist to 'provide us with the best available evidence so we can understand the real challenges'.

The Great Cocaine Roundup

The Green Revolution has another big problem, happening just above the soil and rocks. The yield increases delivered by Borlaug's crop varieties depend upon a number of things. On their own, the new crop types deliver no improvements, but combined with irrigation, fertilisers, herbicides and pesticides, they have transformed the way we feed the world. But as we are seeing, this type of high-input farming comes with problems. As agriculture has increasingly become a battle against nature, nature has slowly and subtly started to fight back. An example of exactly how this might occur can be found within one of the most dangerous and corrupt industries in the world.

Cocaine production is an agriculture of sorts. In the war against this bloodthirsty and destructive type of farming, some of the most effective weapons have come from the field of agrochemistry. For many years glyphosate, a herbicide sold under the brand name Roundup, has been sprayed from the air onto Colombia's coca plantations to destroy crops. Once the valuable crops are sprayed, it can be hard for growers to recover them, so they often revert to less lucrative but marginally safer ways of life.

Around 2004, this strategy started to hit a problem. A strain of coca plant seemingly resistant to glyphosate was popping up across Colombian plantations. Initially, it was widely thought that drug cartels had been dabbling in genetic engineering, creating a Roundup-ready version of their favourite crop similar to commercially available cotton and soya plants. The technology to genetically engineer Roundup resistance was widely available and not beyond the wit of many molecular biologists. Even as a biochemistry undergraduate in the early nineties, I was taught the basic techniques required to genetically modify plants, and could probably have had a go. The CP4 gene that gives plants glyphosate resistance was well known and commercially available. Reputedly, Colombian drug cartels had been offering $10 million to any corrupt scientists willing to engineer a glyphosate resistant variety (I somehow missed the call).[14]

But extensive testing on samples of the new Boliviana Negra variety that was showing resistance seemed to say otherwise. There was no evidence of the CP4 gene, and none of the expected tell-tale traces normally left in the genome by artificial manipulation. It seemed that coca plants had developed resistance all by themselves and drug dealers would be able to continue selling their cocaine as GMO-free to their many affluent, health-conscious American customers.*

Although the genetic change seems to have occurred naturally, the odds are that local farmers helped considerably. Many millions of coca plants in Colombian plantations were sprayed over the years, and it seems that somewhere, someone got lucky. A single plant must have randomly mutated resistance to glyphosate and been spotted by an eagle-eyed – and for some reason hyper-alert – coca farmer. This plant was then quickly cultivated as a new herbicide-resistant variety, spreading by word of mouth across the region's farms. Soon, most of Colombia was growing glyphosate-resistant coca. When the authorities sprayed plantations, they were simply providing free weed control and probably improving yields.

This herbicide resistance had occurred faster than most plant scientists thought possible, which may have been a lucky break.† Or it may be that nature's ability to adapt to difficult circumstances is more powerful than we really know. Evolution, although often categorised as a slow plodding process that takes millennia, can occur incredibly rapidly under certain extremes. Unfortunately, much like the regularly sprayed Colombian plantations, our high-input farming systems have created just such circumstances.

Rise of the Super Pests

The problem with using large amounts of pesticides and herbicides is that they can create an environment where the usually

---

* Unfortunately, with all that glyphosate around, they won't be able to sell it as organic.
† There is another possibility. It could be that plant scientists used an older technique of blasting seeds with radioactivity to cause random mutations, then selecting for Roundup resistance. If the Colombians had contacted me, this might have been my first approach, being cheaper and less dependent upon obtaining the specific genetic material, something likely to raise suspicions. It is however quite time-consuming, depends upon a fair bit of luck, and Colombian drug cartels are not exactly known for their patience or understanding.

slow process of evolution rapidly speeds up. If a single factor is inhibiting all growth, once positive adaptations occur, they tend to shine very quickly. Over the years, as use of herbicides and pesticides has increased, so has the occurrence of weeds and pests resistant to them. If a plant or animal can adapt to life within our chemically laden farms, it can suddenly find a huge evolutionary niche to exploit. Sometimes, this can be devastating.

A number of factors have made these problems worse. Selective breeding of plants for yield and quality has made them extremely tasty, not just for us but for pests. Often, the presence of natural chemicals that act as pesticides has been bred out of agricultural plants due to the bitter taste. This means that when pesticide resistant bugs do develop, there is an all-you-can-eat buffet of the most delicious food imaginable, and nothing else is in the queue. When this happens, fast-breeding pest species have the potential to replicate more rapidly than an unrestricted population of blue tits.

Perhaps even more worryingly, as increasing numbers of agro-chemicals are being banned due to safety concerns, there is an ever-smaller chemical arsenal available to farmers. This lack of diversity means that the development of resistant species is likely to happen even more frequently. It also doesn't help that agronomy tends to be highly risk-averse. When it comes to spraying with chemicals, there can be severe short-term consequences if you decide not to do something, such as losing a whole year's crop to an infestation you failed to control. This means that many chemicals are over-sprayed regardless of the long-term impact, making the development of resistance even more likely.

Simon Leather is a Professor of Entomology at Harper Adams University, studying biological pest control. In his view, the single biggest problem facing global agriculture is the loss of conventional molecules. For various reasons, the arsenal of chemicals available to farmers is shrinking, and there is a great deal of work to be done when it comes to filling that gap in a way that maintains food production and protects the environment. With increasing numbers of weeds and pests developing resistance, the need for alternatives is increasingly urgent. It is also something that is expensive and difficult to address. Professor Leather told me that the cost of developing a broad spectrum pesticide is around $200 million and can take ten to fifteen years. In his opinion, 'The pipeline really isn't very full. The high cost means that new pesticides are only registered for big crops like wheat and maize. There is some really interesting work on pheromones, but these tend to be very species specific, so don't work out economically.'

Currently, there are a number of serious threats to global agriculture from the development of resistant weeds and pests, and no chemicals effective in controlling the cabbage-stem flea beetle, which is affecting rapeseed crops throughout Europe. Cabbage loopers with resistance to Bt toxins are causing widespread damage to a number of US vegetable crops.* A variant of Panama disease resistant to modern fungicides is devastating banana plantations around the world, destroying the livelihoods of millions of people, with the potential to wipe out that crop completely. Glyphosate-resistant water-hemp is increasingly being discovered in US maize and cotton fields, as are many other glyphosate-resistant weed species. The Colorado potato beetle, which is capable of severely damaging potato crops, seems to be particularly adaptable, having developed resistance to fifty-six different chemical insecticides. Western corn rootworm, a persistent maize pest that could potentially decimate crops around the world, has started to develop insecticide resistance in some heavily sprayed areas of the US. And wheat rust, the fungal disease that inspired much of Norman Borlaug's initial breeding work, regularly produces new resistant varieties

---

* Bt toxins will be covered later on in the book, but they are highly effective natural toxins used as insecticides. As well as being sprayed onto crops (including in organic agriculture), some plants have been genetically engineered to produce them.

with the potential to cause global food shortages. In total, around six hundred species of pests and over eight hundred weeds are known to have evolved resistance to one or more chemical treatments, a number that is predicted to grow significantly over the next ten years.[15]

As well as resistance, there are other impacts of pesticide overuse. Herbicides and pesticides are designed to destroy life, and so it's not surprising that they come with all sorts of dangers. In particular, neonicotinoids, developed by Shell and Bayer in the 1980s, are a class of insecticides similar to nicotine, the naturally toxic substance produced by the tobacco plant. The huge advantage of neonics, as they became known, is that they can be applied as a seed treatment before planting. This enables them to protect the plant as a young seedling without the need for spraying fields, meaning that the chance of environmental contamination is greatly reduced.*

Neonicotinoids were also thought to have low toxicity to many beneficial species, but over years of use a number of problems emerged. Neonics are applied to seeds with a sticky substance, and then coated with a talc to prevent them sticking together. It seems that for some methods of planting, where seeds are blown into the ground through a compressed air system, the talc could be blown off, taking some of the insecticide with it and contaminating the surrounding environment. To make matters worse, some previously undetected contamination seemed to be getting into the pollen and nectar of more mature plants and affecting populations of pollinators, particularly bees. Although the contamination was generally a very low dose and not immediately killing insects, there did seem to be a number of non-lethal effects over time, and a damaging effect on population numbers. But as with seemingly everything in the study of insects, the one

---

* Some neonicotinoids are sprayed, but seed application greatly reduces the need for this.

thing everyone seems to agree on is that there are still huge gaps in our knowledge and much that we do not know.[16]

Despite, or perhaps because of this uncertainty, most neonics have now been banned or heavily restricted in the EU, as well as in most US states. This has been widely seen as a positive move, but as with many such issues, whether or not it is beneficial depends largely on what, if anything, is used to replace it. Neonics reduced the need for widespread spraying, and in some applications were relatively safe, but the blanket bans have not accounted for this variation. Simon Leather is sceptical about the ban: 'When the government panicked about pollinators, the funding went to ecologists, not people in applied agriculture. When people have no agricultural background, their recommendations are often unrealistic, sometimes harmful. Neonics are gone now, but no work is being done to see if this has actually benefited pollinators. I doubt that this will ever be studied.'

Pesticide and herbicide resistance will be a constant problem for agriculture, an arms race between farming and nature that will stretch on for as long as we grow crops. Contamination of the environment by substances that are by their nature toxic will also be a constant problem, especially for natural ecosystems that are already fragile. There is certainly a need to control and limit pesticides, and to prevent environmental contamination, but before we start calling for everything to be banned, it is worth remembering that without these chemicals, agricultural yields would drop by around forty percent.[17] * In a world where hunger is a growing threat, this might not feel like progress.

Bring the Outside In

In the production of food, largely because much of it happens outside, there are a number of costs that we call externalities

---

* Even today, thirty-five percent of crops are lost to pests before they are harvested.

(because they are external to production). For example, when a farmer sprays fertiliser onto a field of wheat, the cost of the chemicals is internal, paid by the farmer and factored into the price that we pay for bread. Even if some of the fertiliser runs off the field, the cost is still internal, because the farmer has already paid for it. But when it comes to the damage that the fertiliser does to waterways miles from the farm, those costs are external because, generally speaking, farmers do not have to pay to clear up the damage caused to rivers, lakes or marine life. But inevitably, someone, somewhere has to.

Jules Pretty is Professor of the Environment and Society at the University of Essex and an adviser to the UK government. His work focuses on sustainable agriculture and our connection to the natural world. As he explains, 'We pay for food three times. Once at the till, once in tax and subsidies, and a third time to clean up the mess. In the UK, it costs hundreds of millions of pounds every year to remove pesticides and fertilisers from the water supply, which we pay for in our water bills. Poor people end up paying more for this, essentially making it a regressive additional charge.'

The full cost of environmental harm caused by the burning of fossil fuels is paid neither by those who pull it out the ground, nor by those who do the burning, meaning that there is little financial incentive to do less of either. The cost of rainforest destruction is not built into the price of palm, beef or soya, meaning that farmers will continue to destroy forests in order to produce them.

Tragically, even though virgin rainforests have immense value as a natural wonder, a carbon sink, a provider of pollinators, a source of pharmaceutical breakthroughs, a store of valuable genetic material and a provider of novel crop plants, that value is nearly impossible to realise if all you have is a chainsaw and a family to feed.[18] For countries, companies and individuals that are focused upon survival, competition and short-term economic growth, plunder is pretty much inevitable. In fact, given that economic growth is a proven path to improving almost every facet of your life, it is really the sensible thing to do.

In agriculture, the cost of these externalities can be immense. Professor Tim Benton is Dean of Strategic Research Initiatives at the University of Leeds, working globally on the challenges of providing sustainable, nutritious diets. He told me that the external cost of food is five times the value of the food industry. In his uncompromising view, 'We are going to be buggered if we don't change that. Despite all we know, we are not acting as we need to. Politically, it has become absolutely toxic to say we need to make food more expensive. Politicians, farmers and consumers, everyone is locked into the system. It is like we are stuck in an international game of prisoner's dilemma and no one will shift the dial.'*

It is unrealistic to expect developing nations not to aspire to economic growth. But on a national level, that growth is largely measured by increases in GDP (Gross Domestic Product), which does not take into account the destruction of non-renewable resources, and makes for really bad accounting. In fact, in pure GDP terms, polluting the environment is considered to be an activity that adds value, creating economic growth if money has to be spent clearing up the mess. Countries that stop burning fossil fuels, spray fewer pesticides, preserve forests and invest in soil health fall behind in the economic race. Governments, so often hog-tied by short-term political cycles, will be damned by voters if their economies fail to grow. Those with morals and vision will lose. Those who disregard the future will win.

* The prisoner's dilemma is a demonstration of how two completely rational people might not cooperate, even though it would be in both their interests to do so. It happens essentially because humans seem programmed not to compromise on their own self-interests, even if that means everyone burning in a dumpster fire. A 1990s UK quiz show called *Golden Balls* was based on a version of the prisoner's dilemma, thought by most economists to be irresolvable. It is worth seeking out footage of a contestant called Nick Corrigan, who developed a risky strategy to beat the system.

And on the farms, for as long as costs are still external to the price of food, the farmers who over-spray, waste water, degrade soil and pollute waterways will make more money than those that don't. So long as the price of food does not reflect the true cost of making it, we will continue to destroy the planet. And so the only logical solution is to internalise the externalities. We need to bite the bullet and start paying more for our food.[19]

This is of course the great dilemma. Cheap food has been an immense force for progress, both socially and economically. In the last fifty years, the developed world has finally got the world that it wished for, one where almost all of us live without hunger. As the proportion of time and income spent searching for food has decreased, lives have improved immeasurably. Many will claim that the real issue is that we now spend far too much on property.* Decreases in food prices have coincided with increases in land values, and greater proportions of our income are now spent on rent or mortgages, with relatively tiny amounts now going towards sustenance. But what then is the solution? It's not clear that we have much to gain from devaluing property, which would send the global economy into an unstoppable downward spiral.

Externalities are hard to standardise, and even harder to change. The externalities of fertiliser use will differ from field to field, depending on the amount of run-off, the type of soil and the surrounding water system. Some ecosystems are clearly more valuable than others, but not in ways that are easy to measure. And even though the external cost of nitrogen fertilisers is now far greater than the economic value of the increases in yield they deliver, we still need that increased yield to keep the world fed.[20]

A food system that results in mass hunger would also have externalities, and these will be grimly realised if millions more have to face it. Hunger creates an enormous health burden,

---

* Top tip: when speaking at any food sustainability event, saying this is a sure way to get a cheap round of applause.

damages economic productivity, increases the need for humanitarian spending, and leads to rises in global conflict. Professor Elsa Murano is Director of the Borlaug Institute at Texas A&M University. As a young graduate student she worked with Norman Borlaug, and she now travels the world, continuing his legacy on behalf of the institute that bears his name. She told me, 'Norman Borlaug's legacy was to lift people out of both hunger and poverty. He understood that you need to do both. You prevent conflict through agriculture. Peace cannot be built on empty stomachs or human misery. Poor farmers with no hope or no future are a breeding ground for rebellion.'

Unrestricted growth is a bad thing. Uncontrolled externalities are a terrible thing, and may have poisoned our planet for ever. But in a world that has unknowingly drifted into what looks like the start of a global famine, dramatically raising the price of food for everyone might be equally bad. If we are to pay more for our food, then there will need to be assurances that the richer nations will meet most of the cost, and the vulnerable people of the world will be protected. It will require an already distorted market to be bent even further out of shape so that it is dedicated to the prevention of global hunger. It will be a hard road, requiring every society on Earth to become fairer and more compassionate.

The problem is, it seems incredibly unlikely that we are about to enter a period of heightened fairness and compassion. We cannot come to agreements on fossil fuels, or even comply with the ones we have already signed. Many already see this as an unstable, divided and frightening era in which isolationism and selfishness are on the rise. If your future depends on modern society rapidly transforming into something fluffy, compassionate and caring, it is unlikely to be realised.

So what then? Keep our fingers crossed? Brace for impact? Write off humanity to make way for a race of hyper-intelligent crows?

We will continue to grow and do harm, but as the externalised costs start to impact our lives, we will begin to change because we have no other choice. The rest of this book is going to look at a few of these slow, incremental changes. Some are at the cutting edge of technological innovation, others revivals of ancient and forgotten arts. Some will transform the industrial farming of developed nations; some will benefit the tiniest subsistence smallholdings. And whilst some are beautiful, simple and likely to be embraced by all, others are controversial and likely to prove divisive over the coming years.

But first there is a big, stamping elephant in the room that we need to deal with. A book like this cannot ignore the increasing numbers of people suggesting that one simple change, that we could make right now, would transform the problems we have discussed. Incredibly, this change could be made without damaging our health, or letting anyone go hungry. In order to feed a growing population, cool down the planet, and at the same time make the world a more compassionate place, surely we just need to give up meat.

7

Meat Is . . .

If we're not supposed to eat animals, how come they're
made out of meat?

– Tom Snyder

Oakley's World

It is often said that UK agriculture is split in two. The east of the
country is full of crops and nutrient deficient, whilst the west is
covered in animals and swimming in shit. If only there was a
cheap way of moving the shit from west to east, our food system
might be a lot more productive, and the eastern soil considerably
more carbon-rich.

It's far from a fifty-fifty split. Despite supporting rich pasture,
most British agricultural land is not fit to grow crops on. Sixty-
seven percent is only good for producing livestock, and this is the
predominant farming activity in these areas. Most of the thirty-
three percent that can produce grains, fruits or vegetables does
just that, and the majority of this is in the east.[1]

There are exceptions. One of them weighs about 750 kg and
is staring at me as I write. Oakley is a fourteen-month-old
Limousin bull who regularly tries to eat the young shoots of a
small tree in my garden that overhangs his field. He is a familiar

face, and bounds playfully over to say hello whenever any of us are around. He seems to have a particular connection with my daughter, who has made him a minor star on social media. In some small way, his regular, calming presence helped her in the long recovery from anxiety.

Although still young, Oakley is shaping up to be quite a magnificent beast. He is muscular, bright eyed and full of energy, although perhaps about a hundred or so kilos underweight based on breed averages, something which might well determine his future. If he is lucky, he will be sold off to another farm as a thoroughbred bull and eventually be put to work servicing a field of thirty or so cows and heifers. If this happens, he will probably live for around fifteen or sixteen years, fathering calves across a few different farms.* If things don't work out quite so well – and with a market that demands genetic perfection there is plenty that might go wrong – he will make the thirty-mile journey to a nearby slaughterhouse in a few months' time, and could even be served up as steak in a restaurant near you.

Oakley and the ninety other Limousin cattle in his herd are exceptional because they are located in Lincolnshire on the eastern side of England, an area more known for arable production. This is partly because his field was home to a military base in World War II, and regular ploughing might dredge up old munitions, making pasture a safer option. But it is also because the family that farm this land, who also produce a number of arable crops in the surrounding fields, believe that a mixed farming system is preferable, and find huge synergies in doing the two activities side by side. It helps that Oakley and his kin are raised for breeding and pedigree, something that requires more skill and close attention than cows being produced solely for meat or milk, but also delivers a bit more value per hectare.

---

* Bulls are often moved between different farms to avoid the practical difficulty of keeping them separate from cows or heifers they have fathered, something best avoided to prevent inbreeding. For this reason they are often moved every four to six years.

Only twelve percent of UK land that is suitable for arable farming is currently used for grazing, and an even smaller percentage is under permanent pasture like Oakley's.[2] This surprisingly small area is something over which great ideological battles are currently being fought. Some see Oakley as a shining light that might define a better food future, delivering medium-scale mixed agriculture, full of biodiversity, variety and life. Others see him as a symbol of gross inefficiency, taking up valuable resources, burping the planet to death, and wastefully using land that should be churning out crops. This presents a serious dilemma. Should we share our agricultural land with nature, embracing the sort of small-scale biodiversity found in the trees, grass and hedgerows of Oakley's field (a process known as 'land sharing')? Or should we take the 'land sparing' approach, squeezing the maximum yield out of each piece of productive ground, and hope to return the rest to nature?

I am torn whenever Oakley comes to visit, but not because of any moral concern over meat consumption. Despite a brief flirtation with vegetarianism in my early twenties, I have no qualms about his eventual destination should he not make the grade as a pedigree bull. I love beef, and equally enjoy other meat and dairy products. Speaking as a chef, they provide flavours and textures beyond anything vegetables can provide. Meat is at the heart of much great cooking, and is central to many of my favourite dishes. Although much has changed since I last set foot in a restaurant kitchen, working on the meat section was always a source of status, the premium position reserved for the most talented chefs. I also strongly associate cooking and eating meat with sharing and family, particularly the traditional British roast dinner, which remains my favourite meal. All told, I have to admit that I have a large cultural bias in favour of meat, and strongly believe that I could not live in a world without cheese.

Like most people, I have moral, welfare and safety concerns when it comes to meat and dairy production, and I have seen many examples of poor practices in both industries in the UK and abroad. But on this particular farm, Oakley and his friends always seem far happier than most of the UK's wild animals who, as we have already discussed, spend most of their short lives hungry and afraid. When he does eventually go off to slaughter, I am confident that it will be quick, humane and performed by people who genuinely care about such things. In contrast, the deaths of almost all wild animals are brutal, painful and involve a period of prolonged suffering. Humans are the only meat-eating creatures to have even the slightest concern for the welfare of the animals they consume. Although there is room in many cases to do better, I am confident that Oakley's life and death will be managed as well as they can be.

Given this, any concern anti-meat campaigners have for Oakley is presumably more about his liberty than his ultimate fate, imagining that he would rather spend his life running free than be contained within a field or barn. I am not sure that this is the case, especially on this sunny spring day when he seems quite content, aimlessly chewing the cud and quietly contemplating the Springer Spaniel on the other side of the fence. Liberty for wild creatures comes with far greater horrors than the field, barn or even the slaughterhouse, with hunger and violent predation ending the vast majority of lives early. For humans, who value freedom so highly, this might be an acceptable trade-off. But we must make sure we do not project our values onto creatures who may well have different priorities.

The reason I am torn is because the scene in front of me today, with magnificent pasture-fed beef cattle magically producing nutrient-rich food from the grass, is one that I love. It is something I grew up around, and it feels right to me, especially when the end product is so delicious. But the more I have learnt about the impact of food production, the harder it has become to justify this sort of extensive livestock farming.

Can Oakley really be the scourge of our planet? How is it that cows gently grazing in picturesque fields have become as emblematic of climate change as oil wells, exhaust pipes and coal mines? Although Oakley does occasionally burp in my face when we are discussing life over the fence, can his emissions really compare to the other environmental scourge visible from my house, the huge coal-fired power station on the bank of the nearby River Trent?

The writer and livestock farmer Simon Fairlie describes this dilemma well. In an article for the online magazine *The Land*, discussing the comparisons between livestock and transport emissions, he says, 'Many a farmer has glanced at the endless stream of cars on the motorway spewing gas from their exhausts and planes blazing trails across the sky, then turned towards his cows peacefully grazing, letting out the odd burp and depositing all that useful manure, much as they have done for thousands of years, and thought "that can't be right."'[3]

Fairlie is an intelligent and informed writer on environmental matters, and presumably knows the reasons why these emissions are comparable. Cattle are farmed on an almost unimaginable scale around the world. Around one quarter of the Earth's ice-free surface is used for grazing, which makes livestock farming by far the biggest use of land by any human activity. There are over one billion Oakleys burping out methane worldwide, roughly the same as the number of motor vehicles on the roads. And whilst cars and trucks clearly emit greenhouse gases at a much faster rate, unlike Oakley they are not running the whole time, and crucially take up far less land.[4]

Meaty Dichotomy

The big problem with the debate about meat is that it quickly falls into two camps. On one side, there are those who can never condone the killing or servitude of an animal. For them, consuming flesh is cruel, messy, dirty and wrong. We now have a society that can easily exist without the need to kill in the name of food production, and continuing to do so purely for pleasure is utterly immoral.

On the other side there are those that love meat and dairy, seeing it as a joy, part of their culture, even a God-given right.

Meat is nourishing, wholesome and good. We evolved as meat-eating creatures, with cooperative hunting essential in the development of our societies and the evolution of our remarkable intelligence. To give up on it now would be to abandon what makes us human.

These beliefs are firm and entrenched. They can easily come to form an enormous part of the identity of those that hold them. Although social media is far from the real world, it is telling how many people have 'vegan', 'plant-based', 'carnivore' or 'meat lover' as a prominent part of their profile or biography. Many people literally consider what they have for their tea, or more often what they choose not to have, to be the most interesting thing about them. Dietary choice has, in many cases, replaced religion as the primary way people signal who they are to the world.

Someone who already thinks that meat is morally wrong will be more likely to accept the idea that it is harmful to health, destructive to the environment, socially divisive and driven by a morally corrupt industry. But if you spend too much time looking across rich green pasture, chatting about life to friendly beef cattle, or even if you just really love steak, you might be inclined towards positive beliefs about meat's nutritional content, exquisite taste, environmental benefits and place in a diverse, sustainable food system. This is sometimes known as the 'unity of the virtues', a common fallacy that can easily lead towards the adoption of false beliefs. The writer and religious scholar Dr Alan Levinovitz told me:

> 'The unity of the virtues' [is the fallacy] that all virtues depend on each other, so if something is good in one way then it must be good in all ways. I see this as a kind of wishful thinking, that results from an implicitly (or explicitly) theological understanding of properly organized systems. If a system is harmonious, like, say, an ecosystem, then it makes sense that it will all work together perfectly, as if organized by a deity.

When it comes to meat, this can be especially problematic. When passions run high and people's identities are challenged, complexity and nuance tend to fly out of the window. When almost all of us have strong, pre-existing views about the food we eat, truly objective information about its environmental impact is hard to find, and even harder to recognise.

This is a great shame. The future of life on this planet is very much at stake, and no one seems to be able to agree on anything. Is meat the scourge of climate, or an essential part of sustainable agriculture? Is global veganism the only chance of saving us, or the route to a global health crisis? Can livestock save our soils by enriching them with vital carbon, or are they responsible for degrading land in the first place?

The Price of Flesh

I might have to ask Oakley to close his ears for a bit, because by any measure, the impact of livestock production on our planet makes for pretty horrific reading.

The global production of meat and dairy uses eighty-three percent of world farmland, and produces sixty percent of all the greenhouse gases related to agriculture. But incredibly, animals only provide eighteen percent of the world's calories and thirty-seven percent of the protein. In the US, this inefficiency is even greater, with beef alone using half of the agricultural land, yet only providing three percent of the calories.[5]

Most animal agriculture involves feeding plants to animals, and this is an extremely inefficient way of producing food. Animals inconsiderately use a lot of their energy for running around, thinking about Springer Spaniels or producing enormous amounts of shit. This is particularly the case for beef. When compared to peas or soya, producing a kilogram of beef protein releases 150 times the greenhouse gases, uses 6 times more water, and takes up over 100 times as much land.[6]

When it comes to livestock and climate change, the focus often falls on the notorious methane-rich burps of cows, sheep and other ruminants. Animals such as Oakley have bacteria in their stomachs that help them digest their food, and these bacteria produce methane as a by-product, which Oakley promptly burps out. As we have already discussed, methane is a potent greenhouse gas that contributes significantly to global warming. The more beef cattle there are in the world, the more methane enters the atmosphere, and the hotter the planet becomes. It is thought that the methane produced by ruminant animals makes up two thirds of all the greenhouse gases attributable to agriculture. Cows are literally burping the planet to death.

On top of that, animals also produce greenhouse gases from the other end. Their manure emits nitrous oxide, an even more potent agent of global warming, as well as a small amount of additional methane. Add to that the emissions required to produce the food that livestock eat, including the energy required to make nitrogen fertiliser and the carbon released from the soil, and the total rises even further. All told, livestock account for 14.5% of human-produced greenhouse gas emissions, as much as the whole of transport.[7]

Animals also consume about a third of all of the world's cereal grain, and in developed countries this figure is closer to seventy percent. Around one billion tonnes of human-edible food is poured into livestock troughs every year, enough to feed around 3.5 billion people. Much of this is grown on land that could easily be used for producing crops for humans, resulting in an agricultural system that is highly inefficient. If we got rid of all dairy and meat production tomorrow, we would in theory produce enough food to keep everyone from hunger using just a quarter of the land that is currently farmed.[8]

Although the focus is so often on cow burps, in reality the biggest environmental impact of livestock is land use. Meat production, and especially beef, is spectacularly inefficient when it comes to land, and as demand increases around the world, pressure to convert tropical forest to pasture becomes immense. Seventy percent of previously forested land in the Amazon is now used for pasture, and much of the rest is currently being used to grow feed crops for animals. Seventy percent of the rangelands in the world's dry areas have already been degraded by overgrazing, compaction of the soil, or erosion. Livestock damages an astonishing amount of land worldwide, contributing not only to global warming, but also to loss of biodiversity, problems with water cycling, desertification and huge declines in soil fertility.

Meat production is already putting the world under serious pressure, yet demand is showing no signs of slowing down. Consumption has grown from fifty million tonnes in 1950 to over 300 million tonnes today. Although in many developed countries demand has reached a plateau, worldwide it is increasing at around three percent per year, a far higher rate than human population growth. The nutrition transition, when low-income countries increase in wealth and start to spend more on food, is characterised by an increase in the amount of meat that people eat, a trend that is extremely robust across many different cultures. As global rises in prosperity continue apace, with many low-income economies set to achieve greater wealth over the next thirty years, it is thought that global meat consumption will increase by eighty percent by 2050, and the amount of beef being eaten will nearly double. These increases might well be unstoppable, and have the potential to be even higher. Meat is the food that the world aspires to, a near-universal symbol of wealth, prosperity and status. As the food historian Rachel Laudan explains, 'Meat eating is not just a matter of taste or the environment, it's a foothold, it's a stake in the rich, modern world. It's a sign that they too can leave behind the hierarchical societies of the past and be full citizens and enjoy what we already enjoy in the United States.'⁹

There are huge global disparities between meat consumption worldwide, driven by a variety of cultural and social factors, the largest of which is wealth. But this means that it has a near-unlimited potential to increase. Although US levels have fallen slightly in recent years, they are still nearly three times the global average. If a US-style diet remains something that the world actively desires, we are in for some serious trouble.

Things Get Intense

Although at a personal level meat is representative of a better future, globally it is devastating, and not just because of the climate impact. As worldwide meat production has increased and intensified, animals are being packed increasingly close together and humans are coming into contact with them far more often. As a result, the prevalence of killer diseases is likely to increase rapidly. Diseases such as avian flu, swine flu, COVID-19 and Ebola already cause 2.4 billion cases of human illness every year, killing well over two million people. Widespread over-use of antibiotics in intensive farming systems has led to fears of resistant bacteria developing, with the potential to create untreatable global pandemics.[10]

There have been dramatic increases in the number of animals raised in intensive systems, with nearly eighty percent of all chicken and pork production now taking place in feedlots, along with an increasing amount of beef and dairy.* This sort of intensive farming can pollute local environments and water systems if waste is not well managed, with nutrient-rich effluent often causing the same sort of dieback as nitrogen fertilisers. It can lead to social issues as well as environmental ones. Intensive mega-farms are almost always located in the poorest regions of a country, often within the heart of ethnic minority communities. They pollute the air, poison the water, and often expose poorly paid minority workers to horrific and dangerous working conditions.[11]

---

* Feedlots are animal feeding operations designed to maximise the efficiency of muscle gain in livestock. They are generally large, often indoor, and will usually involve packing a large number of animals into a small space.

The welfare of intensively raised animals is rightly a concern, although it is sometimes a little too easy to damn systems that do not meet our aesthetic ideal of what farming should look like. Our Disneyfied image of animals happily grazing in picturesque fields feels as if it should confer higher welfare, but it is dangerous to make such assumptions. The best intensive systems take great care to monitor, understand and improve the well-being of livestock, largely because this makes for greater productivity. Often it is only intensive systems that are doing this work, and the best farms are making huge investments in research and technology to make animals happier and more comfortable. It is bad farming that causes bad welfare, and although this can happen in large intensive systems, it is also possible on picturesque free-range smallholdings.

Our perception of what good welfare looks like is often skewed. Videos of vegan activists raiding farms to snatch piglets from intensive pens are frequently lauded on social media by supposed animal rights supporters, yet anyone who knows the first thing about animal welfare will tell you that ripping these animals away and cuddling them as if they were pets causes both mother and young huge distress. We are frequently told that slow-grown, outdoor-raised chickens have a happier life, but often the difference between the two is that one takes forty-seven days to reach maturity, and the other takes fifty-eight. There is precious little evidence that the bird that had access to a cold wet field for an extra eleven days before slaughter was any more content.

The greatest advances in animal welfare are unlikely to come from banning intensive systems or drawing arbitrary lines in the sand regarding how animals are raised. We would do far more for the welfare of animals if we worked to improve the pay and conditions of livestock workers, and started to value meat more highly. Animal produce has been devalued and commoditised over the past sixty years, meaning that some poor practice is now inevitable. The only way this might change is if global demand falls significantly, and producers start to receive more income per animal.

In the Red Corner

As we have already discussed, land use change is one of the biggest causes of environmental damage, and meat production is the most significant driver of land use change. But tellingly, land is a factor that many meat advocates often choose to ignore when performing calculations. The figure I mentioned earlier, that livestock account for around 14.5% of all human-produced greenhouse emissions, is generally accepted as correct, backed up by numerous academic studies and contained in reports from the IPCC and the FAO.[12] Yet vastly differing figures are thrown about, muddying the water and creating much uncertainty.

On the pro-meat side, a figure of four percent is often repeated, coming from a US Environmental Protection Agency (EPA) report on climate and correctly asserting that only four percent of US greenhouse emissions are directly related to livestock production.[13] Another study, funded by the US Department of Agriculture (USDA), modelled the impact of different food systems and showed that the total removal of animals would only reduce greenhouse gas emissions by 2.6%.[14] These numbers are often triumphantly waved at vegan environmentalists by meat-loving carnivores on social media, along with gratuitous pictures of recently barbecued rare steaks, eaten on camera (presumably to 'own' the 'soy-boy libtards').*

Numbers like these can be very powerful, but they also create confusion. If you are already inclined to like meat, 4% or 2.6% temptingly absolves your favourite food from blame, helpfully coming from reputable sources and, to the best of my knowledge, reasonably accurate. But in truth, these figures are statistical sleights of hand, and their use is designed to deflect from the truth.

---

* Soy-boy is a common insult hurled at environmentalist vegan types by right-wing meat eaters. It has amusingly been used against me more than once. I am in the unusual position of being regularly insulted by both vegan extremists and meat industry apologists, which shows that I am at least doing something right.

Given that the USDA's job is to represent US agriculture, it can hardly be considered an independent voice on such matters, but assuming the figures are accurate there are still a few important points to note. Firstly, they only cite US numbers on climate change, which is a trick popular with anyone wishing to minimise the impact of meat production. Although the US produces plenty of meat, its impact is far lower in national percentage terms than the rest of the world, simply because the US, with its coal-fired factories, lack of environmental regulations and piss-cheap fuel, is one of the most carbon-heavy economies in the world. A 2.6% reduction in total US greenhouse gas emissions is hardly something to wave away as insignificant, and 4% of US emissions represents an awful lot of gas.

But there is another important reason why US figures are frequently used to dismiss the impact of livestock. In North America, as most available land has already been converted to agriculture and little natural habitat remains, changes in land use are not considered within the emissions data. But meat is clearly a global commodity, and our national food choices cannot be considered in isolation. Meat production is highly inefficient when it comes to land, and if one country increases consumption, that has a global impact, placing pressure on already sparse land resources around the world. There is currently no spare grazing land anywhere on Earth, so the inevitable result of any increase in demand is deforestation, something that will only happen in countries that still have forests left to cut down. This is by far the greatest environmental impact of agriculture, but is completely invisible if you look at US, European or UK figures in isolation. Whenever people decide to eat more meat, the global requirement for agricultural land increases. And when that happens, they start up the chainsaws in Brazil, Indonesia and the Congo.

When global land use change is taken into account, the US diet is thought to contribute more to climate change than transport, with most of that impact driven by animal production. The world shares the sky, so to see global warming as anything other than a global problem is reductionist and absurd. Believing that single nations can isolate their dietary choices is wishful thinking by an industry trying to absolve itself from blame.

In the Green Corner

Most people reading this book will be familiar with headlines such as these:

> Avoiding meat and dairy is 'single biggest way' to reduce your impact on Earth – *Guardian*, May 2018

> Give up meat completely or become a 'flexitarian' to save the planet – *Telegraph*, October 2018

> Vegan diet would slash climate emissions – *The Times*, January 2019

Given the evidence presented so far, it is hard to dismiss them, but these headlines still ignore an awful lot of complexity and nuance regarding meat and dairy production. They also ignore the very real issue that, much like a zero growth economy, global veganism is not actually going to happen.

Campaigners for veganism are also prone to exaggeration and mistruths. Most famously, a claim that animal agriculture is responsible for fifty-one percent of global greenhouse emissions regularly does the rounds, and was at the heart of the popular but bizarre Netflix documentary *Cowspiracy*. This unintentionally hilarious film details its belief that all global environmental groups, including Greenpeace and the Rainforest Action Network, are involved in a conspiracy to hide the real truth about climate change: that the majority of global warming is actually down to the production of meat.

The fifty-one percent figure has previously been parroted by Ethan Brown, the Chief Executive of the vegan burger manufacturer Beyond Meat, and the animal rights group PETA. Much like the 4% and 2.6% figures on the pro-meat side, it is not entirely made up, being based on a 2009 report from the Worldwatch Institute, a Washington-based environmental research group.[15] But again, in isolation this number does not represent an accurate analysis of the true picture, largely because it includes the carbon dioxide that livestock breathe out as part of their respiration.

It is true that all animals, including humans, breathe out carbon dioxide, a potent greenhouse gas. But there is a very good reason why this is not generally included in global emissions data. All the carbon that animals exhale originally comes from plants, and all plants capture that carbon from the sky. It is true that Oakley emits a little bit of CO_2 every time he breathes out, but the grass he eats has previously captured that CO_2 using photosynthesis. This creates a perfectly balanced system of carbon recycling, which means that animal respiration does not contribute to a net increase in greenhouse gases, and arguably decreases it, as a one-tonne ruminant retains quite a lot of carbon in its bones, fat and muscles. Net increases in atmospheric CO_2 only occur when stored carbon, either from fossil fuels or the soil, is burnt off in some way, or if carbon dioxide is converted into methane, a more potent greenhouse gas. The fifty-one percent figure is almost universally recognised by climate and environmental scientists as flawed, and despite what the makers of *Cowspiracy* might think, the Rainforest Action Network are not the biggest supporters of animal agriculture.

There are certainly vested interests on the vegan side of the debate, including Netflix documentary makers, vegan advocacy groups and a few high-profile vegan start-ups, some of which have been prone to hubris. But it is also true that the meat, dairy and cattle industries have had a huge effect on policy, particularly in the US, where lobby groups rival fossil fuels and tobacco for influence. The meat industry is worth $186 billion in the US alone, and $1.4 trillion worldwide, with a number of huge global players keen to influence both nutrition and environmental policy. During the 2013 US presidential elections, the livestock industry contributed $17.5 million to federal candidates to ensure its interests were represented, and it is estimated that it spends a further $10–12 million on lobbying every year.[16]

In 2015, US livestock representatives successfully lobbied for national nutrition guidelines to be changed against the will of the scientific advisory committee, who had recommended that the environmental impact of meat should be considered. The industry's counter-argument was not one based on science. Cattle lobbyists simply insisted that recommending Americans eat less meat would be bad for business, and placed enough pressure on the administration to have the guidelines changed. This included a direct threat by a cattle-friendly congressman to withdraw funding from the department if they did not back down. Later that year, a law was passed by Congress prohibiting the next dietary guidelines committee, due to sit in 2020, from considering the environment at all. And when the questions that the committee would be considering were announced in 2019, it was mysteriously predetermined that they would not be making any recommendations about consumption of red or processed meat, whatever the evidence.[17]

Marion Nestle sat on the 2015 committee whose independent recommendations were overturned by cattle industry lobbyists. She told me: 'The 2020 guidelines committee has just been appointed and two members were nominated by The Cattlemen's Beef Association. This year for the first time, federal agencies have set the committee's research agenda. Environmental issues – sustainability and climate change – are off the table and will not be discussed by this committee.'

But despite this industry resistance, and even though at the time of writing the US has a climate change denying president with his own brand of steak, calls for the world to eat less meat are becoming overwhelming, backed by an enormous body of academic research and numerous internationally funded reports. Study after study is suggesting our current food consumption patterns are destructive, and eating less meat is absolutely key if we want a more sustainable food system. So, should we all just give up meat to save the planet?

Guess what? It's complicated.

Time for the Boring Old Nuance

Although calls for a largely vegan diet seem sensible in light of the data, the reality is not so straightforward. For a start, an estimated one to two billion people rely on animals for their livelihood, and in much of the world's drylands, it is the only viable form of agriculture. It is all very well telling people to give up beef and switch to a more rain-dependent form of food production, but the reality for many is that if they did, they would starve.

It is also true that the majority of world agriculture happens in mixed farms, with over half of all food coming from systems that produce livestock and crops side by side. This is not surprising, as there are many valuable synergies between the two. It is only relatively recently that arable and livestock farming have become so geographically separate in developed economies, where a relentless drive for efficiency has led to extensive monocropping and the sort of agricultural dichotomy that we see in the UK.[18]

In most of the world, animals supply far more than just milk, eggs and meat. They provide labour, pulling ploughs, transporting goods and controlling weeds. They consume otherwise useless crop residues, transforming waste into valuable, protein-rich food. They supply hides, wool and essential soil enrichment, with one cow producing up to seventy kilograms of manure per day, enough to feed an entire hectare of wheat.* When farmers cannot afford or access expensive chemicals, this free fertiliser can mean the difference between starvation and plenty.

---

* If you think the 70 kg estimate sounds like a lot, I invite you to spend some time in my garden when Oakley is stood at the fence.

Perhaps even more importantly, in privileged countries, it is hard to appreciate the vital role that owning a few livestock can play in improving lives. For many, animals provide security, independence and freedom from hardship. Known as the 'bank on four legs' in parts of Africa, goats and cows are sources of income, savings and insurance, built up in times of plenty and drawn upon in times of need.[19]

Even in developed nations, the picture is more complex than it first appears. Feedlot animals can consume material that isn't fit for humans and would otherwise be disposed of, including crop residue, silage and the waste products of milling and seed oil production. They can even use up by-products of the alcohol, dairy, canning and fruit juice industries, most of which would otherwise have to be incinerated. In a circular food system, animals can play an important part, turning items we would otherwise throw away into food, and churning out a number of useful commodities at the same time.[20]

The Swill of the People

In 2001, on the remote Burnside Farm in North East England, a batch of uncooked swill containing imported meat was fed to a barn full of pigs.* The pigs became infected with the foot-and-mouth virus, and before anyone realised, they had been transported hundreds of miles across the country to a slaughterhouse in Essex, coming into contact with many other animals. The resulting outbreak of this highly contagious disease resulted in six million UK animals being slaughtered and burned, costing the economy an estimated £8 billion. It was just one of a series of scandals involving British livestock farming that would undermine public trust for many years.

---

* Swill is scraps of waste food from kitchens or factories, cooked up in water and fed to animals, especially pigs.

As a direct result of poor management on a single farm, the age-old practice of feeding swill to pigs was banned in the UK, a ban that would eventually extend across the entire European Union. This has been extremely damaging to farmers' profits, increasing food costs by an estimated forty to sixty percent. In contrast, swill feeding remains popular across the rest of the world, and in Japan and South Korea forty percent of all food waste is recycled as animal feed. At a time when reducing waste is frequently identified as a key battleground in limiting environmental impacts, many have been calling for the European ban to be overturned. If the practice was reintroduced, the land required for pig feed could be reduced by twenty percent. This would account for an area about the size of Wales (an admittedly outdated measure of land use).

It is doubtful that the swill ban will be overturned anytime soon, given the scars that the foot-and-mouth outbreak left on British livestock farming. Although in Japan and South Korea there have been no similar disease outbreaks, the process there is tightly regulated, with all swill being cooked according to strict protocols to ensure any pathogens are destroyed. UK swill feeding prior to 2001 was supposed to be under similar strict control, and Burnside Farm had been inspected shortly before the outbreak. It would only take one lazy, complacent farm to cause another catastrophe, and there is evidence that this might be hard to prevent. A recent survey of UK smallholdings found that a quarter of pig farmers are still feeding uncooked waste to animals despite the ban, indicating that cultural differences might make continued regulation advisable.[21]

But the problem with swill, and the negative environmental impacts of the ban, provides an insight into the bigger issues surrounding our production of meat. For most of the history of agriculture, the role of animals has been to help create a more circular food system, one in which nothing goes to waste. But as livestock farming has changed in recent years, especially within the large farms of developed economies, it seems to have lost its way.

Tiny, Useless Nails

How can livestock be both highly wasteful, and an essential part of an efficient agricultural system? The answer lies in an apocryphal story about nail production in Soviet Russia, highlighting the important difference between measures and targets.*

There is an old tale that Soviet nail factories used to be measured by the number of nails they produced. If there was ever a danger of missing monthly targets, something that didn't play out well for those in charge, they would switch production to making thousands of tiny but completely useless nails, just to keep up numbers. When officials cottoned on, they changed the targets so that they were defined by the total weight of nails produced. Predictably, factories started producing a small number of enormously heavy, equally useless nails. This was depicted in a famous Russian cartoon of the time, with a factory manager being proudly congratulated for exceeding his tonnage, with two giant nails visible in the background.[22] The moral of the story is that capitalist factories would soon close if they started producing useless things. A market system should hone the industry down to the most popular and profitable producers, and only the most relevant and efficient methods of production would remain.

Or at least that is the theory. In reality, targets can be a blight everywhere. I once worked at a thoroughly capitalist food factory, where overzealous middle managers became obsessed with reducing the number of reportable accidents as part of a health and safety drive. One of the most effective ways the factory found of achieving its targets was to insist that if anyone in the development kitchens suffered an injury that required first aid treatment, they would be subject to an involuntary drug and alcohol test. This involved them being marched off to a special room where

---

* I apologise that communism appears to be getting such a hard time in this book, but remember that in the last chapter I blamed capitalism for destroying the natural world and setting us on a course for wholescale environmental destruction. So swings and roundabouts.

they would have to sit for the rest of the day whilst they waited for a surly employee from the drug testing company to visit the site. They would then have to endure a humiliating test procedure, complete an intrusive interview about their personal life, and lose an entire day's work. This was the case even if they had only nicked their finger whilst chopping onions. If it needed so much as a plaster, you had to have the test.

The result, not surprisingly, was a sharp drop in the number of reported accidents. The reality in the kitchen was that people did still occasionally cut and burn themselves, but when they did, they would go without first aid treatment. Blood flow was secretly stemmed with toilet roll, burnt skin surreptitiously cooled down under a tap, and wounds left open to infection until the end of a shift. If the purpose of the new policy was to reduce the reporting of accidents, it was a resounding success. But if the intention was to improve the health and safety of the workforce, it was a dismal failure. The factory became a slave to its targets, and chose to ignore the harm they were causing.

I never managed to successfully challenge this policy, or a number of similarly ridiculous ones, choosing instead to wait a few years before cowardly exposing them in a book about a completely different subject. I am certain that most people reading will have similar examples, where the imposition of targets and a blind devotion to achieving them led to unintended consequences. It blights government policy, particularly when there is a high degree of central control, but it also damages large businesses, especially when middle managers are charged with achieving a specific metric above all else. In economics this is known as Goodhart's law, which states that once a measure becomes a target, it ceases to be a useful measure.

Agriculture can be viewed in a similar way. Over thousands of years, a system emerged, with animals working in synergy with plants to produce a variety of foods in a sensible, efficient way. This was a complex and imperfect system in which animals played a diverse and important role. But as agriculture intensified, the efficiency of production became paramount, rapidly turning from a useful measure into a damaging target.

In the twentieth century, as refrigeration and cold supply chains rapidly changed how people ate, food production became more centralised. Labour shortages after the Second World War drove the need for more intensive indoor rearing of animals, particularly in the US. Feeds were nutritionally optimised, leading to faster, more efficient growth. Barn raising meant fewer losses from disease or predation. Packing animals into feedlots meant greater efficiency. The synergistic benefits of raising animals alongside production of plants were complex and hard to measure, and so were ultimately ignored.

To make matters worse, subsidies for grain and corn pushed down prices, making it far more efficient to feed them to animals, rather than messing around with nutrient-poor pasture, silage and hay. Despite the fact that this was a wasteful use of arable land, it was the best way to meet the increasing demand for cheap meat and dairy products. Then the Green Revolution happened, creating an illusion that there would always be enough grain, reducing prices even further. To compound things, large-scale beef and dairy production was increasingly subsidised directly in the name of further food security, with farmers paid to produce as much as they could, whatever the eventual costs.

A truly emergent system, one allowed to develop without subsidies or targets, would never have produced perfectly good cereal crops only to pile them into animal troughs. But market distortions and the postwar targeting of efficiency meant that it did exactly that. Before long, we were locked into a cycle of consumption and excess from which we couldn't escape.

Whatever you think of it, this drive for efficiency was quite remarkable. Improvements in livestock yields over the past seventy years have been as transformative as any seen for plant crops during the parallel Green Revolution. Since the introduction of artificial insemination in the 1940s, breeders have been able to take a more scientific approach. Complex algorithms have replaced instinct and the breeder's eye. Accurate measurement of how efficiently feed is converted into flesh has led to animals our grandparents would barely recognise.

In dairy cattle, there has been a 443% increase in milk production per cow. There are now far fewer dairy cows producing far more milk, using less feed, less water and considerably less land. Remarkably, even though it was never the target of this drive, the current US dairy stock has thirty-seven percent of the carbon footprint it had seventy years ago.[23] In 1958 it took 5.4 kg of feed to raise a 2.3 kg broiler chicken. Today, it only takes around 3.75 kg, largely due to improved breeding techniques producing birds that grow four times faster. If new techniques had not delivered these improvements, and efficiency was stuck at 1950s levels, the US would require an extra forty million cattle and thirteen billion chickens to keep up with demand, as well as thirty billion kilograms of additional feed.[24]

In recent times, the prospect of genomic selection has raised its head, with breeders now able to analyse the genomes of animals as well as their physical traits, peeking under the hood of selection. This new technology means that we may not be anywhere near peak efficiency, with another revolution yet to come. Although care must be taken to ensure that genetic diversity is maintained, it is thought that the livestock efficiency train has a good distance left to run.

Whether or not these increases in yield have been positive is a matter of great debate. Getting animals to slaughter more quickly reduces their total greenhouse emissions, and beef raised on pasture produces considerably more methane than beef fed on grain. By their nature, increases in efficiency tend to reduce the climate impact of livestock, leading to lower land requirements and less emissions. But when efficiency or emissions become targets instead of measures, we can lose sight of the role animals should be playing within an agricultural system. Improvements in efficiency inevitably lead to lower prices, increased consumption, more production and so more pollution. Other issues, such as animal welfare, social justice, waterway pollution and local livelihoods, start to be overlooked.

Welcome to the Cheap Meats

By almost every measure, beef is a horribly inefficient way to produce food. Yet there is an astonishing amount of variability. The worst twenty-five percent of beef produces half of the greenhouse gas and uses sixty-one percent of the land. If efficiency is the only goal, then a sensible strategy would be to remove that twenty-five percent. Yet efficiency is generally poor where the land is unproductive, animal mortality is high, and access to modern feeds, breeding techniques and veterinary care is almost non-existent. If you take away that twenty-five percent in the name of meeting efficiency targets, you are taking away the only livelihood of some of the world's most vulnerable people. Inefficient cattle are raised on terrible land where there are few alternatives. In many cases, people are simply eking out a meagre living in places that would otherwise be entirely unproductive. In doing so, the livestock they raise take a very long time to grow and develop.

For this reason, there are huge disparities around the world. An animal such as Oakley, raised in the UK and fed mostly on pasture, will probably produce around 20–25 kg of CO_2 for every kg of meat. The global average is more like 28 kg, and the worst probably around 110 kg.[25] These differences clearly matter when we are looking at what sort of agriculture we want, and also present huge opportunities for progress and improvements, but specifically targeting them is a dangerous game to play.

They also reveal a great deal of uncertainty. Measuring the methane emissions from a herd of cows is much harder than measuring the gases coming from a power station chimney, particularly when cattle are raised in so many different ways. Should we assume that the cows slowly growing on Central African drylands produce emissions at exactly the same rate as the rapidly maturing feedlot stock in the US? It all depends upon the soil type, the rainfall, the breed, the food, the method of production and about a million other things. Averages are frequently used to damn livestock farming as a whole, rarely taking into account that animals often play a vital part in improving the overall efficiency of a complex system.

Averages are particularly unhelpful when it comes to cows, which produce a large number of non-meat by-products for use in many different industries, including hide, hair, gelatine, fertiliser, cosmetics and paint. Generally, it is only the moo that gets wasted when an animal like Oakley goes to slaughter, but his efficiency will be assessed solely by the amount of muscle meat that he yields.

Averages also often miss that dairy herds produce a lot of meat, as spent cows, inadequate bulls and male calves usually end up at the butcher's. When different diets are modelled, vegetarian patterns (i.e. including dairy) are sometimes found to be the most environmentally efficient, yet this would presumably result in an awful lot of spent animals being needlessly incinerated, surely not the most efficient use of a perfectly good food source.

And even the greatest harm, the destruction of tropical forests to create new pasture, is not quite as simple as it first appears. In the Amazon particularly, deforestation often has a good deal more to do with land rights than cows, with conversion to pasture simply being the most convenient way of occupying land for long enough to take ownership. If we are not careful, in focusing so tightly on cattle, we may miss the real reasons for the destruction, shying away from policy decisions and law changes that would stop forests from being destroyed.[26]

Often, a small number of livestock can increase the production capability of a given area of land. A 2016 study modelled the effect that different diets had on the number of people that US agricultural land could adequately feed. The study showed that, contrary to the headlines, a vegan diet could actually support *fewer* people than a number of omnivore scenarios.[27] Modelling of agricultural land use in New York State shows that several types of vegetarian diet would use *more* land than diets containing a small amount of meat.[28] And when a metric known as the Land Use Ratio is used, measuring the amount of human-edible protein that can be produced from a hectare of land, dairy production is considerably more efficient on certain soil types than even the best plants.[29] So the answer to which is the most efficient way to produce food is very much: 'it depends'.

People often make unfair comparisons between meat and vegetables, contrasting the worst animals on the poorest land with the most efficient plants on the best. There are many examples of highly efficient plant crops, and a good environmental argument that we should base our diet on these. Soya, lentils and chickpeas are extremely good ways of producing protein. Wheat, corn, palm and sugar cane are fantastic for growing large amounts of calories on relatively small areas of land.* Compare those crops to animals and there is a striking difference, but none of us restricts our diet purely to these crops.

There are plenty of widely grown plant foods that are terrible in terms of protein per hectare, or calories per unit of CO_2, but rarely get any criticism. Most plant foods are associated with the release of soil carbon, overuse of nitrogen fertilisers, high energy inputs, insecticide contamination, biodiversity loss, transport emissions and deforestation. Many crops are absolutely terrible for the environment. A widely reported 2015 study showed that lettuce, aubergines, celery and cucumber had a greater impact in terms of greenhouse emissions per calorie than bacon.[30] Yet only a fool would attempt to ban them. Increasing consumption of fruits and vegetables is one of the best ways to improve dietary health, and it is perhaps the most common nutritional recommendation around the world. It is ridiculous to assess fruits and vegetables in terms of impact per calorie, because we do not eat

---

* This is perhaps another example of why targeting agricultural efficiency alone is a mistake, because we would need everyone to eat a lot more sugar. As an aside, lots of sugar production, from both cane and beet, is still subsidised around the world, including in the UK. Considering that almost every government is trying to work out how to reduce people's sugar consumption, this is pretty crazy when you think about it.

them for the calories, and rarely for protein, instead seeing them as valuable sources of micronutrients, flavour and variety.

So perhaps we should start looking at animal products in the same way. They provide valuable nutrition, give us much pleasure, and have immense cultural importance and a unique flavour. Dairy, meat and eggs are among the most nutrient-dense foods available. Problems occur when these foods start to dominate our diets and we see them as staples, rather than the occasional treats they should be. Meat should not be damned, but its role in our diets and our food system must change. If we are to have a sustainable future, it really has to.

Few would dispute that raising livestock animals is a very good way of producing high-quality protein, or that they supply a range of valuable micronutrients that are difficult to get from other sources. Vitamin B_{12} is essential in our diets, with deficiency leading to devastating neurological problems, yet there is no natural plant-based source. It is extremely difficult to get complex omega-3 oils from plant foods, and although these are not completely essential, there is increasing evidence that it is a good idea to consume at least some from animal sources. Although there is plenty of calcium in vegetables, it is often in a form that is hard for humans to absorb, and a little from animal foods can go a long way. Perhaps most crucially of all, iron is far more bioavailable in animal products than plants, meaning that a small amount of meat is often highly beneficial in the prevention of anaemia. Professor Steve McGrath is the Head of Sustainable Agriculture Sciences at Rothamsted Research. He runs a number of Gates Foundation funded 'geonutrition' projects around the world, looking for ways of increasing nutrient availability in people's diets through changes to agricultural methods. He explains:

> About two billion people are short of iron and zinc in their diets. Iron really is a bit of a pig. Red soils have tonnes of iron oxide, but it is not easy to get it into plants. There is no simple solution. In the West, we can use chelates, but

they are really expensive.* Some people say we should just
select grain varieties that have high concentrations of iron,
but it's not that simple.

Professor McGrath believes that the best approaches involve
using more diverse crops, particularly pulses, and including a bit
of meat or dairy if people can afford it. The iron contained in
meat, known as haem iron, is far easier for humans to absorb,
meaning that a small number of animals in an agricultural system
can do a huge amount for nutrition status.

For vegans in privileged countries, with access to a diverse
range of good-quality plant-based foods, these issues are of little
concern. If you have more than enough vegetables, can easily
obtain supplements or fortified foods, and have a good ground-
ing in nutrition science, you are unlikely to have any issues.† But
in other parts of the world, where nutrient deficiency affects
billions of people, animal produce can make all the difference.
Modelling of dietary change is complex, with a great deal of
nuance and a huge number of unknowns. Best-case scenarios
tend to assume that if people stop eating meat they will switch
to the most environmentally virtuous options, trading steaks and
burgers for chickpeas and soya. This is unlikely to be the case,
and even if it was, in some parts of the world it would be
impracticable.

But there is little doubting that on a global scale, current
methods of livestock farming have become far too focused on

* Chelates involve bonding a metal ion to an organic compound, which makes it
slightly easier for plants to absorb.
† A number of dietitians and nutrition scientists have expressed concern that the
omega-3 oils from plant sources are extremely hard to utilise, and raising children
on a vegan diet might put them at risk of not getting enough, something that can
cause issues with brain development in children. Many suggest taking fish oil
supplements, although obviously these are not vegan (clue's in the name). Although
this is perhaps a bit beyond my pay grade, evidence seems to point to this being a
serious issue and, personally, I would be worried about a child raised in this way. I
would suggest that anyone wanting to raise young children on a strict vegan diet
seeks out the services and advice of a supportive dietitian.

efficiency and price, rather than considering the wider role animals might have in food production and health. For as long as we concern ourselves exclusively with production targets to meet the rising demand for meat, we will continue to produce it in a terrible, unsustainable way. The only sensible alternative is to work out exactly how many agricultural animals are optimal for an efficient, circular food system, and then look at the fairest, safest way of making them available for everyone.

This approach may upset people at either end of the debate, but despite the controversy, most people who work on these issues understand that animals have a vital role to play in global agriculture, and also agree that we currently consume far too much meat, especially across the Global North.

Most people.

Because in every debate, especially one where passions run high, there are always extremes. And the unity of the virtues has led many to claim that not only is meat safe and benign, but that it is capable of saving the world.

A Savory Interlude

As a general rule of thumb, whenever you find yourself arguing on social media about the environmental impacts of meat, it will take around ten minutes before someone pops up and shares That Video. Often it is left without comment as if it presents a definitive end to any argument. Everything you know about climate change is wrong. Eating meat, and particularly beef, is the only way to save the world.

Allan Savory is a Zimbabwean ecologist, and the video in question is his compelling 2013 TED Talk entitled 'How to fight desertification and reverse climate change'. In twenty-two minutes, he explains that rather than being the environmental scourge of the planet, beef cattle can potentially provide a solution to most of the world's environmental problems. By increasing beef consumption, changing the way we manage grazing, and allowing cattle to work the land in a way that mimics nature, we can remove enough carbon from the atmosphere to return it to pre-industrial levels. 'Only livestock can save us,' Savory memorably claims. 'There is no other alternative left to mankind.'

The talk is dramatic, thrilling and, for anyone who loves a nice steak, utterly convincing. People from Prince Charles and Michael Pollan to the Organic Consumers Association praised it shortly after its release, and it has been viewed millions of times. The heart of Savory's claims is that by increasing the numbers of cows per hectare and managing their grazing so that they remain bunched onto small areas of land, we can mimic the natural grazing patterns of wild animals. Wild herds travel in tight groups and move around quickly to avoid being eaten, and this behaviour promotes the development of sustainable grasslands. It enriches the soil by breaking up the surface, applies plenty of organic fertiliser and the odd carcass, encourages grass to grow deep roots, and prevents the formation of desert. It can even, so Savory claims, transform the world's deserts into rich pasture.

Perhaps most importantly, this sort of transformation would lock carbon into the soil, which, as we have already discussed, has enormous potential to remove large amounts of it from the atmosphere. Converting the world's deserts into grasslands would be transformative for our ability to produce food, but would also have a huge impact on global warming. Few people get to the end of Savory's talk without an enormous sense of positivity and hope (and perhaps a craving for a burger). A former politician, Savory is a powerful and passionate speaker with a missionary zeal, and clearly believes that his work might just be capable of changing the world. He shows a number of powerful images that detail the astonishing transformations that this sort of grazing can achieve.

But in the words of Carl Sagan, 'extraordinary claims require extraordinary evidence,' and Savory's claims about livestock being able to reverse climate change probably require more than a few unverified photos of his exploits.* His views are at odds with reports from the FAO, the World Health Organization, the IPCC and the World Bank. In one corner, we have most of the world's climate, environmental and agricultural scientists suggesting we need to dramatically reduce beef consumption. And in the other, a charismatic Zimbabwean ecologist is saying that we need to increase stocking rates by 400%. Is there any truth to Savory's claims? The answer is almost certainly a little more complex than a definite no, but claims that his methods are humanity's only hope of salvation are vastly overplayed.

Savory did not magically surface in 2013, and his techniques have been bubbling around for many years, largely promoted by the work of his various for-profit institutes. Key to understanding why they have not been more widely embraced by the scientific community is that they have proved incredibly hard to replicate. Savory insists that this is because his methods are 'holistic', meaning that they cannot be studied using normal experimental techniques. In 1990, commenting on many years of failed attempts to reproduce his results, he claimed that 'the scientific method never discovers anything. Observant, creative people make discoveries.'[31] We can safely assume that Norman Borlaug and Fritz Haber would disagree.

Savory believes that his work is consistently overlooked in the battle against climate change because reductionist science cannot comprehend it. He has frequently claimed that 'holistic management does not permit replication.' I would suggest that if a process cannot be replicated it has little chance of transforming the world, and a number of prominent scientists agree. Professor Dave Briske from Texas A&M University has been a consistent critic, stating that Savory's claims are 'not only unsupported by scientific evidence, but often in direct conflict with it'.[32]

---

* Savory has since claimed that he never suggested his grazing methods have the potential to reverse climate change, although the title and content of his TED Talk would seem to be at odds with this.

But Savory also has a number of high-profile advocates and supporters, including several farmers who have successfully adopted his methods. Many claim that the sort of grazing Savory advocates has transformed their land, most notably Joel Salatin, who Michael Pollan featured in his book *The Omnivore's Dilemma*, and Hunter Lovins, who passionately defended Savory's work in a 2014 *Guardian* article after George Monbiot had criticised it in the same newspaper. Lovins memorably attacked Monbiot as someone who 'lies awake at night wondering if what works in practice can possibly be true in theory', before detailing her personal experience in transforming a thousand-acre plot.[33]

I have never transformed a thousand acres of degraded land into a productive farm, but I have spent many years investigating the practices of charlatans and cranks in the world of food. Perhaps the most important thing you learn is that the majority of people who sell false hope do so with the best intentions. Be it detox, homeopathy, celery juice or the alkaline diet, most advocates truly believe in their methods. The most successful will have an army of adoring followers, all giving dramatic testimony regarding how the miracle worked for them. Often there are compelling before and after pictures, much like those in Savory's TED Talk, although I am more used to these showing improvements in abs rather than transformations of scrubland.

Also common is an assertion that it is not possible to analyse or study techniques using the scientific method. I have seen the claim that something is 'a holistic process that defies replication' enough times to be wary. I have also frequently heard the challenge that if a real-life experience shows that something works, why on earth do we need science to prove it? Why worry if something doesn't work in theory, when it obviously works in practice? So said the advocates of bloodletting, trepanning and exorcism.

There will always be advocates for whom Savory's techniques have worked, but perhaps missing from the picture are many others for whom it has not been successful. Professor Andres Cibils from New Mexico State University claims to have identified a number of ranchers Savory worked with, most of whom said that they had 'tried it and either modified or abandoned it because the results were a train wreck'. Much like with health, the variability and complexity of agriculture allows for some apparent successes to occur. People generally don't like sharing their failures, but every time the technique appears to succeed, it creates a passionate advocate who will shout about it from the rooftops. This can provide a convincing illusion that something always works, even if it hardly ever does.

In farming, everything is local and everything is complicated. What works well in one place will probably fail in others. This is why we need to be wary of claims that one idea can transform the world, especially when it resists scientific study and replication. Savory's work might simply show that farmers who care about their soil and look for ways to restore it tend to do better than those that don't. Perhaps we knew that anyway.

Seventy-three percent of all the land currently under grazing is suffering from degradation, mostly because it is already overstocked. High-density stocking almost always results in the compaction and destruction of land. But perhaps the real tragedy of Savory's claims is that in certain cases, there might just be something in it. An FAO report into the use of holistic management in Brazil showed that on certain farms, it has the potential to reduce the greenhouse emissions of livestock by eighteen percent.[34] Hardly world-saving, but definitely significant. In certain circumstances, good grazing practice can increase soil carbon and improve the land, and even has some potential for removing carbon from the atmosphere.

Pete Smith is Professor of Plant and Soil Science at Aberdeen University and Director of Scotland's Centre of Expertise on Climate Change. He is widely recognised as a world expert on the potential for soil improvements in mitigating climate change. On the claims made for this sort of rotational grazing, he told me:

I can see a mechanism where soil carbon could increase, especially in some dry countries, but there are some enormous claims being made on the potential for carbon capture. The hype is a long way ahead of the science, and any suggestion that we can do this and carry on using fossil fuels is absurd and dangerous. The claims are being made long before the science is in, and they might lead people to think we aren't in the middle of a climate emergency, which we definitely are.

The suggestion that eating more cows is going to reverse climate change is pure fantasy. For a start, there are only five billion hectares of potential rangeland around the world, and the maximum amount of carbon they could possibly hold is around 1.25 billion tonnes. To reverse climate change, we would require them to take up over thirteen billion tonnes every year, an order of magnitude higher.

Even if all the world's grazed land could achieve its maximum potential, there is another issue that advocates for cattle often choose to ignore. Even when some carbon does get locked up in the soil, the land soon becomes saturated, providing a one-time hit of atmospheric carbon removal as an area of land improves. Because of this, pasture can be considered an important carbon sink, but is not an infinite carbon drain. Once established, pasture does not pull any more carbon from the sky, yet the cattle grazing on it continue to produce methane indefinitely, meaning that any benefit of carbon capture is lost within a few years.

Although ecosystems can be completely circular and self-contained, in agriculture humans are breaking the cycle by definition. If grazing animals are pulling nutrients from the soil, and humans are removing those animals for milk or meat, eventually the soil will become depleted. You cannot just keep on taking from the land. Unless we can limit our population growth and change our demand for food, we are going to run out eventually.

Meaty Issues

Meat raises the passions like almost nothing else. But whilst it's important to debate the nuances, we must be careful not to sleepwalk our way towards disaster. Virtually no one who understands these issues is arguing that we should be eating more meat, and the current consumption patterns in every developed economy are completely unsustainable. Equally, no one I have spoken to is lobbying for the worldwide implementation of vegan diets, understanding that this is unrealistic, unhealthy and in many parts of the world, unsustainable. In truth, almost everyone arguing about burps and farts agrees about where we need to be, eating less meat and being more careful and considered about the way that it is produced. So instead of passionately arguing about the difference between fur and hair, we need to hurry up and get on with changing things.

The best solutions depend on increasing the amount of meat, eggs and dairy in the diet of the world's poorest nations, and dramatically reducing it across the developed world. At some point, consumption should meet in the middle, at a level that balances planetary and individual health. We are still a long way from knowing what that level might be, although a number of attempts have been made in recent years.

But arguing about how much is perhaps irrelevant if we do not also have ways of making that transition happen, somehow equitably distributing a limited amount of animal produce in a way that does not mirror the huge wealth inequalities across the world. This will be difficult to achieve, but as the future of humanity depends upon it, we have to have hope that it is possible.

A criticism often levelled at anyone campaigning for food system change on environmental grounds is that they are apologists for fossil fuel companies, passing the blame onto innocent cows, stood peacefully chewing the cud in picturesque fields. But when you know the facts, that criticism is absurd. All on its own, our current food system is on course to alter the planet for ever. Without a substantial reduction in the number of animal products that we consume, within the next few decades, agriculture will raise global temperatures by two degrees, destroy all of the world's forests, and drive a million species to extinction. Although power generation, industry, transport and construction will add significantly to that harm, and in many cases exceed it, if you work in food and do nothing but pass on blame, you really need to stand aside and let the grown-ups take over.

Improvements in agricultural efficiency are likely to be important, but they will not be sufficient. They might allow us a little more time before we hit the wall, but they cannot stop us from doing so.[35] We desperately need to change consumption, shrinking down the powerful meat and cattle industries, something that they will fight every step of the way. It is going to take every ounce of our collective creativity, skill, influence and strategy. We will need to completely restructure our food system, and at the same time work out a way of protecting the most vulnerable people from harm. When it comes to food, this is perhaps the most difficult battle we are likely to face.

Well, one of the biggest battles. Because across the next two chapters we are going to enter into an increasingly strange world, where the fight for the future of food takes some bizarre and surprising turns.

8

Local and Organic

Much that passes as idealism is disguised hatred or disguised love of power.

— Bertrand Russell

As we have seen already, assessing the sustainability of a single food item can be incredibly confusing. As a consumer, this can make any attempt to eat in a more environmentally friendly way extremely challenging. What people really need are simple signposts to guide them towards better choices. But as soon as a measure becomes consumer facing, food marketers will make sure that it rapidly turns into a target. Traffic light nutrition labels on UK food packaging were well intentioned, but they became useless the moment they were used as targets because companies found ways to game the system. When it comes to the environment, if you want to choose meat with the lowest greenhouse gas emissions, highly intensive barn-raised chickens are the way to go. But there are several good reasons why this might not be a 'better' option for the environment as a whole.

To make things easier, two influential signposts have emerged, selling themselves, at least in part, on their sustainability credentials. To save the planet, we should eat local food. And if we can't eat locally, then we should always choose organic produce. Both local and organic are kinder on the planet, taste good and are better for our health. Right?

Unfortunately, when we dig down into how the local and organic food movements came about, things get very dark very quickly. So much so that we might start to wonder if we should be basing our food choices on them at all.

But first, a little bit about the troubled history of my favourite food of all: potatoes.

The Other Revolution

There was a great agricultural revolution that occurred way before Norman Borlaug set to work in his Mexican test fields, and it was down to a single crop species. The potato, introduced into Europe from the New World towards the end of the sixteenth century, swept across the continent, transforming agricultural productivity as it went. Potatoes yielded between two and four times more calories per hectare than cereal grain, as well as being incredibly simple to grow and harvest, requiring little more than a shovel and a few days labour every year. They were easily stored by burying them underground for several months without the need for expensive barns, and often produced crops from otherwise unproductive land.

But perhaps more importantly, getting potatoes from the field to the plate required far less effort, equipment and skill than grain crops, with no need for milling, drying or baking in an oven. A simple pot over a fire could turn this bountiful crop into a delicious, filling, nutrient-packed source of energy. At a time when very few people had a kitchen in their homes, this was a big deal. European peasant populations that adopted the potato were thought to be stronger, healthier and less prone to nutrient deficiency than their wheat-eating counterparts.

Potatoes transformed European agriculture throughout the eighteenth and nineteenth centuries, freeing rural labour to move into the urban centres and helping to create the human force that powered the Industrial Revolution. When potatoes arrived in Europe, they allowed Europe to change the world.

But just like the Green Revolution, there were a few issues. Potatoes were highly susceptible to disease, and fungal infections could easily devastate crops. For this reason it was vitally important that countries and communities did not become too dependent upon this miracle food, and maintained a diverse agriculture that could see it through times of shortage. Wheat had fuelled Europe for many centuries, and it remained the dominant staple in most regions. Potatoes were generally the favoured crop of the poorest people, and when they occasionally failed, it was important that bread was available to make up the shortfall.

For one country, circumstances made maintaining such crop diversity particularly difficult. By the 1840s, Ireland was Europe's poorest nation, made destitute by years of abuse under English rule. Rural Ireland had been divided up between Scottish and English Protestant landowners, many of whom had never visited the country. They simply milked Irish land for profit, passing on management responsibilities to local agents, who would in turn divide it up between tenant farmers. In a drive to maximise profits, land was broken into smaller and smaller plots, with distant landowners often demanding extortionate rents.

Nearly half of plots took up only two hectares or less by 1840. These plots were often farmed by large families with many mouths to feed. With traditional crops or livestock it would have been impossible for people to live off such a small area, especially in the south-west of the country, where rainfall was too high to grow wheat, oats or barley reliably. The most sensible thing to raise would have been a combination of root crops, grain and livestock, but few farmers had enough land to do this.

The only crop that could feed entire families off such tiny plots was potatoes, and so these became the dominant source of nutrition for much of the country. As the brutal land ownership regime squeezed farmers into the most meagre living imaginable, potatoes became the gossamer thread holding them above the chasm of starvation. Tragically, it would not hold out for very long.

Many had a different view of the Irish problem, especially wealthy Protestants on the other side of the Irish Sea. In England, the Irish condition was widely thought to be a natural product of their flawed character. The Irish were considered idle, stupid, irresponsible and, worst of all, relentlessly Catholic. Potatoes, so the thinking of the day went, were the laziest way to farm the land, requiring the minimum labour to produce food. They were also a crop without all the pleasing Protestant religious metaphors associated with the production of grain and bread.

Throughout England, particularly among the rich landowning classes, it was widely believed that the Irish were breeding like rabbits, pausing only occasionally to feast on this devilish New World crop. When potatoes were hit by disease, these workshy Catholics would go cap in hand to their English neighbours, expecting to be bailed out once again. Few admitted that it was the cruelty of English landowners that had locked so many farmers into this cycle of relentless poverty, and potatoes were grown not through idleness, but because they were the only way of keeping bellies full.

Our old friend the Reverend Thomas Malthus was particularly vexed by the Irish problem, and it is widely thought that his famous essay on population growth was inspired by it. His obvious disdain for the Irish tendency towards 'virtuous attachment' was seemingly passed on to his students and followers, something that would play out in deadly fashion a few years down the line.

Local Food for Local People

Malthus wasn't just a repressed, xenophobic English cleric who believed humanity was doomed. He was an important economist and thinker, with a great deal of influence on the government of the day. Apart from falsely predicting catastrophe, he is perhaps best known for his support of the Corn Laws, legislation passed in 1815 that imposed tariffs on imported grain.* Like many at the time, Malthus believed that if foreign grain, particularly that being grown in the vast new farms across the Atlantic, came to the UK without restriction, British farming would rapidly become uneconomical. As a result, farmers would go out of business and food security would be undermined, leaving the country uniquely vulnerable to attack. Despite the rise of free trade economics, Malthus believed that British agriculture must be protected, something that he would argue until his death in 1834.

I made a similar point earlier in this book: if you cannot produce enough food to feed your country, there might be a price to pay during conflict. But the Corn Laws were also designed to protect the status quo for wealthy landowners who made much of their income from tenant farmers. The laws artificially raised the price of basic foods, keeping rural workers in poverty whilst landowners counted their cash. Whilst the aristocracy domi-nated the UK parliament, there was an interest in keeping the price of bread high and the common people hungry. But in the 1840s, three powerful forces were sweeping across Europe that would change things forever.

Industry, Revolution and Blight

Richard Cobden was a Manchester-based industrialist who represented the first of these forces. As new industries devel-oped, it became possible to create great wealth without the need for large tracts of inherited land. Cobden was a self-made man who considered the landed aristocracy a blight on the country: lazy and arrogant, they stood in the way of Britain's future as a powerful industrial force. In the Corn Laws, he saw an issue that might just shift the balance of power, and finally put the aristo-crats in their place.

* In nineteenth-century England, the term 'corn' referred to any grain crops and not just maize.

Cobden argued that whilst the price of bread was kept artificially high it trapped workers in pointless toil on unproductive and inefficient farms. Repeal the Corn Laws and imported grain would free this labour to work in the highly profitable mills and factories of the North. As food became cheaper, the extra money in the workers' pockets would fuel new spending on consumer goods, so driving new industries and increasing the country's wealth.

It was perhaps also the case that along with many of the new industrialists, Cobden felt that if food prices fell they could get away with paying factory workers less, and so drive greater profits for themselves. But even so, his Anti-Corn Law League managed to create huge support for repeal. The prospect of cheaper food, especially during the 1840s when much of Europe was entering a period of economic hardship, was always going to be a popular one.

Cobden entered parliament in 1841, and regularly debated against the Conservative government of the day for the Corn Laws to be repealed. Prime Minister Robert Peel was an advocate of the free market, but he was also influenced by the teachings of Malthus and felt agriculture to be a special case. It did not help that Peel's Conservative Party was almost entirely composed of aristocratic landowners whose incomes would be severely hit by a repeal of the laws and an influx of foreign grain.

Peel himself was no wealthy landowner; he had worked his way up through the civil service, becoming the first UK prime minister not to come from the landed gentry. He gradually started to be worn down by the logic of Cobden's arguments, and came to support repeal. In one memorable exchange, after a passionate speech by Cobden calling on Conservatives to give up feudal privileges in the mercantile age, Peel was stunned into silence. He tore up his notes, turned to a colleague and said, 'You must answer this, for I cannot.'

Peel would eventually commit political suicide, crossing the house to vote with the opposition and repeal the Corn Laws. In doing so, he split the Conservative Party in two, destroying it for a generation. He was ousted from power shortly afterwards, making way for a new government led by Lord Russell from the opposition Whig Party. It was a crucial moment in British politics, representing a shift in power from aristocratic landowners to new industrialists. A seemingly obscure argument about the price of grain went on to shape a nation. And at its heart, as with so much profound political change, was a battle about hunger.

Peel's reasons for this act of political self-destruction have been debated ever since. Was it the action of a man angered at his own party's selfishness, or a stand for the right of the common man to his daily bread? Maybe it was, as many have since suggested, an astute move to avoid the second force that was shaping Europe: the coming threat of revolution.

The 1840s was a time of great unrest, and in tipping the political balance away from rich aristocrats and towards the working man, Peel may have avoided a popular uprising. Just a few years later, much of Europe would fall into revolution and bloodshed. Repeal was a quiet, bloodless and very British revolution that alleviated some of the country's gnawing hunger and sense of injustice. Although it still sticks in the craw of many British Conservatives, they should perhaps be thankful that, unlike much of Europe, their ancestors never had to face a more violent threat.

But there was another factor that may have forced Peel's hand. Because a third force was busy sweeping across Europe in the 1840s, different but no less powerful than the other two. This one was a microscopic spore that would go on to brutalise a nation.

As prime minister, Robert Peel already knew exactly how serious potato blight would be should it hit Ireland. It first appeared on American farms in the early 1800s, and by 1844 had travelled on ships across to Europe. Once there, the spores hitched a ride on the wind, sweeping rapidly across Europe's extensive potato fields. Unlike other diseases, blight could wipe out an entire crop, turning the majority of affected potatoes into a brown, inedible mush, oozing with slime. It destroyed a huge number of European potatoes, eventually reaching Ireland in 1845. In its first year it would infect a third of the Irish crop, leaving many of Europe's poorest people desperately hungry and vulnerable.

Peel made a number of convoluted attempts to help the people of Ireland once blight arrived, although he stopped short of providing direct food aid. The Irish potato blight was part of his justification for repealing the Corn Laws, arguing that it would allow cheap grain to be imported, driving down prices and letting the power of the free market prevent famine. It is widely thought that this was little more than an exploitation of circumstance to justify a policy that he was going to force through anyway. But although Peel could certainly have done more to help in the early days of blight, he was broadly sympathetic towards the people of Ireland, and thought that steps should be taken to avoid famine in a land that was, after all, under direct British rule. The government that replaced him in June 1846 held a different view.

The management of the Irish blight problem was soon handed to a civil servant called Charles Trevelyan, who had studied under Malthus and shared his intense distaste for the Irish people. Along with many British politicians at the time, Trevelyan saw blight not as an urgent crisis, but an opportunity to reshape Ireland into a better country. In refusing to provide aid, they would induce a Malthusian catastrophe and reset the population, creating a new order. The lazy, feckless, potato-dependent Catholics would be wiped away like an infection, and a new stronger people would grow to replace them. This might sound unbelievable, but Trevelyan defined the blight as 'the sharp but effectual remedy by which the cure is likely to be effected. God grant that the generation to which this opportunity has been offered may rightly perform its part.'

Blight hit again late in 1846, this time much harder, destroying over three quarters of the crop. The following year, known as Black '47, would be one of the darkest in Irish history. Despite the Corn Law repeal, cheap grain never arrived, largely because much of Europe had been devastated by the same disease, and had little left to export. Even if it had arrived, those most in need would never have been able to afford it. They grew potatoes because they were poor and when their crops failed, they had nothing.

Perhaps most cruelly of all, the lack of imports was largely irrelevant. There was plenty to eat in Ireland, particularly in the east, where lower rainfall could easily support corn, barley, oats and pigs. But this bounty never reached the south or west, even when its people were starving to death. Most of it was exported to England – four thousand ships filled with food left Irish ports in 1847. Grain was fed to livestock, fattening them to produce ham, butter and bacon for the English to eat as a luxury. In those years, English pigs ate better than Irish people, a situation consciously engineered by Westminster politicians.

A million people died and well over a million took flight, reducing the country's population by a third. Tales of hardship and misery became legendary throughout the world, with towns such as Skibbereen becoming synonymous with human suffering. Despite Ireland falling under the jurisdiction of one of the wealthiest and most powerful nations of the time, shocking reports led to relief money being raised around the world. It is sometimes claimed that enslaved people on the plantations of North America helped raised funds to feed Ireland. Eventually, intense international scrutiny forced Trevelyan to relent, and famine relief was sent, but help arrived years too late.

Trevelyan and the Westminster government broke the Irish with their cruelty, leaving deep scars across the nation that rightly remain to this day. Perhaps more than any case of mass hunger that we have discussed so far, the Irish famine was the deliberate starvation of people out of a misguided sense of moral superiority. This is the true face of Malthusian thinking.

Beyond the Corn Laws

The Corn Law repeal eventually drove down food prices, encouraged imports from the Americas, and perhaps staved off a revolution in England. Once Irish bellies were full, they fought hard for vital land reforms that prevented the return of hardship. When blight hit again in 1879 it caused some hunger but few deaths, proving once and for all that it was not the blight that had killed so many, but human neglect and cruelty.

But what about the potential threat to national sovereignty from shifting the grain supply abroad? How was that issue ever resolved? The unsettling truth is that before and after the Corn Laws were repealed, Britain was not food secure, and still isn't today. Since the eighteenth century, the UK has been unable to produce enough to feed its population adequately, and it currently imports around forty percent of all the food it consumes. Professor Ian Boyd is the Chief Scientific Officer at the UK government's Department for Environment, Food and Rural Affairs. He told me:

> We could probably provide all the food we need from within the UK, but it would support a very different diet from the one we enjoy now. We have relied on a global food system since the repeal of the Corn Laws, and nothing since then has suggested that this was not a good idea – except perhaps during WWII – even if some people are still arguing that we should go back to a pre-repeal system. The UK food economy is worth around £110 billion, and farming is only about 12% of the total. The rest is processing and the conversion of commodities – many of which are imported – into products with added value. There is nothing in that picture which suggests we should grow everything locally. Depending on the crop, it can be a lot more resource efficient to grow it elsewhere. The UK does not have an abundance of either high quality land or sunlight, both of which are needed for agriculture to thrive.

The idea that our continued sovereignty depends on our ability to feed ourselves is a myth, and a highly pervasive one. Through two world wars, Britain was vulnerable to starvation if the supply of foreign grain was cut off. It was not 'digging for victory' that kept Britain fed, but maintaining naval superiority. There was hardship, shortage, but never mass starvation.

As Ireland showed during its Great Famine, when agriculture focuses solely upon growing enough calories locally, it can create a dangerously precarious food system, prone to collapse and shortage. And as Britain has shown ever since, within a small and limited country, a diverse food supply linked to international trade is preferable, allowing us to specialise in the things we do well, and import what isn't suited to our land.

Our bakeries have long been supplied with imported high-protein wheat, grown on the plains of North America and Ukraine. The majority of the picturesque wheat fields in eastern England produce a crop of such low quality that it is destined for animal feed. We drink wine and consume olive oil from abroad, and eat beef and dairy from rich domestic pasture, which is exactly the way it should be. Despite years of European food subsidies, the UK cannot feed itself, nor, I would argue, should it attempt to.

The evidence to support the notion that eating local food is better for the planet is surprisingly thin. The concept of 'Food Miles' was the first sustainability metric applied to food, and for a while was widely adopted. It seems such a logically sound premise, to reduce transportation by eating things grown near where you live. Shop at local farmers' markets, support local producers, give back to the rural community, and cut down on those gas-guzzling trucks shipping plastic-wrapped produce to giant air-conditioned supermarkets. Think global, eat local.

Sadly, however, despite this near-ubiquitous message, the reality is anything but clear-cut. Even where it is highest, in countries like the US and UK, transport generally only represents around eleven to twelve percent of the greenhouse emissions of food production. The energy required to heat local hothouses often vastly exceeds the energy required to ship produce from warmer countries, and minimising transport often does not minimise the environmental impact. Although some perishable crops such as green beans or asparagus are frequently airfreighted, which does have a much higher environmental impact, often these high-value products provide vital sources of income in developing countries, enabling much-needed investment in agriculture.

Efficiency most often comes through scale. Life Cycle Assessments show that the highly efficient logistics of large supermarkets, with modern trucks, backhauling and economies of scale, have an environmental impact far lower than the ramshackle vans and pickups transporting produce to farmers' markets.* And it is all very well telling people to eat only food from just a few miles away, but in many parts of the world where winters are harsh, this would lead to a pretty grim and restricted diet for much of the year.[1]

International trade in food developed for a reason. Agriculture is a tough way to make a living, and specialisation means that people can get more out of their land. This greater efficiency is hugely positive for the environment. Trade across countries also means that a wider selection of food is now available to individuals, even as globally the number of different crops being grown has fallen. Active trade routes mean that local crop failures are now far less likely to result in famine and death. Food has become cheaper, supply more reliable and production more efficient.

A wider selection of foods from a more diverse area has also benefited people's health. In many areas, deficiencies in the soil can lead to deficiencies in the diet if people are restricted to local produce. In Derbyshire, just a few miles from where I am writing, alkaline soils strongly bind iodine, stopping it from getting into plants. For hundreds of years, goitre, an enlarged thyroid

---

* A Life Cycle Assessment (LCA) is a systematic study of the environmental impact of a product throughout its entire life, from manufacture, transport, use and disposal. Backhauling is about making sure trucks are always full, even on return journeys.

gland caused by iodine deficiency, was known as 'Derbyshire Neck', such was its prevalence in the county. Although it was long thought to be caused by drinking the local river water, the reality was that when people only ate food produced locally, their diets were deficient in iodine, leading to swollen and deformed necks, a high prevalence of neurological disorders, stillbirths and widespread infertility. As food supplies opened up towards the end of the nineteenth century, goitre began to disappear from Derbyshire, long before anyone knew the true cause.[2]

The truth is that from a health, environment and taste perspective, what we eat is far more important than where it is produced. But despite this, a powerful movement has grown up around local food, spearheaded by passionate chefs and food writers. Pioneered by Alice Waters in the US, and developed by the likes of Michael Pollan, Dan Barber and Hugh Fearnley-Whittingstall, local food is championed, chefs are encouraged to engage with farmers, and the best food is thought to be produced by those who regularly get mud on their boots. In many ways, I sympathise. If chefs know and support their local producers, understand where their food comes from, and give carefully produced ingredients the respect they deserve, then surely they will produce better cuisine. But too often, doing what feels right comes at the expense of reason and evidence.[3]

In many ways, our desire for self-sufficiency is a hangover from the rise of nationalism in the 1930s. Mussolini's infamous 'Battle of the Grain' in Italy was a drive to remove dependence upon foreign imports, involving legislation similar to the Corn Laws. In a bid to produce enough wheat to feed the country, thousands of established vineyards, olive groves and orchards were torn up, often leaving land vastly unsuited for cereal crops. Much of Italy's food history and tradition was destroyed, and as a result, wheat was often the only food that people could afford.

Food, agriculture and the natural world can create blind spots where we fail to spot unpleasant rhetoric, allowing bigotry and nationalistic jingoism to sneak in through the back door.

Sometimes, a seemingly benign argument for environmentalism or support of your local community can serve as cover for something very dark indeed.

Blood and Soil

In 2017, at a 'Unite the Right' rally in Charlottesville, Virginia, Neo-Nazi groups were heard chanting the surprising and little-known extreme-right phrase 'blood and soil'. This resurfaced again later the same year during the 'White Lives Matter' march at Shelbyville. Then, in 2019, after the horrific Christchurch shooting in New Zealand, the perpetrator was found to have described himself as an 'ecofascist' in his manifesto. Despite their seemingly liberal and progressive personas, local food, environmentalism and the organic movement have some truly unpleasant roots.[4]

'Blood and soil' was a central tenet of German fascism during the 1930s, which has uncomfortable commonalities with subsequent local food movements. Despite Haber and Bosch's best efforts, lengthy blockades meant that by 1917 many in Germany were going hungry, often taking to the streets in protest. Hitler strongly believed that losing the home front in this way had lost Germany the Great War. He was well aware that a nation will doubt the legitimacy and competence of its leadership the moment bread fails to reach the shelves, and on taking power, the Nazi regime pursued food security, especially as they planned for conflict.

The idea of 'blood and soil' was based on a book by Richard Walther Darré, a Nazi physician who would later become Hitler's minister of agriculture. As well as being a eugenicist and selective-breeding advocate, Dr Darré was a local food enthusiast, and argued that only food specifically grown on German soil was suitable for the German people. He claimed that the supposedly superior Aryan race had a deep connection with the landscape and produce of its homeland, and must be fed from there alone.

Key in Darré's writing was an idolisation of German agricultural workers as the backbone of the country, something that tapped into a pervasive early-twentieth-century distrust of urban living. This is classic retrograde, appeal-to-nature bullshit, a theme that sadly persists in much environmental and food writing today. It imagines a perfect, Edenic state somewhere deep in the country's medieval past which modern humanity has recklessly ruined. According to this vein of thinking, purity and value can only be regained by returning to the countryside, a simpler world without the confusions of mixed ethnicity and bustling crowds. Only truly naturalised people can exist within a country's natural landscape.

Blood and soil informed much Nazi ideology. Hatred of cities was often a coded reference for hatred of Jewish people, who throughout Europe had been prevented from buying land and so largely lived in urban areas. A mystical connection between the German people and their soil ran directly counter to the lives of nomadic Jewish and Romany populations. Non-sedentary groups were cast as inferior, uprooted, inhuman.

Blood and soil meant that outsiders could never truly belong in a country. Anyone considered non-German was using up vital resources and should be immediately removed. In *Mein Kampf*, Hitler outlined how foreign policy should centre on obtaining more land to grow food for the German people. Particularly in his sights were the extensive wheat producing areas of Russia's 'bread basket', Ukraine.

A belief in blood and soil meant that Germans were persuaded to eat only domestic produce. People were encouraged to consume less animal produce, bake rye bread instead of using imported wheat, and consume whole grains to prevent waste and excess. A tenuous link between local food and good health was created, based on a bizarre but remarkably persistent blend of nationalism and soil worshipping spirituality. Laws prevented anyone without German blood from farming the land, excluding them from infiltrating the rural idyll. Inspired by Darré's book, the natural and local food movements became hugely popular, a patriotic choice to help propel the country into a bright future. The reality was that the German people were being secretly prepared for war.[5]

Of course, for legal reasons I do not believe that all local food advocates are closet Neo-Nazis, and many local food movements have emerged without poisonous political associations. But it is always worth questioning why we favour local foods, and often wrongly assign them a whole unity of virtues. It does not take much for passionate support of local produce to slip into a call to exclude dangerous foreign elements. A love of a country's food, nature or produce can be a profound and beautiful thing. But it can also be the acceptable face of insular nationalism, leading otherwise reasonable people to sit on common ground with ideologies they despise. Local food can be a source of great pleasure, but choosing it does not set you on a path to spiritual betterment.

We should produce the best food we can within a given region, and trade with the rest of the world to ensure the best diet for all. This is the system that has developed and flourished as the world population has grown, with global order gradually emerging from local chaos. There is no reason to believe that the landscape around us, defined by arbitrary national borders, is capable of providing everything we need for our present or our future. In many cases, we know that it barely provided for our past.

Local food can be a valuable buffer against external supply problems, much like the bank on four legs in Central Africa. Connection to local farms can also help people foster a better understanding of how food is produced, which is not to be sniffed at. But for a properly functioning food system, the world should grow grain only where grain grows best, graze cattle on the right sort of pasture, and produce maize where the Sun shines brightly. The environmental cost of transport is almost always outweighed by the efficiency of producing the right species in the right soil and climate. As for food sovereignty, we never had it. If the world powers decide upon a global conflict tomorrow, I dearly hope we have enough time to worry about the price of grain.

Planet Organic

I said at the beginning of this chapter that we are going to be looking at two of the most common signposts used to assess a food's sustainability, and addressing why both of them are deeply flawed. Now that we are moving on to the organic movement, at least we can leave behind any troubling Nazi connections.

Ah. About that . . .

Biodynamism

> If the blonds and blue-eyed people die out, the human race will become increasingly dense . . . In the case of fair people, less nourishment is driven into the eyes and hair; it remains instead in the brain and endows it with intelligence. Brown and dark-haired people drive the substances into their eyes and hair that the fair people retain in their brains.
>
> – Rudolf Steiner, *Health and Illness Volume One*

Rudolf Steiner was a powerful and politically connected Austrian philosopher perhaps best known for founding Waldorf schools and creating a bizarre alternative health system known as Anthroposophic Medicine.* What is less well known about him is that he was a rabid anti-Semite and racist who created a pseudoscientific theory of root races to justify his ideas about Aryan superiority, and believed that the persecution of Jews was part of their 'inner destiny'.

Towards the end of his life, in 1925, Steiner also developed a theory of agricultural practice called biodynamic agriculture.

---

* By 'alternative' I mean that it has no basis in logic, evidence or reason, and doesn't actually work. If you like the sort of medicine that is effective at treating disease, it is not really an alternative.

Much of this was entirely sensible and ahead of its time, focusing on the importance of continued soil fertility rather than crop yields, a rejection of chemical fertilisers, and viewing the farm as an ecosystem rather than a food-growing medium. But other parts of his biodynamic doctrine were bizarre: Steiner believed in reincarnation and astral forces, and this extended to his theory of agriculture. Invisible cosmic rays were thought to affect the soil, and the Earth was believed to breathe twice a day. The sowing of seeds needed to coincide with patterns found in astral charts, often requiring work by the light of the Moon.

'Preparation 500' was a key factor in biodynamic farming, made by packing cow manure into the horn of a steer, burying it, digging it up a few months later, mixing it with water, stirring it and then spraying it onto the field. Steiner helpfully explains that a cow's horns are actually antennae to help it communicate with the astral plane, and farmyard manure is permeated with ethereal forces, meaning that when they are combined and buried, some special stuff happens. But you have to be careful – the magic is only released if you stir the rotten faeces in a particular rhythm. Preparation 500 is still used on the five thousand or so biodynamic farms that exist around the world today, so someone, somewhere is actually stirring rotten shit right now.

It was through biodynamic farming that the Steiner organisation most influenced the Nazis, finding common ground with a love of naturalness, distasteful racial theories and a belief in the occult. Rudolf Hess was a particularly ardent fan, and many of the Third Reich leaders were strong advocates of biodynamic agriculture. Steiner's thinking strongly influenced the so-called Green Wing of the Nazi Party, and a biodynamic plantation was set up at Dachau to produce naturopathic materials for 'experiments'.* Strangely, much of this information fails to make the

---

* Probably better described as 'brutal, inhuman torture' rather than 'experiments'. But at least the Nazis wasted a bit of time stuffing shit into cow horns and reading pointless astral charts.

websites of the various biodynamic associations around the world.[6]

Biodynamic farming would go on to influence organic movements across Central Europe after the war. Although many abandoned the more bizarre aspects of Steiner's thought, and his vile racism is largely forgotten, biodynamic agriculture still exists in its pure form today, including magic horns filled with shit, astral charts and planting by the Moon. The growth of biodynamic farming was paralleled by the development of similar movements around the world, a few of which did not require the coexistence of poisonous political ideologies.

A few. But not quite all.

Tarka the Black Shirt

Published in 1927, Henry Williamson's *Tarka the Otter* is a gentle tale set in the North Devon countryside, detailing the adventures of an anthropomorphic river mammal. Over the years, *Tarka* has become one of the UK's favourite and most enduring books about the natural world. It is so beloved that it has never been out of print, and was once narrated by David Attenborough on audio cassette (remember them?). Later in his career, Williamson's editors would frequently have to ask him to remove sections of his nature writing, because it turns out that he was not always the kindly, endearing figure that we might imagine him to be.

These days, it seems jarring to think of far right politics and environmentalism coming together. Yet between the wars, the natural world, eugenics and a hatred of urban culture united the political extremes, including the very worst of British fascism. Williamson was a great admirer of Hitler, a keen member of Oswald Mosley's notorious Blackshirts, and formed a group called 'Kinship in Husbandry' with the prominent fascist and anti-Semite Jorian Jenks. Their organisation was dedicated to spreading a belief that new methods of organic farming could restore the moral, physical and economic health of the UK. They championed a form of agriculture that had been developed by Sir Albert Howard, a British botanist who had a pragmatic approach to soil management, based on a so-called 'law of return'. Central to Howard's doctrine was a belief that the new artificial fertilisers were toxic, and agricultural soil should be regularly enriched with animal manure.

Although he was no fascist himself, Howard's organic movement was far from being an early incarnation of a hippy commune. He joined forces with a number of disillusioned aristocrats and Christians, united in a belief that new forms of industrial farming were against God and destroying the natural world. The early organic movement was funded by the same money that had supported the Corn Laws. The landowning class, although still wealthy, had been marginalised by the industrial age. The organic movement provided an opportunity for them to rail against progress, demanding a return to a glorious past.

Key within the early movement were figures like Lord Northbourne, who coined the term organic, and Lady Eve Balfour. Balfour imbued the early British organic movement with a mysticism that often discredited it, leading to advocates being excluded from serious conversations about how to improve farming. Then, in 1946, Balfour teamed up with the fascist Jorian Jenks to form the Soil Association. Jenks continued to spew hate and bile throughout the 1940s and 1950s whilst editing the Association's journal. Although the Soil Association did start moving towards the political left shortly before Jenks died in 1963, they maintain a strong support of local food movements and a deep organisational distrust of international trade.[7] *

---

* A similar organic farming movement spread across the US via the very different figure of Jerome Rodale, a self-made entrepreneur who was heavily influenced by Howard's work. Rodale was widely attacked as a spiritualist and kook by US farmers, and held a Balfour-like belief in a mysterious life force within the soil. His reputation was not enhanced when, at seventy-two, he died of a heart attack

Organic Today

The Soil Association is now just one of 283 organic associations around the world, championing organic methods and providing accreditation for farms. But what exactly is organic farming? And crucially, is it a good signpost for sustainability? Because if it actually reduces the environmental impact of food production, most of us would probably forgive its embarrassing past associations.[8]

Globally, organic is a reasonably broad church, but generally speaking it describes farming methods that involve minimal use of pesticides, no artificial fertilisers, no genetically modified produce, free-range animals, and no routine use of antibiotics. Much like the sensible parts of the biodynamic movement, it is focused on building soil health, treating the farm as an ecosystem, and minimising disruption with chemicals. Good organic farms will use compost and manure to build up soil carbon, plant a diverse set of crops, and attempt to manage pests naturally.

Advocates claim that organic is a more natural method of farming, and so is bound to be better, both for people's health and for the environment. This sounds convincing, but does it really stack up? This is an important question, because the majority of people purchasing organic food do so for these perceived benefits.

From an environmental perspective, the evidence in favour of organic certainly doesn't look great. Many different studies have been conducted, but the balance seems to show that per unit of food, organic farming produces more greenhouse gases, uses more land, has higher rates of nutrient run-off, causes more eutrophication of water systems, and is worse for acidification of

during a television interview, shortly after drinking his own recipe of asparagus boiled in urine and claiming that he was going to live to be a hundred.

soil.* Energy use is generally lower in organic systems because there is no need to manufacture nitrogen fertiliser. But as energy is one of the smallest environmental pressures created by food production, this is really only a marginal benefit.[9]

These results may be surprising, but they have been widely replicated and are reasonably consistent. Obviously, there is some variance between different food types: for instance, organic pulses, beans and fruit create lower greenhouse emissions, whereas organic vegetables are worse for energy use, largely because weeds are controlled using flamethrowers.† Eutrophication tends to be higher in organic systems, because although manure improves soil structure, it also provides less control over nutrient release, with large amounts of nitrogen and phosphorus running off when rainfall is high.

Organic often fosters good biodiversity on farms, with many different species living in and among crops, but this effect is largely down to the low yields found in organic systems. If methods are introduced to increase yields, biodiversity decreases accordingly, meaning that one of organic's most touted benefits is probably just a side effect of its greatest weakness.[10]

Low yields are the huge, unspoken problem when it comes to organic production. On almost every farm, more land is required to produce the same amount of food. This is particularly the case for crops such as wheat or maize. Organic wheat yields are around twenty-seven percent lower on similar ground, and organic maize produces thirty-five percent less. When the additional effect of land use is taken into account, it pushes organic production even further into environmental deficit. Organic peas, usually among the better performing crops, were found to have a fifty percent bigger climate impact than conventional ones

---

* Sometimes organic looks better if assessed per unit of land, but as this is a book about preventing hunger, I feel it is best to concentrate on impact per unit of food. Organic usually performs far worse when assessed in this way because of the lower yields.

† I've never really understood how this counts as working with nature.

when calculations accounted for land use differences.[11] In fact, organic farming is pretty much indefensible when it comes to land use.

It all comes back to the issue of 'land sharing' versus 'land sparing'. Should we maximise farm yields at all costs and transform the spare land created into wild spaces, or should we accept lower yields and encourage on-farm biodiversity? Although data always tends to favour the land sparing approach, often this is not as clear-cut as it seems. Hanna Tuomisto is an Associate Professor in Sustainable Food Systems at the University of Helsinki who specialises in the life cycle analysis of food production. She told me:

> People assume that organic is better, but when you look at the data, it is not evidence based. But it does depend on what you are looking at. Theoretically it is better to intensively farm less land, but in reality that is not what happens. There is no good evidence to show that intensive farming leads to more land becoming available for biodiversity. If agriculture intensifies, the prices drop and demand rises. Even if food demand is limited, demand for land will shift to other agricultural uses such as biofuel. It might actually be good to pay more for organic food and ensure we have more biodiversity where there is farming.

In an ideal world, we would all have the foresight to set aside land for wildlife, but in practice, we put to use any land that might make us money. So this is just one more area where the theory collides with the real world.

One other point is rarely discussed in conversations about organic farming. Contrary to popular belief, organic farming does not expressly forbid the use of all pesticides in the way that is sometimes implied. It simply restricts what can and cannot be applied and attempts to limit use. Many different pesticides are used in organic systems, including some of the most toxic, such

as copper sulphate and rotenone.* Even a few synthetic chemicals are sometimes allowed if they are the only way of controlling
a particular pest. This is a huge bone of contention within the
organic industry, with many believing in an absolute ban, leaving
crops to perish if pests cannot be naturally controlled. But clearly
such a system would increase prices and further reduce yields,
digging the knife even further into organic food's Achilles heel.[12]

On average, organic does tend to win when it comes to stored
soil carbon, which is an extremely important environmental
metric. But this is only because a lot of conventional agriculture
is catastrophically bad at keeping carbon in the soil, rather than
any intrinsic advantage of organic methods. After all, there are no
tools for retaining soil carbon available to organic farmers that
conventional farmers cannot also use. The opposite, however, is
not necessarily true.[13]

No Till Problem

The development of no-till farming systems has been a quiet revolution in agriculture in recent years. Originally developed in
drought-prone regions of Australia and the US as a way of helping
with water retention, it is a system that removes the need for
ploughing the land, using special planters that sow grain and
seeds with minimum soil disruption. It has been remarkably
successful, with no-till and minimum-till systems spreading
rapidly around the world. It allows crops to be grown with far less
work, far less fuel, and far less soil disruption. Combined with a
clever use of cover crops and rotations, it is also an extremely
effective way of restoring soil carbon, as well as preventing erosion.
Many consider it to be the holy grail of sustainable agriculture.

---

* The EU did recently attempt to ban copper sulphate because of a high toxicity
and cancer risk, but had to relent because of the lack of alternatives available to
organic farmers.

But when it comes to organic no-till, there is a problem. One of the main reasons for ploughing is to get rid of weeds, and without weedkillers such as glyphosate, no-till isn't an option. Without ploughing or chemical control, weed suppression requires either back-breaking labour, plastic sheeting, or an extensive, fast-growing cover crop that will outcompete any weeds. These sort of cover crops can work in some circumstances, but they come with their own issues, providing little protection from perennial weeds, and often delaying crop growth. Organic no-till is still possible in some cases, but it is always far more challenging and often not feasible at all. If the world were to go organic tomorrow, or even just ban glyphosate as some European countries already have, one of the most promising new sustainable farming practices would be largely lost.

Generally speaking, organic systems were designed in temperate European and US farms, meaning that organic certification often requires the implementation of practices that are not suitable elsewhere. This can cause many valuable new ideas to be rejected out of hand. For instance, the use of biochar, charcoal created by burning organic matter at low temperatures in special ovens, is another tool for sequestering carbon in the soil. A practice first developed in the Amazon thousands of years ago, biochar can be made from almost any carbon-containing waste, including wood, grain, crop residue, leaves and even plastic bags. It can be buried into the soil, improving long-term carbon storage and enriching the land at the same time. But organic regulators have a difficult relationship with biochar. The crop scientist and writer Dr Sarah Taber told me:

> Biochar should be adopted, but organic certification people have decreed that it needs to be made from wood for it to be organic. There is a mindset in organic that only traditional European practices are allowed. It's often just a feel-good factory for white folks. They talk a good

sustainability game, but they are all about preserving cultural privilege. It's almost a vehicle for covert white supremacy.

Too often, organic farming is not based on the best available new evidence but on a toxic mix of cultural privilege, mysticism and a rejection of modernity. If it really is a righteous effort to improve the soil, the movement must resist the retrograde desire to return to an imagined past. Despite the pitfalls, much about organic is entirely sensible. It recognises the importance of soil health and structure, appreciates the value of stored carbon, and was way ahead of its time in doing so. It looks at the farm as a system, rather than a hydroponic medium for plant growth. It finds new ways to control pests and weeds, many of which may help combat the increasing threat of pesticide resistance.

Organic production is innovative, and because of its limitations, it often manages to find novel solutions. Many clever insights into the use of varied cover crops originally came from organic farms. The sort of complex crop rotations that enhance soil health and productivity stem from organic. In the same way that Formula 1 produces technical breakthroughs that eventually filter down into road cars, organic can be a hotbed of testing, insight and creativity.

But it will never feed the world, and here's why.

Half the World Away

Crucial to the organic movement is a complete rejection of artificial fertilisers, including nitrogen produced by the Haber–Bosch process. But just remember for a moment William Crookes's dramatic speech to the British Association in Chapter 2. We were starting to run out of nitrogen in the late nineteenth century, when the world population was only around 1.6 billion. Farming back then was largely what would now be termed organic and although a few technologies have sprung up since, exactly how many people could the world support without being able to capture bread from the air?*

This calculation is difficult, but it has been done. It is possible to capture atmospheric nitrogen using legumes with their special fixing bacteria, but there are limits on the amount that can be fixed per hectare, and we cannot live on beans. To grow enough food, especially the large amounts of cereal crops required to feed humanity, something else would be needed to enrich the soil. Guano and mineral reserves would swiftly run out with the hugely increased demand. Animal manure and compost only recycle nitrogen from one place to another, never actually adding any more into the system.

Vaclav Smil performs this calculation in his book *Enriching the Earth*, and similar work elsewhere has produced almost identical results.[14] Without nitrogen fertiliser, we might be able to feed up to four billion people on frugal diets with little meat or dairy. On our current diets, the limit would be around three billion. The problem with side-by-side comparisons of modern-day organic versus conventional yields is that they only reflect a post-Haber world where nitrogen is never going to run out. If organic was the only system, it quickly would. Add to this the impact of removing pesticides, without which it is thought that agricultural production would fall by another forty percent, and it is a pretty grim picture.[15]

There is no way around this for organic advocates. However good the productivity or profitability of individual farms, on a global scale that sort of farming would hit a wall very quickly. The shocking truth is that if you want the world to go completely organic, you need to decide which half of the population you are prepared to kill. Our progress has had a cost, but in accepting and understanding this, we should not overlook its considerable benefits.

---

* Congratulations to everyone who remembered that chemically altered superphospate was widely used at this time and is not allowed in organic systems.

Organic will, perhaps sensibly, remain a tiny niche within the food systems of rich and privileged countries, currently covering only 1.4% of world farmland. That a few wealthy people are willing to pay more for organic's restrictive practices is probably a good thing, as it allows this type of production to inspire wider changes to the way we farm. If, as many have suggested, Europe were to go completely organic, it might just be able to feed itself sustainably, but the huge reduction in yields would have reverberations around the world. An organic Europe would cause huge damage to tropical forests and ecosystems in distant lands. To suggest this path is the embodiment of isolationism, a parroting of early fascist propaganda that betrays organic and local food's dark past: stop the world, we want to get off.

But interestingly, in recent years some potential solutions have started to emerge that might just provide answers to organic's big problems. New technology is providing a vision of a future where the nitrogen issue is removed from the equation completely, finally making Haber–Bosch irrelevant. Fields of wheat could be grown with little need to spray or enrich the soil at all, preventing nutrient run-off and stopping eutrophication in its tracks. The fossil fuel energy of nitrogen fixation would be removed completely from the system, and organic or near-organic farms would finally be capable of feeding the world.

This sounds like something that the movement might be keen to embrace. But instead, it is the one thing that they fear the most.

9

GMO

It may be that this solution is not the final one. Nitrogen bacteria teach us that nature, with her sophisticated forms of the chemistry of living matter, still understands and utilises methods which we do not as yet know how to imitate.

> – Fritz Haber, receiving the Nobel Prize
> for Chemistry in 1919

'If I had one of these ready now, it would pretty much change the debate,' Professor Giles Oldroyd tells me as we discuss one of the most contentious issues in food. I suspect he may well be correct, although the plant he is describing is still a little way off. 'We'll definitely have them by 2050,' he says, although he won't be drawn into anything more specific about his Gates Foundation funded project. But his tone gives away his excitement: a generation of miracle plants might be considerably closer than that.

Some of the oldest plant fossils on Earth show evidence of interactions with a group of fungi (specifically 'arbuscular mycorrhizal'), suggesting that they were incredibly important in the development of complex life. These strange fungi have a symbiotic relationship with most plants, including all modern crop species, interacting with roots to provide a network of fine filaments that expand out into the soil. The fungi play a particular role in helping plants take up phosphorus, making this hard-to-access nutrient a little more available.

But it is not mycorrhizal fungi that have Professor Oldroyd, a plant biologist at Oxford University, so excited about the future. As already mentioned, some plants have the ability to form interactions with other types of microorganisms. Of particular interest are legumes, which grow root nodules that provide a home for nitrogen-fixing bacteria, giving these plants the ability to capture nitrogen directly from the air.

As Fritz Haber found during his years of experimentation, the bond between atoms that form molecules of nitrogen gas is extremely strong and very hard to break. The ability to do so is unusual in the natural world largely because it is so energy expensive, but also because in any closed ecosystem nutrients are recycled and there is little need for extra nitrogen. But as we have discussed, agriculture is not a closed system, so if other crops could fix their own nitrogen it would be transformative for world food production. Remarkably, with the development of new technologies, it seems that this might soon be possible.

Giles Oldroyd explained to me that although the ability of legumes to associate with nitrogen-fixing bacteria is a complex process with lots of steps, it is actually very similar to the process that enables all plants to interact with mycorrhizal fungi. This means that most of the biological mechanisms required already exist in almost every plant. In fact, there are only about three genes that are specific to nitrogen-fixing plants, compared to around 120 for the entire mycorrhizal association.

The reason why this is so exciting is that if that small, select number of nitrogen-specific genes can be introduced into major crop species such as wheat or corn, they could potentially fix their own nitrogen. If this can be done efficiently enough, it could make chemical nitrogen fertilisers obsolete, as each plant would take what it needs directly from the air. Once this is possible, it would mean that the use of phosphorus and potassium could be hugely optimised; mycorrhizal fungi and bacteria would grow freely around crop roots; carbon would be returned to the soil; and the whole of modern agriculture would be revolutionised. We would be talking about wheat that can fertilise itself.

It is almost impossible to overstate the potential impact of such a breakthrough. It could transform food production in the developed world, where excess fertiliser use is so damaging, but also in developing countries, where lack of available nitrogen is such a limiting factor. But although they would almost certainly change the face of modern food production, the fact that they would be GMOs, genetically modified organisms, would create a whole world of problems. The likelihood is that making this one change will also necessitate changes to a host of other genes. Breaking the nitrogen bond requires an awful lot of energy, with as much as twenty-five percent of all the solar power captured by legumes being lent to bacteria for that reaction alone. If wheat is to fix its own nitrogen, it would almost certainly need more energy than it can currently capture through photosynthesis.

But even this sort of transformation might be possible using different types of genetic modification. It turns out that the photosynthesis of most plants is extremely inefficient, and a number of programmes are currently under way attempting to increase the energy capture of different crops, helping to turn more of the Sun's energy into food.[1] It is thought that increases of forty to fifty percent are not just possible, but highly likely in the near future.

There are other projects looking at different methods of nitrogen capture, including the direct transfer of a nitrogen-fixing enzyme from bacteria into plants.[2] It has also recently been discovered that some varieties of wild maize have previously unknown methods of fixing nitrogen, with aerial roots secreting a sticky mucus-like substance that harbours special bacteria.[3] Although some advances might be made using conventional breeding, it seems likely that in order to address the nitrogen fertiliser issues that the world is facing, genetic modification will provide the solution.

This is not going to be a discussion of whether GMOs are safe because that has already been established. There is no credible source of information regarding the potential for GMOs to damage human health, and plenty of evidence of benefit. GMOs have been widely consumed by millions of humans for over twenty years, and there has not been a single verified case of harm. This is certainly not for want of people looking. The 'evidence' against seems to be based upon a few 1950s B-movie horror plots, and the use of the word 'Frankenfood'. Claiming GMOs are unsafe is as ridiculous and unscientific as denying climate change, although for some reason far more socially acceptable.

GMOs are completely safe according to the World Health Organization in 2014, the American Association for the Advancement of Science in 2012, the European Union in 2010, the British Royal Society in 2009 and countless others.[4] In 2016, 134 Nobel Prize winners wrote an open letter to the environmental organisation Greenpeace asking them to ditch their campaign opposing the introduction of Golden Rice.[5] Golden Rice is a potentially transformative genetically modified rice variety containing Vitamin A, developed as a non-profit humanitarian project to prevent devastating deficiency diseases in the developing world, including childhood blindness. Along with numerous other anti-GMO organisations, Greenpeace have campaigned to keep this crop from people in desperate need, seemingly for ideological reasons alone. Passions run high when it comes to GMO, and often seem to trump logic, sense or even compassion.

The safety of genetically modified foods is hardly surprising, because there is no known mechanism by which eating them could cause harm. We eat genetic material of some sort in every meal, and it is digested down to be unrecognisable before it reaches our bloodstream. Genes are regularly transferred between organisms naturally, with even our own genomes containing much DNA of non-human origin. Fears about genetic modification are based on misinformation, misunderstanding and the concerted efforts of a number of campaigning individuals determined to undermine this technology at every step.

Many of their reasons for doing so are similar to the naturalistic fallacy that we saw in the early years of the organic movement, with resistance to change, fear of the seemingly 'unnatural', and an often unshakable belief that a return to the past is the key to a better future. By and large, those resisting GMOs are drawn from organic associations, misguided environmentalists, campaigning chefs and a few 'real food' advocates. Occasionally, however, the anti-GMO rabbit hole takes some surprising twists and turns, with the involvement of large corporate players and some truly bizarre individuals.

We shall explore them a little later, but first, it is worth explaining exactly what GMO means, how widespread it is, and why so many are fighting so hard against it.

Going Nuclear

Since the 1920s, long before the structure of DNA was discovered, scientists have been successfully altering the genes of crop plants. Mutation breeding, where seeds or young plants are exposed to radiation or DNA-altering chemicals, was first attempted nearly a hundred years ago, but ramped up after the Second World War as governments tried to find peaceful applications for their burgeoning nuclear technologies. Millions of seeds were exposed to powerful radiation, mostly gamma rays or X-rays, in order to produce a range of mutants. Researchers would then search through the resulting plants to see if they had produced anything interesting or useful. Mutants have even been obtained by sending seeds up into space and exposing them to cosmic radiation.

There were a number of early successes for mutation breeding, producing high-yielding crops, disease-resistant plants and numerous new varieties with special properties. When Norman Borlaug's dwarf wheat varieties were first introduced into India, local researchers used mutation breeding to produce varieties more suited to the local cuisine. Most commercial red and pink grapefruits were originally produced by exposing conventional grapefruit seeds to gamma rays. Golden Promise Barley, a highly prized variety used in several premium Scottish malt whiskies, was also produced in this way, debuting in 1967 and remaining popular, often sold as an exclusive 'heritage' crop.

For some reason, despite sounding like the terrifying origin story of an obscure Marvel superhero, this sort of breeding never encountered much public resistance. There are over three thousand varieties from 175 different species registered on the mutagenic plants database, and their use is allowed in organic farming. This is of course quite sensible. Although the initial radiation exposure is fraught with danger, future generations of seeds will not be contaminated or harmful in any way.[6]

The main problems with mutation breeding are practical ones. The mutations produced are entirely random, requiring researchers to search painstakingly through many thousands of young plants looking for something useful. There is no way of guiding the process if you are after a particular trait, and no way of ensuring that the mutations produced are not detrimental in other ways. It is very much like giving millions of monkeys a typewriter and hoping that one of them churns out a work of art, or even just an amusing tweet. Given this, something more specific was needed, and the answer was to come from the world of molecular biology.

As understanding of molecular genetics opened up in the 1980s, the potential for genetically modifying plants started to be realised. A genetically modified organism is any living thing that has had its genetic material deliberately altered using a specific set of techniques. Scientists have been deliberately altering the genomes of bacteria in this way since the early seventies, and in 1978 the first human insulin was commercially produced from genetically modified bacteria, revolutionising the production of that drug. Since 1990, the vast majority of rennet, the enzyme used to make dairy proteins coagulate in cheese making, has been produced from genetically modified microorganisms. Rennet was traditionally made from the stomach of an unweaned calf as a by-product of veal production, making it both limited in supply and morally questionable, especially for vegetarians.*

Genetically modified plants started to be produced in the early 1980s, and in 1994 a tomato variety called Flavr Savr was the first to be approved for sale, having been modified to ripen more slowly and last longer on the shelf. A tomato puree made from Flavr Savr was an initial success in UK supermarkets due to its competitive price, but towards the end of the 1990s public resistance was growing and Flavr Savr was eventually withdrawn from sale.

This resistance was stepped up throughout the European Union in the mid-nineties when genetically modified soya started to be imported from the US. European regulators demanded that the GM varieties be kept separate, leading to an acrimonious and long-running dispute. A few years later, perhaps sensing an opportunity to resist cheap foreign imports and protect the interests of local farmers, the EU doubled down, bringing in some of the most stringent GMO regulations in the world. Approval for GMO foods in Europe has been almost non-existent ever since, with several member states, including Germany and France, banning them altogether.

Gene Editing

One of the problems with conventional genetic modification is that it tends to plonk new genes randomly into the genome with little direction or control. The resulting organism can have issues if this random placement knocks out something useful, but it

---

* Unweaned veal refers to (usually) male calves separated from their mothers immediately after birth. This separation does cause the animal distress, but is an inevitable consequence of dairy farming, so if you like milk, butter or cheese, it is probably not something you can afford to be too squeamish about. Veal calves can be raised with good regard for their welfare and often are, but there is also evidence of cruelty and poor practice in the industry.

also produces a genome different to anything found in nature. In recent years, however, a number of new 'gene editing' techniques have meant this process can be performed far more accurately. Scientists can now undertake highly targeted genetic alterations, turning off specific genes, making repairs to genetic abnormalities, or swapping different versions of a gene from one variety into another, dropping it in exactly the right place. The resulting plants or animals are often genetically identical to the sort of organisms created by selective breeding, with the advantage that the same results can be achieved without the painstaking years in the test field that Norman Borlaug endured. These techniques have transformed the field over the past ten years, opening up a new world of possibilities for both medicine and agriculture.

For a while, many scientists held out hope that plants produced using gene editing would be given a different status to other genetically modified foods, especially if they were no different to selectively bred varieties. This hope proved misplaced. Campaigners were still more scared of the new Frankenfood than the good old organic seeds that grandpa used to irradiate, and in 2018 the European Union ruled that they would not be treated any differently to other genetically modified crops.[7]

There are actually very few genetically modified crop plants currently being grown commercially. The two most common types are those that have been developed to be tolerant to glyphosate, the herbicide sold under the brand name Roundup, and insect-resistant varieties using the Bt gene. Bt comes from a bacterium with a very specific toxicity to insects but not to humans, something that has been sprayed onto fields as an organic-approved pesticide for many years. Adding the Bt gene puts this insecticide into the plant cell, causing it to be resistant to many devastating pests.

'Roundup Ready' soya, maize, canola (also known as rapeseed), sugar beet and cotton are commonly grown, as the resistance means that competing weeds can be easily controlled with glyphosate, one of the most effective and least environmentally toxic of all herbicides. Bt maize and cotton have also proven incredibly successful, providing a high level of insect resistance without the need for spraying. By 2017, eighty percent of all cotton, seventy-seven percent of soya, thirty-two percent of maize and thirty percent of canola being grown around the world was genetically modified.[8]

There have been a few other successes. A drought-tolerant maize has shown a lot of promise in the US and Africa, with the potential to provide essential resilience in a changing climate. Potatoes resistant to disease have hugely reduced crop wastage. The Hawaiian papaya industry was saved from being completely wiped out by viral infection after a resistant variety was developed, something that was only introduced after a concerted campaign by activists trying to prevent it.[9] An insect-resistant aubergine with the Bt gene was introduced into Bangladesh despite protests from European and US campaigners, and has hugely increased the incomes of many poor farmers in that country, as well as reducing exposure to pesticides.[10] And a version of cowpea carrying the Bt gene has recently been introduced in Nigeria, where it is a hugely important food crop prone to devastating losses from insect infestation.[11]

Many more plants are awaiting approval by regulators. There are potatoes with the ability to produce less acrylamide, a naturally occurring toxin that forms when they are cooked at high temperatures. The introduction of bananas resistant to Panama disease has been delayed by anti-GMO campaigners in Uganda, despite the disease devastating the livelihoods of thousands of farmers. A new variety of cassava, a vital staple in much of Sub-Saharan Africa, has been developed to contain high levels of iron and zinc to help combat vitamin deficiency, and Ugandan scientists have also created a banana with increased vitamin A.[12] All these, and hundreds more with the potential to reduce environmental impact, increase productivity or improve nutrition, are developed and ready to go.[13]

But despite this, there is a great deal of resistance. The early development of GMOs was tainted by some seemingly underhand commercial tactics by large corporate players such as Monsanto, whose new seeds often locked farmers into high-input farming. With companies allowed to place patents on modified plants, it became illegal to replant seeds saved from previous harvests as was traditionally the case, meaning new seeds had to be purchased every year. Commercial pressure to grow the high-yielding GMO varieties meant that farmers were practically forced to buy seeds from a small number of giant international corporations, often having to take on large amounts of debt in order to do so. When these crops started to be widely implemented in poorer countries, this debt could often be devastating, especially in years when harvests were poor.

But there is a great deal of irony in the blanket resistance to GM technology that has resulted. By and large it is focused, with some justification, on distrust of a few large companies.* But the increased scrutiny, onerous legislative hurdles and coordinated campaigns from pressure groups have played into the hands of large operators such as Bayer and Syngenta.† Dr Sarah Evanega is a plant biologist and Director of Cornell Alliance for Science, a pro-GMO advocacy group that works around the world. She told me that the main beneficiaries of anti-GMO activism have been the big companies. 'If you hate Monsanto, the worst thing you can do is ramp up the regulatory burden.' Dr Evanega believes that public and small private sector businesses have largely abandoned GM technology because of this burden, leaving a small number of large companies to dominate the market.

---

* Monsanto, along with a number of other chemical companies, historically manufactured the notorious Agent Orange, as well as DDT, the controversial insecticide used to control mosquitos. The fact that DDT was widely regarded as safe when launched is often held as evidence that scientists can never truly know how safe such things are, and the campaign against DDT, the dangers of which were first brought to light in Rachel Carson's book *Silent Spring*, is generally thought to mark the beginning of modern environmentalism, and its movement away from fascist ideology.

† The chemical giant Bayer purchased Monsanto in 2016.

In Evanega's opinion, activities to stifle the introduction of these plants are harming our ability to feed ourselves sustainably: 'Agriculture has a major impact on the environment. We need better tools to make it cleaner and leaner. We have GMOs now, we should use them. You can stand in the way, but if you are standing in the way of something that is going to prohibit some of the biggest harms of agriculture, how can you call yourself an environmentalist?'

There are currently only twelve types of genetically modified food crops being widely grown worldwide, yet even with this small number, the environmental benefits have been significant. A 2014 meta-analysis of 147 studies showed that introduction of GMOs has led to pesticide use being reduced by thirty-seven percent and yield increases of twenty-two percent. The greatest gains were experienced by farmers in developing countries, particularly from insect-resistant crops.[14] In the UK, where the introduction of GMOs has been blocked by European regulators, a lack of these tools has left the country more dependent on pesticides and its farming less competitive.[15]

Herbicide-tolerant crops have been shown to reduce the need for tilling, improving carbon sequestration and soil quality.[16] Reductions in pesticide application from the use of Bt corn and cotton actually result in significant increases in pollinator and insect diversity, because the intervention is less indiscriminate, and reduces damage to nearby natural habitats.[17] It also significantly decreases the exposure of agricultural workers to unpleasant compounds, particularly in regions where their use is not well regulated.

Frustratingly, there is a lot more in the hutch when it comes to GMO crops, particularly from universities, independent institutions and small businesses. Excessive costs, public resistance and regulatory burdens mean that we will never see the benefit of many of the breakthroughs we have already made. Some of the bigger projects will almost certainly reach the market. C_4 rice, utilising a more efficient method of photosynthesis borrowed from maize, could revolutionise the production of that crop.[18] But many others will never see the light of day, as widespread resistance means that ideas are shelved before completion.

Dr Kim Hammond-Kosack is a geneticist focusing on plant pathogens at Rothamsted, currently involved in a project looking at the future of wheat. She told me that her philosophy is always to try to put the solution in the seed, explaining that farmers currently growing standard varieties have to manage production with chemical sprays:

> My work is adding traits to crops that will reduce the chemistry going onto the field. We go through older varieties found in stock centres such as the Vavilov Institute in St. Petersburg, looking for useful traits and then breeding them in. We are also currently working on a transgenic wheat solution for a floral pathogen, which will be the first transgenic wheat.

As well as reducing chemical applications, this work can help solve problems that cannot be otherwise addressed. In areas of particularly high rainfall, chemicals often get washed away, meaning that solutions in the seed are the only way forward.

On the effect that the anti-GMO campaigning has had, she told me:

> We would be so much further on if it wasn't for the resistance. There are so many fundamental problems that could be solved. There is so much low hanging fruit.* So many projects get taken to concept, then halted. We can manipulate roots, growth speeds, plant defences, drought tolerance. That knowledge is sitting in a bottle waiting to be opened.

---

* Not literal low-hanging fruit, which given the context I felt was important to mention.

Kevin Folta studies plant genomics as Professor of Horticultural Sciences at Florida University and has a similar view. He told me:

> Every crop has some sort of genetic engineering story that would omit pesticides and fungicides. There is even a gene isolated from wild potato species that works against blight. Something like that could easily remove tonnes of fungicide and insecticide from the environment. Taxpayers are currently paying for great solutions that we can't implement.

It is ironic that solutions that could reduce chemical applications are so roundly resisted by supposed environmental campaigners many of whom demand blanket GMO bans. This is stifling progress now, often preventing developing world farmers from accessing crops that could revolutionise their lives. In the future, it may prevent access to seeds that could make global agriculture many times more sustainable, unshackling it from the need for so much chemistry to be applied to the field. When the door to this future becomes available, it will be interesting to see how many campaigners demand that it stays firmly shut.

Rise of the Frankenpigs

An area where there is even more resistance is the development of genetically modified animals. The only genetically modified animal currently approved anywhere in the world is a fast-growing salmon known as AquAdvantage, commercially produced and sold in Canada. It took around $60 million and twenty-five years to bring to market, and it has still not been given approval in the US due to resistance from a group of Alaska senators.*

---

* Personally, after burning $60 million, I would have spent a tiny bit more and paid someone to come up with a better name. Perhaps something that doesn't sound like a storyline from the *Terminator* movies.

Only a few tonnes of AquAdvantage have been sold so far, making it probably the most expensive fish in history.

But despite this lack of progress, genetic modification of animals could transform world food production. Gene edited chicken cells resistant to influenza have been developed by a group of UK researchers, with the potential to greatly reduce the incidence of human influenza outbreaks, saving millions of lives.[19] The same group has already produced pigs resistant to PRRS, a viral disease that costs billions of dollars and a huge amount of animal suffering.[20] And ask any cattle farmer about the process of dehorning animals, and they will admit that current methods, either burning or application of caustic chemicals, are painful, unpleasant, but sadly necessary for welfare and safety reasons. Gene editing has the potential to produce hornless cattle, making this cruelty obsolete.[21]

There is plenty more. Alison Van Eenennaam is a geneticist at the University of California, Davis who runs the Animal Genomics and Biotechnology Laboratory. She has spent most of her life working to improve the productivity and welfare of livestock animals. She told me:

> It has been twenty years of frustration. Animal breeders have not been able to use GMO. The plant GMO resistance has largely blocked it. We can use other techniques, but they are far less efficient. As things are, we still lose twenty percent of global animal protein to disease. We could use gene editing to make PRRS virus resistant pigs. If there is a better solution, knock yourself out, but right now there is no other option.

She also told me that there are currently unused genetic solutions that could prevent mastitis in cows, create pigs that excrete seventy-five percent less phosphorus (so making them more efficient and less polluting) and pigs that are resistant to swine fever.

It is also possible to knock out the testicular development gene, so preventing 'boar taint' without the need for castration.* There are even genetically modified goats that express lysozyme in their milk, something that could help prevent diarrhoea from raw milk consumption, a serious problem across much of the developing world. 'All this is on the shelf research,' she told me.

One of the main reasons for the lack of genetically modified animals is that US regulators have deemed that any changes to animal genomes are classified as veterinary drugs, requiring an even more expensive and onerous approval process. For this reason, research has nearly dried up, despite its potential, and many animals that could transform food production spend their days aimlessly wandering around research centre enclosures.

Resistance Ain't Futile

The potential benefits of GMOs are clear and their safety is a matter of scientific consensus. But resistance to them is widespread, persistent and extremely effective, controlling public perception and strongly influencing policy, especially in Europe. Where exactly has this resistance come from?

A number of environmental groups, including Greenpeace, have been very vocal in their opposition to GMOs. Given the environmental benefits, the potential to increase food security, the reduction in chemical application and the improvements in animal welfare, these attacks often seem misplaced and surprising from supposedly environmental organisations.

Mark Lynas is a writer and environmental campaigner who has written several books about the potential horrors of climate

* Boar Taint is an unpleasant flavour that contaminates the meat of male pigs once they reach puberty, making them unfit for consumption. Traditionally, this has been controlled by castration, but there are justified welfare concerns surrounding the practice.

change, including the influential (and terrifying) *Six Degrees*. In the early 2000s, he was one of a number of activists who travelled around the country destroying and vandalising GMO test crops, including those being grown at Rothamsted Research, and writing articles criticising their use. He has since dramatically changed his mind on this issue, telling me that he longs for the day 'when the organic movement accepts that agricultural products contain genes'. He now regularly criticises the GMO stance of Greenpeace and the Soil Association, organisations that he used to have strong connections with.

One of his greatest concerns is that scientists are fighting an asymmetrical war, and often get destroyed in the media by anti-GMO activists not constrained by the truth. 'Sensational storylines will always defeat objective science,' he tells me. 'GMOs can be used to reduce pesticides and reduce biodiversity loss, but somehow they get pitched as the opposite.' Properly controlled experiments have already generated compelling evidence, but there is a frustrating lack of understanding by those who are set against it. 'Allowing anti-GMO activists to dictate agricultural policy is like putting homeopaths in charge of healthcare. It has meant that you can't have a sensible conversation about GMOs in Central Europe. Policy in Africa has been pushed by a European agenda that "natural" farming is better for Africa, keeping hundreds of millions of people food insecure.'

Key in the environmental movement's resistance to GMOs, and their decision to pitch them as environmentally destructive, has been their funding. From the early 2000s, public fear of GMO crops in affluent countries made it a rich seam of fundraising potential. For a considerable period of time, campaigning against GMO foods in local supermarkets became a more effective way of raising money than campaigning to save unseen rainforests in distant lands, meaning that many activist organisations put huge resources behind it. The misinformed public distrusted GMOs, so they quite logically paid charities to campaign against them, which led to further distrust.

In addition, a burgeoning organic industry jumped on the anti-GMO bandwagon. Now worth $65 billion worldwide, organic brands saw an opportunity to push their own produce. The US Organic Consumers Association, paid for by money from large organic industry players, funds an organisation called US Right To Know, which operates under the tagline 'Exposing what the food industry doesn't want you to know'. In 2015, they targeted fourteen senior US scientists, releasing researchers' personal emails and communications obtained through Freedom of Information requests. In an article for the *Guardian*, three former presidents of the American Association for the Advancement of Science compared these tactics to those of the notorious 'Climategate' scandal, where personal communications were published in an attempt to silence leading climate scientists and cast doubt on the scientific consensus on global warming.[22]

More mysterious is the connection between prominent anti-GMO advocates, yogic flying and the bizarre world of the Maharishi Institute of Management. The Maharishi Institute is a complex multi-billion-dollar organisation with, shall we say, religious leanings, which is strangely tied to the funding and support of anti-GMO campaigning. Central to the movement is a belief that people can be literally taught to fly using meditation techniques.[23]

Two of the most prominent anti-GMO campaigners from the Maharishi school, based in Fairfield, Iowa, where it has a US base, are former academic John Fagan and yogic flying instructor Jeffrey Smith. Both have been prominent in the US anti-GMO movement, writing books, making films, regularly appearing in the media, and even occasionally acting as expert witnesses. They have also worked in collaboration with the Organic Consumers Association on a number of anti-GMO initiatives.

John Fagan, who has been given the title of professor by the mysterious Maharishi Institute, sells what he describes as a new paradigm in agriculture, involving the use of so-called 'Vedic Pandits'. These agricultural gurus wander around fields applying special noises to crops at different stages of growth, apparently to enliven the consciousness of food. Fagan claims that this technique utilises a modern understanding of quantum physics, with special vibrations infusing the plants with information, which is a deeply interesting interpretation of both plant science and quantum physics. He describes these techniques as being 'technically cutting edge'. I describe them as people stood in a field humming.[24]

Whereas Fagan did at least have a background as a scientist before he went Vedic, Jeffrey Smith's primary qualification for talking about agriculture seems to come from his time spent as a dance teacher, a profession he left in order to teach people how to fly using the power of their mind. He has since written a number of highly influential books about genetically modified foods and is a prominent voice in the anti-GMO movement, even being called as an expert witness during the Hawaiian Papaya hearing.[25] In the past, both have had financial interests in the public fear of GMOs. In the mid-1990s, Fagan founded Genetic ID, a large global organisation that tests for the presence of genetically modified produce in foods. Smith spent several years working for Genetic ID as Spokesman and Vice President of Marketing.

Alison Van Eenennaam has been a regular target of anti-GMO activists including US Right to Know. If it bothers her too much, she doesn't let on. She told me:

> We can't seem to win the debate on vaccines, what chance do we stand with GMO? The thing is, if no one is allowed to lie, the data is so strong it is hard to win any anti-GMO arguments. But the organic and natural food industry has a well-paid marketing department. It's the science communicators who are the Davids in this battle. Good people drop out when they get attacked, especially when their scientific reputation is being questioned. As a scientist, often the only thing you have is your reputation.

The attacks on Dr Van Eenennaam were stepped up after she featured prominently in a pro-GMO movie called *Food Evolution*, where she took part in, and won, a public debate on GMO safety. Freedom of information requests were sent out for all the email correspondence of about fifty different researchers. I asked her why she has been such a consistent critic, despite the attacks on her and her reputation. 'I just don't want my kids to grow up in a world where these idiots win,' she replied.

A Note of Caution

I have spoken previously in this book about taking mice to the opera, and why we must be careful about the manipulation of genes. This very much applies when it comes to genetic modification of food. We are unlikely to understand the full impact of adding or knocking out a particular gene straight away, and must be incredibly careful whenever we do. When it comes to the human genome, I would only ever support gene editing in the very small number of cases where certain heritable diseases are linked to mutations in a single gene.

Agriculture is different. We can change the genome of crop plants and study them over the long term in many different circumstances, and if they don't work, we still have a bank of seeds that might. We are only ever looking for crops that do a particular job in a certain set of circumstances. When it comes to animals, I will admit that I am torn. I do think that if there are welfare and safety benefits, the possibility of preventing the next disease pandemic, or the chance of reducing the huge wastage from disease, it is a path worth treading. There is a key difference between this and the modification of the human genome, because animal breeding is generally kept under strict control. Breeders thoroughly understand the need to maintain genetic diversity in the herd, with many preserved heritage breeds serving the same purpose as Vavilov's invaluable seed banks (hello Oakley). And just like crop plants, we need farm animals to do a particular set of jobs in limited circumstances, so they may never need to get ready for the opera.

But if genetic modification of animals becomes a relentless drive for increased production efficiency, creating freakish protein machines with no regard for life quality or welfare, it becomes a far more dangerous path. With an ever-smaller number of global companies controlling the breeding of livestock, particularly when it comes to chickens and pigs, it is sensible to be wary and critical of how this technology is being used. Supporting publicly funded research in universities and public institutes becomes even more important in this case, making sure that the biggest breakthroughs are kept in public hands and the worst excesses of capitalism are regulated.

Who Benefits?

Pertinent to the debate is the lack of appreciable consumer benefit for the current range of GMO crops, especially in developed economies where so few people are engaged with agriculture. The benefits of GMO tend to be felt by agricultural producers, with lower costs, higher yields and less work.

Every new food product has at least some potential for risk, and consumers are being asked to take this on without any noticeable benefit to themselves. Although the food they eat might be slightly cheaper, this makes little difference in affluent economies, as food is already incredibly cheap. The environmental impact might be lessened, but again this benefit is invisible on the supermarket shelf. There is a health benefit for the farmworker who does not have to spray as many insecticides, but even here the consumer does not see the upside.

When the potential for risk is amplified by the media and campaigners, the consumer choice ends up being a clear one.

Individual preference trumps the wider system positives every time. Although no actual risk has been demonstrated, the so-called 'precautionary principle' comes into play. It is unlikely that this would be the case if the new technology directly improved consumers' lives in some way. No one has ever successfully campaigned against insulin being produced by genetic modification, because the millions of diabetics who directly benefit would doubtless tell them where to stick it.

Achim Dobermann, the former Chief Executive of Rothamsted Research, explained to me that EU policies on genetic modification are firmly based on the precautionary principle. Although this sort of caution might sound sensible, in reality if we used the same principle to make decisions on which technologies we are going to allow, we wouldn't have Wi-Fi, mobile phones or cars. These policies have caused huge problems with a potentially important project running at Rothamsted to grow fish oils in plants. Currently, aquaculture is the fastest growing agricultural sector, already using one million tonnes of fish oil every year. As things are, this all has to be harvested from the oceans, meaning that we are catching wild fish to feed farmed ones, depleting global resources on an enormous scale. A plant-based solution could be a huge environmental win, but the fact that it involves genetically modified plants has put up several unnecessary roadblocks. Professor Dobermann explains:

> It has taken years of genetic engineering to make fish oil in a plant and now it is time to start growing. It would only take a few hundred thousand hectares to meet the whole global need. The problem is, there is an EU ban on GM feed. It would grow well in the UK, but getting EU approval is hopeless and the UK government won't do things differently. So you have to go to the US and Canada. This means that a UK-researched crop is being grown abroad, and UK farmers are not seeing the benefit.

It is hard to know where this debate will end. Perhaps a succession of breakthroughs such as nitrogen-fixing wheat, C_4 rice, drought-proof maize and blight-resistant potatoes will change the game. Maybe the pressures of a warming climate and shrinking natural habitats will make their use inevitable. Or perhaps even these technologies will be stubbornly resisted by Western campaigners, whilst people in the developing world needlessly go without.

It seems increasingly likely that combining practices borrowed from organic farming with a new generation of GMO crops designed to limit chemical inputs might hold the key to a more sustainable form of agriculture. It is a shame that many of those who strongly resist GMOs cannot see that they have the potential to make the sort of farming they advocate capable of feeding the world. Almost all the problems and limitations associated with organic production could be countered using genetically altered plants, yet organic farming is the one place they will never be accepted.

There are, of course, valid concerns. Concentrating the entirety of world food production into the hands of a few chemical and seed companies has some terrifying implications. Forcing farmers in the developing world to buy overpriced seeds that might push them closer to destitution should never be allowed. I share a distaste for capitalist forces that value shareholder return over humanity, but still believe that there is no need to throw the baby out with the bathwater. In fact, this is the last thing we should be doing. We should be encouraging, perhaps even insisting, that the benefits of genetic modification are placed in the hands of those that need it the most. We should prevent useful genes from being patented and protected by profit-driven corporations. We should be assisting innovative start-ups in commercialising their breakthroughs, and allowing publicly funded academic research to reach the public.

There is no doubt that genetic modification has the potential to revolutionise food production. Although it needs regulation, there is no reason why it can't be implemented fairly, safely and responsibly. It could lead to a food system with no need for chemical fertilisers, fungicides or pesticides. It could hugely increase efficiency, transform yields, prevent disease, increase biodiversity and improve animal welfare. In some cases it probably would make profits for large companies, but if we could democratise it sufficiently and place the tools of change in enough people's hands, this need not have to be at the expense of progress. To resist this technology in its entirety because companies have used sharp business practices in the past is not only foolish, but inhumane – we would never accept the same logic for pharmaceuticals.

We are stopping a new and much-needed agricultural revolution in its tracks. Almost all of the food we eat has been shaped and genetically altered by selective breeding over the past ten thousand years, often beyond all recognition. All food contains DNA, and many crops have genomes that have been massively changed over time. Most of what we eat has been mutated somehow, often in ways that are far from natural. None of this has ever done us any harm.

For thousands of years, the biological traits that influence the production of food have been created entirely randomly. This situation is far from ideal. We have been relying on monkeys at typewriters, sifting through the dross they produce and occasionally finding something useful. With gene editing techniques, we have finally found our Shakespeare. If fear and scaremongering keep him locked away, it will come at a great cost to humanity. Many will needlessly go hungry as a result.

10

Wasting Away

We waste today, because we think we have tomorrow.
　　　　　　　　　　　　　　　　　　　　　 – Nitya Prakash

Over the next few chapters I shall try to look beyond the catastrophe towards some solutions. This is tough, because the picture
is pretty bleak. One of the most persistent forms of resistance
from various interested parties, be it the meat industry, organic
groups, or libertarians keen to preserve the free market, is a
general sense of environmental whataboutery. People call for
inaction on their favoured issue by claiming that something else
is far worse. Why should I give up meat when billionaire vegan
environmentalists fly around the world in private jets? Who cares
about organic's low yields when a billion Chinese people are
increasing their beef consumption? What about coal power,
pesticides, deforestation, oil spills?

It is undeniably fun to criticise virtue signalling billionaires,
who so often seem oblivious to their own considerable carbon
emissions. When Richard Branson recently took to social media
to share his thoughts about reducing meat consumption for the
good of the planet, many people pointedly reminded him that he
runs an actual airline, giving him one of the largest carbon footprints on Earth. Anger at this sort of hypocrisy is understandable,
but the key to genuine progress is to accept that although Branson
is a tosser, environmental whataboutery is a zero-sum game.

If that is the path we tread, then the meat eaters will just blame the car drivers, the petrol heads will blame the frequent fliers, the holiday reps will blame the coal-fired power stations, the Americans will blame the Chinese, the Chinese will blame the rich people, and nothing will get done. The truth is that everyone can rightly do this, because no single change on its own will be enough to save us. Action on food is certainly not sufficient to stop environmental disaster, but it is essential. So is action on flights, cars, power generation, the construction industry and a thousand other things, but that's not an excuse for inaction on food.

Aside from hypocritical airline tycoons, perhaps the biggest source of whataboutery affecting the food debate is the subject of this chapter. Many readers will be surprised that we have got so far into the book without mentioning it. It is a huge drain on the resources of the planet, but is also emblematic of how difficult change is, because although it is a rare example of across-the-board agreement, progress has been slow and faltering. A quick dip into the statistics provides some shocking indictments of our broken food system, but they also give an insight into how desperately hard it is going to be to improve things.

It is often said that where there's a will, there's a way. But here, despite almost universal will, we just can't seem to find a way.

Wasted

Think about all the shocking impacts of agriculture that we have discussed so far. The poisoned air, the dying oceans, the lifeless soil. The mass extinctions, the plundered forests, the scorched land. The only possible justification for all that destruction is that we have been busy preventing hunger. We have developed a food system productive enough to keep an unprecedented number of humans alive, and without it, there would have been death on a biblical scale. Well done humanity. Sorry about the planet and everything, but what can you do? We couldn't let all those people starve.

Except that a third of all the food we produce doesn't actually feed anyone. It is simply thrown away, rendered unfit for consumption. Which means that a third of all that environmental destruction has been to no other end than filling up the world's bins, which we waste more energy emptying.

This is the shocking truth of our supposedly efficient food system. Over thirty percent by weight, and about one quarter of all calories, ends up in the trash. This waste costs an astonishing $1 trillion every year, and produces twenty-five percent of all the greenhouse gases related to agriculture. If food waste was a country (and what a strange country it would be), it would be the world's third-largest environmental polluter after China and the USA.

It is not hard to see why this extraordinary waste gets called out by campaigners keen to absolve their own particular interest from blame. If we didn't waste any food, it would largely compensate for the lower yields in organic production. If we stopped throwing so much away, the impact of meat would be far lower. Without waste, we would need less land, less fertiliser, fewer pesticides.* The contents of the global bin could easily feed all of the world's hungry people, ending famine, wiping out nutrient deficiencies, and bringing down global food prices to alleviate poverty. So why on earth are we not doing more?

Waste is an easy target to attack, because although there is an argument that food companies and retailers have an interest in encouraging it, no one is publicly campaigning for it to increase. Farmers hate waste. Consumers hate waste. Manufacturers and retailers really hate waste. Consultants are employed to find ways of reducing it. Whole departments of global corporations dedicate their existence to shaving fractions of a percent off the total. But we still throw away one in three plates of food. And we can't seem to stop.

---

* Or less pesticides. Probably fewer pesticides and less pesticides. Fewer scanned better, so I went with that.

In general, in developed countries food waste tends to occur near to the consumer, whereas in the developing world it happens closer to the farm.[1] In rich nations, hyper-efficient, carefully planned agriculture, lean food manufacturing, clever logistics and temperature controlled supply chains mean that little gets wasted before it reaches people's homes. But once food gets through the consumer's door, cheap prices, inappropriate pack sizes and a culture of excess mean that much of it never gets eaten. It seems that the richer a nation gets, the more its waste gets shifted down the supply chain so that the end consumer has to deal with it.

Many would argue that this extraordinary amount of waste is the surest sign that our food system – and perhaps our entire economic system – is broken. I spoke to Professor Tim Benton, Director of the Energy, Environment and Resources Department at Chatham House. 'It all comes down to the fact that all economies base themselves on economic growth,' he told me. 'This is the economic fiction of the past three hundred years. What the **** is the point in making food so cheap that it makes economic sense for people to throw it away?' Admittedly, he was having a really bad day after spending a bit too much time with politicians and policymakers and asked me to moderate his language, just in case his mother ends up reading the quote.

The Farms That Waste

In developing nations, less sophisticated agriculture, poorer food storage, fewer processing facilities, a harsher climate and more challenging transportation networks all conspire to waste more food before it reaches the consumer. Differences in shopping and cooking habits, and an understandable tendency for poor people to value food a great deal more highly, mean that little gets wasted in the home. But even here, things are complicated and the numbers should not always be taken at face value. Dr Megan Blake researches food security and food justice at the University of Sheffield. She told me that the way food waste is estimated can often be extremely misleading. Usually, it is measured for a week or so, and then the results extrapolated to give a long-term picture, leading to a huge potential for inaccuracy. In Dr Blake's opinion, even the commonly expressed idea that people in wealthy countries waste food at home and poor countries waste it all on the field makes all sorts of assumptions and should not be taken at face value:

> How do we know this? It makes it look like farms in wealthy countries are really efficient and developing world farmers don't know what they are doing. But when is food classified as waste? When it's left in the field and goes back into the soil? When it's fed to animals?

Similarly, Jonas Cromwell, a researcher at the University of Sheffield's Grantham Centre for Sustainable Futures who has studied food waste in the burgeoning avocado industry in Tanzania, thinks that a lot of the figures from emerging economies may actually be down to misunderstandings and cultural differences. When I asked him how much food was wasted on the Tanzanian farms he worked with, I expected tales of widespread losses from disease, pests or the inability to bring in harvests. Instead, he presented a far more nuanced picture. 'It depends upon the type of food. With avocados, if there is waste on the farm, it is shared with neighbours, eaten by the farmers, or fed to animals . . . For the export varieties of avocado, they are not well known in the local markets, and cannot be sold, so there can be a lot of excess.'

For many years after their introduction in the colonial era, avocado trees in Tanzania were grown solely for shade and shelter, and the fruit was not considered to be a source of human food. Avocados were known as 'butter for dogs', until the culture changed and they became more valued. But the smaller varieties so valued in the hipster cafes of the US and Europe are still unfamiliar locally, and can't be sold if there is an excess. In time, it is likely that this too will change, as the export varieties become more widely adopted, and local people start to eat them. Given the complexity surrounding this one crop, it does seem unlikely that we really understand the nature of agricultural food waste everywhere in the world.

That said, there are almost certainly technologies and practices that could help reduce farm waste in developing nations, and there is much important work going on in this area. This includes the introduction of better harvesting equipment, more accurate weather forecasting, disease-resistant crop species, higher standards of veterinary care, improved transport networks, better food storage and new processing facilities, including a number of avocado oil extraction plants to use up excess production. Reducing food waste by fifty percent before 2030 is one of the UN's Sustainable Development Goals, and these practices will almost certainly help move towards that aim. Arguably, the bigger challenge exists in more developed nations and economies, because for all our technology, knowledge and desire, we just can't seem to shift the dial.

Hard to Shift

Actually, that is not entirely true. In the UK, the consumer-facing Love Food, Hate Waste campaign run by the government-funded charity WRAP has seen some success. Between 2007 and 2012, it saw a twenty-one percent reduction in food waste through a multi-pronged campaign supported by several major manufacturers and retailers. It is widely thought that this campaign was successful because it had almost universal support across the food industry. WRAP built a strong and motivated coalition, operating at arm's length from government, and had a great deal of credibility with businesses, largely because it worked in partnership rather than trying to impose restrictions and rules. It is a model for successful change that many could learn from.

The campaign had its limitations. In the unlikely event that something similar was successfully implemented across the world, it would still not come close to meeting the Sustainable Development Goal of a fifty percent reduction by 2030. To achieve that, a far more fundamental shift is needed. Whilst campaigns continue to focus on correcting the behaviour of individuals, they are unlikely to create significant and lasting change. The problem of food waste in developed nations is deep-rooted, inextricable from our food system and culture. It is not as simple as food being too cheap.

Professor David Evans researches the sustainability of food systems at Bristol University's School of Economics. In his opinion, most debates about behaviour change are flawed because they focus on the consumer, which in reality is only the tip of the iceberg. 'Lots of campaigners say that the problem is that people don't have the "correct attitude", or "they can't cook," or "they are disconnected from the food system." But under the microscope, we see a very different picture.' In Professor Evans's opinion, it is not the case that people don't care about food waste. In reality they care a great deal, but they also have many other concerns and priorities. This makes it extremely important to consider the wider context in which food is wasted:

A big problem is the pressure to cook with fresh ingredients, using recipes that don't use all of them. The conventions of family meals and freshness are an established way of doing things that is taken for granted. They are organising principles that shape the food system, but they are never unpacked.

Professor Evans's work has shown that the concept of freshness can be extremely problematic. Although freshness in food is almost universally seen as a good thing, signifying wholesome, more natural produce, the reality is quite different. He describes freshness as 'an empty term that carries a lot of weight', but also has many unintended consequences, including additional food waste, the excess energy required for a cold supply chain and the often problematic labour conditions of seasonal agricultural workers.

The conclusions drawn from much of Professor Evans's work deeply challenge many people's notions of what a better food system might look like, and perhaps explain why food waste is such a difficult problem to crack. For many who bemoan food waste, some of the solutions might be extremely unpalatable. As he explains:

> People would not waste as much if there was not the pressure to make family meals using fresh ingredients. We really need to think about how to align conventions with more sustainable diets. Things can change, but in the UK, we have a failure of ambition at thinking about systemic change, so we fall back onto individual behaviour.

Convenience food is routinely vilified as unhealthy and cheap, and family cooking, eating together, and making dishes from scratch, are hailed as being positive behaviours (including by this author on more than one occasion). But this sort of cookery is far more likely to result in food being wasted. As Professor Evans explained to me, the reality is that 'people who eat frozen pizza don't waste food.' The imperative to eat 'properly', taking time to make large home-cooked meals, is often framed as morally superior. There is immense societal pressure, especially on mothers, to perform this function, but the reality is that this is the main source of domestic food waste. Everything that is framed as being the 'right' way to eat – eating with family, cooking for friends, crafting recipes made from scratch – results in higher levels of waste, both from ingredients that cannot be bought in the correct quantities, and the uneaten leftovers that result from this sort of cooking.[2]

It is not that consumers don't care. There is very little that consumers care more about than food waste. It is almost universally felt to be morally wrong, even by those who don't have huge environmental concerns. To frame food waste as a failure of behaviour caused by a lack of moral responsibility completely misunderstands the reasons why it occurs. It is often a result of people doing the best they can for their family and friends. It comes from a desire to be a good provider, and to keep fridges and cupboards stocked with nutritious, healthy food. It comes from anxiety about food safety and people desperately trying to keep up with societal expectations of good parenting.

In reality, the only way to address food waste is to create large-scale systemic change. It will require changes to behaviour, but also to the conventions of society and the infrastructure that controls our food supply. There is a chance that this might mean giving up on many of our existing conventions around eating. If the main meal of the day could be shifted from evening to lunch-time, placing it largely as an out-of-home occasion in workplaces, colleges or schools, then it would almost certainly lead to less waste. Large caterers are far better at managing food waste and limiting environmental impacts. This would also provide more opportunities to improve nutrition, as large companies and institutions could be encouraged to change their practices, through guidance, incentives and subsidies.

This might sound bleak. I have long written about the importance of eating together, sharing meals with those you love, and letting food enhance your greatest moments of celebration and joy. To call for anything else now feels inherently wrong. But we live in a rapidly changing world, and we need to change if we are to make progress.

Plastic Population

A great deal of the food waste in developed countries occurs because food is packaged in sizes that are not appropriate for many consumers. Vegetables, herbs, bread, meat and salad are often sold in packs that contain enough to stretch across several meals, especially for smaller families and households, making some waste inevitable. Walking around the average supermarket, you might assume that every single UK household contains a nuclear family with 2.4 children and half a dog, but the reality of modern life is very different. Nearly fifteen percent of UK households are single-parent families, and another thirty percent are people living alone, meaning that for many shoppers, most of the currently available pack sizes are completely unsuitable. Of course, this leads plenty of commenters to conclude that food being sold in packaging at all is the real problem, harking back to the days when everyone bought their produce loose from friendly greengrocers and butchers.*

Single-use plastic packaging, of the sort that much of our fruits, vegetables and meat is now sold in, has become emblematic of our environmental wastefulness. The pollution of the world's oceans with plastic waste, the effects of which were so powerfully highlighted in David Attenborough's *Blue Planet* television series, is a shameful stain on humanity's record. Yet public strength of feeling has the potential to force through solutions that might not be ideal. It is now sacrilegious for someone interested in the environment to suggest that plastic is anything other than the embodiment of evil, which has some troubling implications. Most worryingly, this anti-plastic sentiment is a trend that many large companies have sought to exploit, often with little regard as to whether or not they are actually doing the right thing.

As with so many of the issues we have discussed, if the amount of plastic we are using ends up being a target rather than a measure, it is likely to lead us way off course. Although there is a desperate need to cut down on unnecessary plastic waste, there are many reasons why a zero-plastic world might not be ideal from an environmental perspective. Dr Christian Reynolds

---

* I suspect I am older than many readers, and I don't remember a world like this. If there ever was one, there is probably a reason why it no longer exists.

researches the environmental impact of food consumption at the University of Sheffield, and has also worked with WRAP as a technical consultant. He told me that, contrary to many people's assumptions, some plastic packaging can improve sustainability, often increasing a food's shelf life by weeks. It is not unusual for the additional food waste created by removing packaging to exceed the environmental impact of the plastic used. There is, however, some uncertainty surrounding this:

> At the moment, the data available isn't able to give us a definitive picture, but we do know that packaging avoidance can lead to more food waste, and a higher environmental impact. Often, single occupancy and smaller households can't get through a standard sized loaf of bread, or a full pack of bacon before they spoil. Split packs can help, yet those often have more plastic. It's really about balance, and finding a sweet spot to minimise waste.

In addition, trying to ban all plastics would not just impact on the packaging found on supermarket shelves. Much of the plastic used in food production is invisible to consumers, but potentially beneficial to the environment. Professor Tony Ryan is a polymer chemist and current Director of the Grantham Centre for Sustainable Futures. He told me that there is plastic at all layers of the food system and much of it is unseen by most food consumers. For example, there are plastics in poly-tunnels, seed packs and containers for fertilisers and often these can have a positive environmental impact, especially when it comes to water use. Professor Ryan told me: 'Tomatoes grown in an open field use up to ten times more water than if they are grown under plastic. The greenhouse emissions for transporting fresh fish in plastic crates is about half that of card if the crates are recycled.'

Excessive use of single-use plastics is definitely problematic, but the alternatives touted as solutions are often little better, and occasionally considerably worse. And some of the best ways

forward may require us to use plastics in a different way. Professor
Ryan sees the collection system for single-use plastics as a tragedy of the commons: 'It is cheaper and easier for everyone in the
chain to use a new piece of plastic every time. But there's a lot of
marketing-led greenwash.'

Surprisingly, Professor Ryan explained that glass is often a
terrible alternative, even when compared to single-use plastic,
because the end of life is not accounted for. He also explained
that in many of the popular 'plant-based' plastic bottles available,
it is only possible for about thirty percent of the plastic to be
derived from plants. These supposedly more sustainable options
are made from PET, or polyethylene terephthalate, and only the
ethylene part can be derived from plant sources.

With regard to the options that might actually have a positive
environmental impact, rather than just making wealthy consumers feel good about themselves, commercial pressures often get
in the way. Professor Ryan explains:

> German PET, which is heavier duty and designed for recy-
> cling, is a much better way. But a bottle wash and collec-
> tion is needed, which puts up prices, so the industry has
> strongly resisted it. Big soft drinks companies have worked
> on preventing the mandation of reusable PET because
> they say that people piss in them, and the urea deposits are
> not taken out by low-temperature wash cycles. Vested
> interests will try and create all sorts of excuses not to
> increase costs.

Consumers are made to feel very guilty about plastic. People are
sold guides to going 'plastic free', while excess packaging is
viciously shamed on social media, and anyone daring to use a
single-use straw is made to feel as if they are punching an endangered seal pup in the face. The intense public engagement with
the plastic issue can be a force for good, leading to greater awareness of environmental issues, but we must not let it become

hijacked by those that fail to appreciate the wider picture. Preventing plastic pollution of the oceans is important, but equally, rational use of plastics can help reduce the overall environmental impact of our food system.

Is plastic a bigger problem than food waste? Is it a more serious issue than water stress, or land use? How would removing plastics impact upon disabled or elderly people, who often rely on packaged convenience foods, and cannot prepare everything fresh? Every time a seemingly over-packaged food solution, be it a pre-peeled orange or a pre-sliced cauliflower, is shamed on social media, a chorus of largely ignored disability campaigners try to raise awareness of the importance of such products for their independence, and remind people that not everyone can easily peel an orange, and many people struggle to hold a kitchen knife. Should we make others' lives more difficult so that we can feel better about ourselves?

Campaigners in the UK have been demanding the removal of plastic packaging from the food in supermarkets and that stores become plastic-free. This is a laudable aim, but in practice such solutions can mean that stores simply have to remove the plastics used to protect produce during transportation before they reach the supermarket shelf. The food landscape many people demand is one that shifts waste back up the chain, with more spoilage in store, and packaging being disposed of out of sight. If the only thing we are reducing is our guilt, it does not feel like the sort of progress we need.

The greatest leaps forward in addressing the problem of plastic pollution are unlikely to be found in a complete ban, or the mass shaming of anyone drinking through a straw. They will come from the implementation of joined-up recycling systems, better waste management, the exposure of corporate greenwashing, and a more nuanced understanding of what best practice looks like. In the UK, the kerbside collection of plastic waste varies from region to region, meaning that manufacturers have little hope of knowing what the best options are to minimise their environmental impact. 'Zero to landfill' means little if everything you dispose of gets incinerated. Compostable waste is only positive if it actually gets used for compost. The greatest impacts of packaging lie not with consumer choice, but with the way in which waste is managed around the world. It is this boring, unglamorous and largely hidden battle that we should be fighting.

To remove plastics completely would take away a tool that can, in a number of cases, lessen the environmental impact of food. It would also take away convenience options that vastly improve the lives and independence of many people, unfairly punishing those who have less choice than the rest of us. That does not mean that all plastics should get a free pass, but we must be careful to distinguish between middle-class pretensions and rational efforts to create a better world. Plastics have become the visible symbol of all that is wrong with consumer culture, but that is perhaps only because the truly terrifying monsters are largely unseen. If we focus only on the threats that fill our eyeline, we are in danger of being blindsided by the real dangers.

Too many problems that are framed as a matter of individual choice actually require widespread systemic change. That is not to say that individual engagement is unimportant. The desire not to waste food taps into something fundamental about being human. Seeing plastic pollute the oceans has left an imprint of shame on the world. If we mobilise this feeling effectively, it can provide a catalyst for wider systemic change. Motivated consumers can campaign for a better system, fight for a better world. We just need to ensure that we are fighting for the sort of change that genuinely moves us forward.

11

The Protein Alternative

Never doubt that a small group of thoughtful, committed
citizens can change the world; indeed, it's the only thing
that ever has.

– Margaret Mead

The Ice Kings

In 1806, Boston businessman Frederic Tudor hatched an ill-
advised plan to export some of New England's plentiful winter
ice to the Caribbean, hoping he would find a lucrative market
cooling down the rich European settlers of Martinique. Tudor
was widely thought to be crazy at the time. Ice was something
that belonged in cold countries during the winter, and had no
place in warm, tropical climates. Most people were unsure what
anyone would do with ice in the Caribbean, other than just
observe it as a rapidly melting curiosity. Unable to find a ship
willing to carry his temporary and seemingly useless cargo, he
invested a huge amount of money buying his own vessel, filled it
with local ice, and off he sailed.

Perhaps surprisingly, when his ship reached Martinique,
much of the ice was still intact. But once there, he struggled to
persuade any of the residents why they might want this chilly
new commodity, and before long the unsold ice had melted away

in the Caribbean sun, leaving little more than a puddle of broken dreams.

Despite this initial failure, Tudor persisted, convinced that there was a fortune to be made. Over the next five years, he made a series of similarly ill-fated attempts, losing a huge amount of money and landing him in debtors' prison three times. Even then, he refused to give up, instead focusing his efforts on transporting ice to the Southern US states. A born marketer, he developed a number of innovative strategies to persuade people that they needed ice in their lives. He would provide the first delivery for free, teach restaurants to make ice cream, work with doctors to help them bring down patients' fevers, and persuade bars to offer cold drinks alongside ones at room temperature to see which their customers preferred. Before long, imported ice went from being an unknown and unwanted curiosity, to an accepted part of everyday life. Tudor achieved the capitalist dream: making millions of people desperately need something they didn't even know they wanted.

Over the next fifty years, the nascent ice industry boomed with Tudor at its head, shipping millions of tonnes all around the world, employing thousands of people and developing new technologies to harvest, ship and store the now essential commodity. Tudor became known as the 'Boston Ice King', making himself a huge fortune.[1]

But change was coming. Towards the middle of the nineteenth century, a Floridian doctor named John Gorrie was plotting a cold revolution of his own. His obsession with building cooling and chilling machines meant that, much like Tudor, he was widely derided and mocked. After all, why would anyone go to the cost and hassle of making their own ice, when supplies from cold climates were seemingly limitless? Gorrie died in 1855 shortly before his dreams of a new industry were realised, but in 1868, the first ice factory, based on the technology he had pioneered a few years before his death, opened in New Orleans.

At first the new ice-making machines were unreliable and expensive, and struggled to challenge the huge trade in transported ice. It was pejoratively referred to as 'artificial ice', with many people at the time refusing to believe that such chilled sorcery was possible. It is said that a Mississippi preacher who reported back on a visit to one of the new ice factories was told to step down from his position after his congregation assumed he had been possessed by the devil.

It would take until after the Great War for people finally to embrace the new factory-made product, and before long the century-old trade in transported ice became obsolete. Ice became more affordable and available as a result, moving from being a luxury to a domestic essential. Factory-made ice was delivered to thousands of American homes throughout the year and kept in kitchen ice-boxes, meaning that for the first time, consumers could safely store fresh food all year round.

In tandem, the dairy, meat and seafood businesses flourished and grew. Ice-cooled trucks and trains allowed perishable fresh produce to be widely transported for the first time, so that once-exclusive local delicacies could be enjoyed across the nation. More and more ice plants opened to fill the increasing demand, and many fortunes were made. The food landscape of America was changed forever, allowing more produce to be traded, farms to specialise production, and diets to increase in variety. Cheap, factory-made ice fuelled the expansion of American cities, allowing a wider and healthier selection of foods to be eaten by the growing population. Shopping habits changed as fresh food could be stored many times longer than before, paving the way for supermarkets and other large retailers. The ice train seemed unstoppable. Until it suddenly stopped.

Through the 1950s and 1960s, domestic fridges and freezers became cheaper, more reliable and small enough to fit into home kitchens. Very quickly, demand for factory-made ice dwindled. Thousands of plants closed their doors. The ice trade was a short-lived industry that transformed the world, then melted away, leaving barely a trace.

The really curious thing is that the people involved in the harvesting or manufacture of ice did not see the changes to their industry coming before it was too late. Ice harvesters were replaced by the new-fangled factories and their strange artificial product, no doubt railing at how inferior and unnatural it all seemed. A few years on, after ice producers had convinced themselves that expensive and hard-to-maintain domestic chillers would never catch on, they were forced to close the factory doors.

The ice business seemed so essential and irreplaceable that no one stopped to think about what it was they were actually selling. They thought they were selling frozen water, but in reality their product was the ability to keep things cold. If they had seen their business as chilling consumers' goods rather than trading in ice, they might have invested in the future. Perhaps we would be putting our milk into the kitchen Tudor, or getting some frozen peas out of the electric Gorrie.[2]

Big change is like that. Often people see it coming, but deny and deflect, even when the rising tide is lapping around their ankles. History is full of people who thought that the future was just a fad, and insisted it would never catch on. It always pays to keep your eyes wide open, and know exactly what it is your business sells.

In the past few years, a number of people have hinted that a new ice factory might be creeping up on one of the world's largest industries, perhaps with the potential to make it obsolete. From an environmental perspective, there is an argument that this might be no bad thing. Indeed, environmental considerations may well be something that contribute to the demise of the industry.

Certainly, there is a wind of change blowing that is getting hard to ignore. But is there really a chance that livestock and meat, a $1.4 trillion global industry supporting the livelihoods of between one and two billion people, might go the way of ice factories, video rental stores, encyclopaedia salesmen, telephone sex lines, and the many other businesses that failed to adapt to change before it was too late?[3]

The Protein Alternatives

In recent years, a number of innovators have been asking if there is a way of creating something that does the job of meat, but made from different ingredients. Others have even suggested that we might be able to produce real meat without killing any animals. As we have already discussed, current levels of global livestock production are deeply problematic from an environmental perspective and come with obvious animal welfare concerns. If the world's seemingly insatiable demand for meat could be supplied without the need for animals, and the replacements are less environmentally damaging, then a whole load of problems would be overcome all at once. In the absence of effective ways of stemming global demand, is it time to look at creating better alternatives? Is it time for Meat 2.0?*

Although products along these lines have been around for some time, this quest has been stepped up over the past few years, becoming perhaps the largest trend in food. What was once the preserve of a small number of companies and a few niche brands has very much entered the mainstream. Get it right, and the prize might be enormous. Fail, and the future of the planet is at stake.

Meat and animal produce provides thirty-seven percent of global protein and eighteen percent of calories, with the rest coming from plant-based foods.[4] It is entirely possible to get all of our protein requirements from vegetable sources, and many people already do, particularly in the world's poorest nations. But as economies develop and people find new wealth, they almost invariably gravitate towards meat. Meat and dairy are not only delicious, but they are also reliable sources of high-quality protein that is easier to absorb than many vegetable sources.

---

* I use this phrase purely because it is the sort of banal corporate speak that I am certain will wind up my editor.

Before we go any further, I do need to declare my interest. Over the past couple of years, much of my non-writing work has focused on developing meat-free, vegan and reduced-meat products for the food industry. This is largely because, having sold a few books, I am in the fortunate position of being able to pick and choose the work I do these days, and firmly believe this is the most valuable thing a development chef can be doing right now. If we can create products that rival or exceed the taste of meat, with similar or improved nutrition and a smaller environmental footprint, it could potentially transform global food production. Once meat alternatives are good enough, we can begin to address the true cost of animal-produced meat, perhaps even using monetary incentives to reduce demand. If, as seems inevitable with such blunt financial instruments, this results in the poorest people in society being unable to afford to eat meat often, at least they will be able to eat food that is cheap, nutritious, culturally appropriate and tastes good.

Unfortunately for the environment, but perhaps fortunately for my ability to get paid work, making plant-based products as delicious as meat is a difficult task. In part, my assessment in this chapter is based on personal experience, but I have also spoken to a number of key players in the industry, particularly about the difficulty of measuring environmental footprints and about the behavioural shifts required to make change happen.

For now, the big question is, can these alternatives become as transformative of the protein industry as refrigerators were with regard to ice? Or is meat so unique that it can never be replaced?

Hail Seitan

Perhaps the most surprising fact about the world's food supply is that if we suddenly swapped all the beef we eat for soya, global demand for soya would fall significantly. The reason for this seeming paradox is that the vast majority of soya currently grown is used in animal feed, and animals, particularly cattle, are really inefficient at making edible protein. We would have a far less destructive food system if humans ate more soya themselves, decreasing the pressure on land, and cutting out the emissions of all those burping cows.

Of course, it is not quite that simple, especially as cattle are often eating the by-product of soya bean oil production, but soya protein is often the development chef's first port of call when trying to replace meat. Traditional products such as tofu and tempeh, made from fermented soya beans, are high in protein and can be useful in some circumstances, but these have a distinctive texture and flavour that only have niche appeal. Perhaps more interesting are the many types of isolated soya protein now available, which can be shaped, formed and given different textures.

Soya protein doesn't easily form the same fibrous structure as meat, but you can make passable burgers, sausages and 'chicken' nuggets from it, as well as ground meat dishes such as chilli, lasagne or bolognese. Environmentally, soya is something of a powerhouse crop, with high protein and calorie yields per hectare, relatively low water usage, and the important ability to fix its own nitrogen.[5]

The biggest issue with soya is its flavour. Although many consumers enjoy it, it has a strong beany characteristic that a significant number of people find extremely unpleasant. To an extent this can be masked using natural flavourings, but it is often overpowering, especially in savoury products.

There are other issues: most of the soya grown worldwide comes from GMO strains, which limits its popularity; it is also associated with large-scale monoculture and tropical deforestation, particularly in Brazil, which makes many people wary. But it is worth remembering that every time we swap out beef for soya, we actually reduce the demand for soya beans around the world.

Peas are also a nitrogen-fixing crop, and are extremely valuable when grown in rotation, making them another environmental powerhouse. They do not suffer from the GMO stigma that plagues soya, and are far less associated with global deforestation. They are also, particularly in Western eyes, a little bit more acceptable as a food ingredient.

Pea protein can be extracted fairly easily, particularly from yellow pea varieties, and these pea protein isolates have improved in quality in recent years. Much like soya, pea protein tends to have a strong beany flavour and a slight off note, but can be made to produce some interesting textures, and takes on flavour well. A number of the most recent vegan and vegetarian burgers have been made from pea protein, including the famous Beyond Burger, which is eighteen percent pea. The strong, distinctive savoury and grill flavours of the Beyond product are almost certainly an attempt to mask the flavour of the pea protein.

Pea seems to have it all, with the potential to replace soya as the alternative protein of choice. Recently, however, there have been reports that suppliers and producers are struggling to keep up with demand. Soya has the advantage of already being grown in immense quantities globally, with no agricultural production increase necessary if people start to swap it for beef.* But the scale of increased pea production required to make even a small dent in the $1.4 trillion market for meat would involve addressing a number of unknowns.

A surprisingly large amount of the world's protein comes from wheat, which has, excluding soya, a higher protein content than any other staple crop. It is possible to extract this protein and do various things with it, including making the same sort of isolates produced from pea and soya. Wheat protein has traditionally been used as a meat substitute for many years across a number of cuisines, with a flavoured version being sold as Mock Duck in Chinese supermarkets, and as Seitan in many vegetarian and health food shops. It can be made fairly easily at home from

---

* Although the likelihood is that new factories to manufacture soya protein isolates would be required.

wheat flour, simply by washing away the starch with water, leaving an insoluble protein mass. If you have a bag of flour in a cupboard at home, you could make a passable vegan meat replacement for dinner tonight, although to be honest it is quite a lot of effort for minimal reward.

The two big issues with wheat protein are the taste, as it has a strong mealy flavour that is difficult to mask, and the fact that it is basically pure gluten, something that increasing numbers of people are trying to avoid. But wheat protein can be very useful if you want to create firm meaty textures, and bind other protein ingredients together.

One of the oldest meat replacement brands is Quorn, launched in the UK in 1985, which is derived from a unique ingredient. Quorn products are based on a form of mycoprotein, made by growing a specific type of single-celled fungus in large fermentation tanks. This results in a largely flavourless, high-quality vegetarian protein with interesting textural properties, closely resembling the fibrous structure of chicken. Mycoprotein can make some of the most realistic chicken-like products on the market, and does not suffer from the strong, beany flavour found in most soya and pea versions.

Over the years, the Quorn brand has largely focused on its health benefits, developing products such as sausages and burgers that are much lower in fat than their meat equivalents. This focus has led to a perhaps deserved reputation for products that are more worthy than delicious, but this has not stopped Quorn expanding rapidly in many countries around the world.

For many years, all Quorn products were vegetarian rather than vegan, as the company struggled to find an alternative to the egg white used to bind the mycoprotein together, but more recently they have managed to create an acceptable vegan version. In 2019, a vegan sausage roll, made from Quorn and produced for the UK bakery chain Greggs, proved to be one of the most popular and impactful product launches of the year, receiving a huge amount of media coverage and starting national conversations about meat consumption. It also upset Piers Morgan, which is of course the dream of every food product developer.[6]

Lentils, Pulses and Chickpeas

In the debate about alternative proteins, too little attention gets paid to the real vegetable stars, crops such as lentils, pulses and chickpeas. When it comes to almost every single sustainability metric, these are by far the best options for meeting the protein requirements of the world. They fix their own nitrogen, work well in rotation with other crops, have extremely high protein yields per unit of land, are incredibly water efficient, can easily be stored for a long time after harvest, and make a number of delicious dishes across a wide variety of cuisines, including hummus, perhaps the world's greatest food. They also contain lots of dietary fibre (especially compared to meat, which has none), something most of us could do with eating more of.

Amid all the clever scientific breakthroughs, smart new product developments and futuristic visions of a new food system, perhaps one of the best things we can do for the environment and our health is eat a lot more of these unglamorous, unheralded, and in some cases forgotten, ingredients. If I were writing a sustainability diet cookbook, pretty much every recipe would be based on these types of plants, and there would be an entire chapter on hummus. Fortunately, this is something I am going to spare the world from, although I have no doubt that many similar books will be popping up over the next few years, including at least two from Jamie Oliver (perhaps to assuage his guilt after signing a £5 million promotional deal with Shell in 2018).[7] If these books are not all about lentils and chickpeas, please ignore them as the authors clearly don't know what they are talking about.

Alternative Alternatives

There are a few others worth mentioning. It is possible to extract protein from potatoes, but there is so little in there that it is barely worthwhile. Rice protein can also be isolated, but has a bitter flavour that is hard to disguise. Hemp protein does get used in some sports and nutrition products, but again has an overpowering taste and is unsuitable for most applications. The reason that many protein drinks and snacks are sweet and strongly flavoured is because most extracted protein tastes vile and needs masking.

There are a couple of relatively new options that might prove interesting in the near future. Lupin protein has a strong, unpleasant taste, but some new varieties have been developed that seem to be addressing this. Lupins are not well known as a food crop, but products made from this legume can provide passable alternatives to soya-based drinks and desserts. This is particularly interesting as lupins are capable of growing on poor quality marginal land that is not suitable for much else, and can also thrive in climates where soya is not as easily grown, such as Northern Europe.

Perhaps even more revolutionary, a Finnish company called Solar Foods has announced that by 2021 it will be manufacturing a high-protein flour based on a bacterium that does not require any land to grow, as it is capable of creating all the sugars it requires from the air. Most fermentation products, including Quorn, require feeding with glucose derived from plants, and so even though they are grown in factories, their production still uses large amounts of agricultural land. According to early reports, this new product only requires energy, nitrogen, water, carbon dioxide and a few added nutrients. If the energy can be made from sustainable sources such as solar or wind, this might end up being one of the most carbon-friendly proteins of all. Here's hoping it doesn't taste awful.[8]

How to Replace Meat

How exactly do you create something that resembles meat from vegetable-based ingredients?* The slightly uncomfortable truth is that much of the insight into how to achieve this comes not from tech-savvy food pioneers based in Silicon Valley, but from the shadier end of the meat industry. For many years, manufacturers have had an interest in finding ways of replacing meat with better value alternatives such as soya and pea, which often provide a lot of the protein in the cheapest, nastiest processed meats. Obviously, because things like pea and soya are very different to meat in terms of flavour and texture, you can't just swap meat for an equal quantity of vegetables. Producers use a number of ingredients and techniques to hide the fact that there is very little meat in some processed products, and many of these methods have been adopted by the new generation of vegetarian and vegan producers. It is not surprising that this trend is an appealing one for the industry. When these techniques are used to reduce the amount of meat, the result is a cheap, low-value product. But as soon as the amount of meat hits zero, you are suddenly able to charge a premium.

For structure, some sort of gelling agent is required to hold the protein together. Carrageenan, an extract of seaweed, is used in some cases, but one of the most useful ingredients is methylcellulose. This is a type of cellulose extracted from woody plants that has been chemically altered so that it forms a loose gel, which gets firmer on heating. This means that methylcellulose fairly closely replicates what happens to meat and eggs as they cook. When used properly, it allows you to

---

* Technically, I mean vegetable, fungal and microorganisms. I am also excluding insects here because I have never really worked with them, and my pathetic Western sensibilities mean that I still find the prospect of a maggot burger (that's what it is folks, whatever you call it) a long way from being acceptable to consumers. We shall cover insect farming briefly in Chapter 12.

create a burger or sausage that can be formed into a shape when cold, but tightens up on cooking, giving a meat-like texture. The only problem is that because methylcellulose has been chemically altered, it cannot be classified as a natural product, so anything containing it is not able to say it is made from 'all natural ingredients'.

The other big issue is flavour. Vegetable proteins lack some of the delicious savoury characteristics of meat, sometimes referred to as umami. This can be added back in with a combination of monosodium glutamate (MSG) and ribotides (another food additive that provides a different sort of savoury flavour), but these are generally not favoured by consumers, and are rarely used these days. Instead, yeast extracts, usually powders rather than the sticky Marmite paste people are familiar with, are common, and modern extracts come with various different flavour characteristics. A number of other flavourings, largely developed for use in the shadier end of the meat industry to hide the off notes in cheap sausages, have proven extremely effective in a new generation of meat-free products.

In addition, there are a number of natural flavourings that can be used to make vegan burgers taste of beef, vegan nuggets taste of chicken, and even vegetable-based products that taste like fish. These flavours use various aroma chemicals extracted from vegetables to replicate the distinctive flavour of meat. If this sounds like sorcery, the reality is that it might as well be. The processes for creating these sorts of flavourings are closely guarded, and the science behind it incredibly complex. Flavour chemists are very much the magicians of the food industry, with the most talented ones being highly sought after, often working away for years in the same secretive laboratories that produce perfumes and fragrances. But the existence of realistic vegan meat flavours is not a new breakthrough. Those bacon-flavoured crisps that you have enjoyed for years do not taste that way because they are sprinkled with ground-up pig.

Once you have structure, flavour and protein content, the next thing you need is fat. In cheap meat products, rendered animal fat can be added back in, but vegan and vegetarian options require a different approach. It is not as simple as adding a bit of vegetable oil, as in order to recreate the succulence of meat you need small granules of solid fat that melt as the product cooks. Fats such as palm or coconut oil, which are solid at room temperature but melt as they heat, are the most useful.* These can be cooled down so they are very hard, grated or shredded in some way, then added into the mixture, forming small lumps of solid fat that melt during cooking. Unfortunately, both these oils have sustainability issues and contain a lot of saturated fat, which is not ideal from a health perspective.

Obviously, there is more to it than that, otherwise I would be out of a job. A number of techniques and ingredients are used to replicate the fibrous nature of meat, and to make it cook in a more realistic way. Natural colours can improve the appearance of products. Spices and other flavourings can mask some of the less pleasant protein flavours, just as they often do in meat-based sausages. And many companies have attempted to make beef-type products that 'bleed' on cooking, using ingredients such as beetroot juice to replicate the red myoglobin that you get with rare burgers and steaks.

It is now perfectly possible to create vegetable-based food that closely replicates cheap, processed meat products, such as burgers, sausages and formed chicken. A strong industry focus and some clever product development is making these products better all the time, and as a result, a number of people have been well and truly cashing in.†

* I mentioned in a previous book that coconut oil should only be used if you enjoy food that tastes of shampoo. I stand by this assessment, but refined coconut oils are available that have the flavour largely removed from them, and I do sometimes use these in meat-free recipes.

† Not me. My rates as a development chef are extremely reasonable, but please book early to avoid disappointment.

The New Kids

In 2019, the plant-based burger company Beyond Meat launched onto the US stock market in one of the most anticipated IPOs (initial public offerings) of recent years. It did not disappoint. The IPO valued the company at $1.5 billion, climbing to over 160% of that value in the first day of trading. Within a few months, Beyond Meat's shares had increased in value by an astonishing 700%, and the company was worth more than the decades-old soup manufacturer Campbell's.

This extraordinary valuation almost certainly represents a bubble. Beyond has little in the way of new technology, no significant intellectual property, a key ingredient that might be limited in supply, and a recipe that any talented product developer could make a passable copy of in a couple of days. In 2019, Beyond made a net loss of $9.4 million on sales of $240 million, which certainly makes its highest valuation of $12 billion somewhat enthusiastic. But the extraordinary rise of a company that is essentially borrowing decades-old meat industry technology is an indication of the powerful, perhaps unstoppable, rise of these products.

Currently, plant-based meat substitutes are worth around $4.6 billion worldwide, and this is projected to grow to $6.4 billion by 2023. This will still only be around half of one percent of the value of global meat consumption, but it is in serious growth and currently represents one percent of the market if we look at the US alone. Many analysts are now looking towards plant-based milks, which from virtually nothing have grown to around thirteen percent of all milk sales in a very short time.[9]

The Beyond Meat flagship burger is being manufactured by two large producers of ground beef products, who have the technology, knowledge and supply chains to successfully deliver these sorts of products. This is a good indication that, unlike the ice traders, meat producers have realised that they are in the protein business, and really have to get on board with the new trend.

Tyson Foods, one of the world's biggest producers of chicken, has invested heavily in Beyond, and has also launched its own brand of plant-based meat substitutes. Cargill, one of the world's largest beef producers, has put a great deal of money behind a large pea protein manufacturer, and Dutch meat giant Jan Zandbergen has a distribution agreement with plant-based burger manufacturer Moving Mountains. These moves are being encouraged by investors, perhaps in part to avoid the sort of complacency that put paid to ice traders, but also because meat is a highly volatile commodity. The new plant-based alternatives represent more added value, greater price stability, and the potential to create new consumer brands.

The meat industry would almost certainly be more than happy to get animals out of the equation. Livestock are inefficient, messy, polluting, dangerous and susceptible to disease. A clean, modern factory and a few fields of peas might be a welcome change for businesses used to grim slaughterhouses and blood-splattered production facilities. It has been estimated that the three largest meat companies, Cargill, Tyson and the Brazilian giant JBS, are responsible for more greenhouse emissions than some of the largest oil companies, something they may be held accountable for in the near future if governments start getting serious about carbon taxes. Much like the oil giants, meat companies may feel that by showcasing investments in carbon-reducing technologies, they can deflect from the devastating impact of their main activity.

A couple of other new players are worth a mention. Impossible Foods are another plant-based burger company. Their flagship burger is based largely on soya protein, but also contains a novel ingredient known as soya leghaemoglobin, which is produced in the same way as the rennet used to make cheese, by genetically engineering yeast and growing it in fermentation tanks. The resulting ingredient, known as haem, gives the Impossible product a distinctive ferrous beef flavour, and makes the burger 'bleed', replicating the myoglobin in rare cooked beef. Impossible has seen a great deal of commercial success, particularly in catering, and although it is still in private hands it is valued at around $2 billion.

Another interesting use of genetically modified bacteria is being attempted by the US start-up Perfect Day, which is looking to produce dairy proteins in this way, opening up the possibility of milks and cheeses made without the need for animals. Despite the success of plant-based burgers and drinks, there is widespread consensus that all vegan cheese is awful, so any improvements there will be welcomed with open arms.

Culture Shock

Instead of replicating meat with vegetables, a task with obvious limitations, how about growing real meat without the need for killing animals? Theoretically, there is no reason why it can't be done, as scientists have long been capable of growing animal cells and tissues in a laboratory. The production of lab-grown skin grafts, and even heart tissue, is currently at an advanced stage.

To produce meat in a laboratory, you first need to harvest some stem cells, something that can easily be done without killing the animal. You then need to create conditions that will make the stem cells differentiate into muscle cells, place them into a growing medium, allow them some sort of scaffold to form structures on, and provide them with the right conditions to replicate. A number of companies and institutions have been working hard on this, and in 2013, the researcher Professor Mark Post organised a tasting of the first cell-grown burger, produced entirely in a laboratory and derived from the cells of a living cow.[10] Companies such as Memphis Meats, Just, Higher Steaks and Aleph Farms are currently working on commercialising this technology, although at the time of writing none are past the prototype stage.[11]

One of the big issues is the growth medium, which is usually made from serums derived from cow, chicken or horse embryos

– not all that appealing to those seeking vegetarian or sustainability credentials. One of the greatest obstacles to producing cultured meat has been the creation of plant-based growth mediums, and although much of the work has been secretive, a number of companies are reporting that they have already achieved it. That doesn't mean they are cost-effective, because they will require specific growth factor proteins that are extremely expensive to produce.

Producing animal tissues in a lab also requires cells that are slightly different to normal ones, which stop replicating after a few generations. For this reason, care must be taken to select special, so-called 'immortalised' cell lines (effectively cancer cells), or perhaps even genetically modify them. This is an issue that cellular meat companies tend to skirt around, since people might not like the idea of eating a cancer burger.

The production of minced, processed meats such as burgers or chicken nuggets is seemingly not far off, although growing a steak in a laboratory is probably a good deal further away. Steak is a lot more complex, requiring multiple cell types, structures and tissues, but even if this proves possible one day, there are still many issues to consider. In a world where genetically modified plants are referred to as Frankenfood and banned throughout most of Europe, how acceptable is lab-produced GM cancer meat likely to be to consumers? A recent survey suggested that only twenty percent of people would be willing to try it, perhaps limiting its mass appeal. And this is before the technophobic rhetoric of 'real food' advocates and the PR machine of the livestock industry has started to grind into action (I apologise if I have given them any ideas).[12]

Putting PR aside, how sure are we that cultured meat is a more environmentally friendly option? Obviously, sustainability is not the only concern, but it is the focus of this book. The reality is that we don't yet know what the impact of these products is likely to be, and until large-scale production is up and running, it is going to be incredibly hard to tell. Hanna Tuomisto from the

University of Helsinki has conducted one of the few studies looking at the environmental impact of cultured meats, and her conclusion seems to be that it depends on the source of energy.[13] Crucially, when compared to some of the more efficient methods of meat production, it might be hard to make any sustainability improvements at all. Dr Tuomisto told me:

> The energy use is likely to be really high compared to livestock, but it depends on the source of nutrients, and the greenhouse gas emissions depend on the source of energy. If you can run a bioreactor on solar, it would be much lower. For beef production it is hard to reduce emissions, but for cultured meat it is mostly related to the energy source, so a bit easier to control. But poultry is very efficient. You can get 1 kg of meat from 2 kg of feed, which would be hard to achieve even with a cell culture.

The third issue, and one that is rarely mentioned, is one of scale. If we really want cultured meat to make an impact on our food system, then it will need to replace a significant amount of livestock. Currently, a few companies and institutions are investing significant resources into this technology, and can produce a few grams at an enormous cost. Yet in order to replace just ten percent of the meat consumed annually, production would somehow need to step up to making thirty billion kilograms per year, requiring thousands of huge industrial plants all over the world.

To put that figure into perspective, in 2019, Quorn invested £150 million in a factory capable of producing twenty million kilograms of mycoprotein per year, equivalent to about 0.006% of the world's meat supply.[14] Mycoprotein is produced in the same sort of fermentation vessels that might one day manufacture cultured meat, but is an order of magnitude easier to produce, with proven technology, a simple growth medium, and cell lines far more suited to rapid production. Anyone who has spent time culturing animal tissues in a laboratory will tell you that even on a small scale it is very hard to keep things sterile, and the process requires great care and high levels of antibiotics. It is almost certain that cultured meat will be many times more complex and expensive to produce than Quorn, but even if it isn't, meeting just one tenth of the global demand for meat would require well over £2 trillion worth of investment.

Do we really want thousands of industrial plants producing slabs of cultured meat, especially when there is no proven environmental benefit? Do we want a transfer of power in world meat production away from farmers and into the hands of a few global companies, likely to be the only ones capable of the huge investment required to set up production?* Wouldn't it be better to invest some of that £2 trillion persuading people to eat ten percent less meat, focusing on the virtues of lentils and chickpeas? After all, for that sort of money you could enlist the help of 400,000 Jamie Olivers.

There are also important unanswered questions about whether enough sustainable energy could ever be produced to meet the huge demands of a cultured meat industry producing millions of tonnes of product. And even deeper questions about the practical reality of what would happen to all the agricultural land freed up in the process.

Shifting Diets

It has been estimated that if we can replace fifty percent of the meat produced around the world with plant or cellular alternatives, it would reduce demand for agricultural land by thirty-eight percent. Several reports into the global impact of agriculture

* To be honest, the meat industry is already heavily dominated by a few global companies, including JBS, Tyson and Cargill, but cellular meat would be impossible to produce without big money backing, whereas there are many small livestock farmers.

have identified plant-based meat substitutes as vitally important in reducing the environmental impact of our food system. In order to create a more sustainable agriculture, most developed economies need to drastically cut down their consumption of meat, and parts of the developing world need to increase the amount they eat for health reasons. These two moving levels of consumption should one day meet up, hopefully at a point that is sustainable, optimal for health, and perfectly designed to create a circular, efficient food system.

This optimal level for global meat consumption is the source of much debate. If, as many researchers think is sensible, we were to limit meat production to that which can be made from non-human edible feed such as pasture, hay or swill, we would only be able to produce between 9 g and 31 g per person per day.[15] This level is considerably less than the current global average, let alone any increased future demand. Whenever anyone claims that meat is fine as long as it is grass fed, it is worth reminding them that the best estimates suggest we could only produce enough that way to make one or two burgers' worth each per week. Any more than that, and livestock are going to be competing for human-edible food.

In 2018, in an attempt to create recommendations for a diet that is optimal in terms of planetary and human health, the EAT-*Lancet* report suggested that average meat consumption should be around 43 g per day, with only 14 g of that being red meat.[16] This roughly equates to a diet containing one small beef burger and a couple of pieces of chicken every week, leading to accusations that a rich elite of global vegans were trying to impose their liberal agenda on the masses.[17] The World Health Organization has suggested that 70 g per day of red meat, or a burger every other day, is optimal for health, which is perhaps more realistic, but in many people's opinion not drastic enough to save the environment.[18] In the absence of a consensus, the answer is likely to be found somewhere between the extremes.

Whatever the figure, it has not yet permeated public consciousness. The US average consumption of meat is currently around 301 g per day. In Brazil, it is 225 g. In China, 136 g, and set to rise to 150 g by 2026.[19] Globally, per capita meat consumption averages out at 118 g per day and it is predicted that this will increase by nearly twenty percent over the next thirty years, which combined with a growing population will nearly double demand.[20] In order to address the environmental impact of food, we can debate all we like, and could spend the next few decades producing reports, without having the slightest impact on the way that people eat. Behaviour change on an unprecedented global scale is desperately required. We need to create enormous shifts. We also need to maintain diets that are delicious, tempting and humane.

Finding a way to make this happen is perhaps one of the greatest challenges currently facing humanity, yet one that virtually no one is talking about. Huge sums of money are being ploughed into complex life-cycle assessments, satellite images of habitat destruction, and computer modelling of our food system's future impact. But far too little attention is being paid to how we might actually create the huge, global shifts in behaviour required to do anything about it.

12

Behave Yourself

To do good is noble. To tell others to do good is even nobler
and much less trouble.

— Mark Twain

Writing this book has been a long road. I have read virtually every
text and report on the environmental impact of food, spoken to
dozens of the world's leading experts, travelled to different
corners of the world, and spent a few too many hours staring out
of my window thinking about exactly how garden birds are going
to vanquish humanity.*

What has become increasingly clear is that even though we
seem to be hurtling relentlessly towards disaster, there are
reasons to be hopeful. We actually know a lot about the path we
should be taking if we want to feed a growing human population
sustainably. There are many technological, policy and industry
advances that will help, and these are the subject of the next
chapter. But on their own, they are nowhere near enough.[1] What
we really need are major behavioural shifts, the scope and scale
of which we have never seen before. The problem is, despite

* Yes, I know, flying is bad and I am a massive hypocrite, but long-haul flights do
leave me with plenty of time for reading mind-numbingly boring reports on global
agriculture.

countless reports about the desperate need for change, very few people are talking about how this might actually happen. Like a supply teacher struggling to control a rowdy classroom, there appears to be an assumption that if we just relentlessly tell people how pressing the need for action is, they will eventually start to behave themselves.

Food behaviour is far more ingrained than we like to assume, wrapped up in a complex mix of societal expectations, cultural norms, hedonism, economics, nurturing instincts, identity, status and self-interest. It was incredibly hard to alter people's behaviour when it came to smoking, but with food we can expect things to be an order of magnitude more difficult. Unlike smoking, the ideal amount of food that we want people to consume is not zero, and as we have seen, it isn't easy to create simple signposts that indicate how sustainable a food product is. Changing diets requires care, compassion, cultural sensitivity and careful analysis, and it also needs to happen quickly, widely and dramatically.

Humans are not slaves or drones. We can be influenced but, as someone who has worked for large branded food businesses for half his career, I can attest that even when enormous marketing budgets are available, it is incredibly difficult to get consumers to fundamentally change their behaviour in a targeted, predictable way. If it was easy and I knew the secret, I would be relaxing on a gas-guzzling luxury yacht right now, rather than wearing three pairs of socks because I'm worried about how much the electric heater in my office costs to run.

The truth is that many hugely expensive marketing and promotional campaigns miserably fail to alter the behaviour of consumers. A lot of inexpensive and poorly thought-out strategies succeed way beyond expectations, often propelling previously unknown brands into the public eye. The elephant in the room is that consumer behaviour is frequently confounding, with marketers having to find patterns in randomness to justify their roles. Tiny increases in sales will be attributed entirely to marketing activity, yet huge declines will be put down to 'unseasonal

weather' or 'phasing', one of many terms used by commercial
managers when they haven't a clue what's going on. Unfortunately,
a whole industry is founded on the premise that human behaviour is malleable, and a sector of the media has devoted itself to
exposing how evil food corporations have us all in their thrall.
This makes for good copy, but is far from the truth. Anyone who
has experienced the panic, incomprehension and incompetence
that thrive at the top level of food companies, or the hubris and
misinformation that emanate from advertising and marketing
organisations, might have a different view.

The capitalist market for food is the complex aggregate of a
billion thoughts and interactions, and anyone claiming that they
can affect it with any degree of consistency or accuracy is hawking snake oil. The biggest global corporations rarely attempt to
create new food brands, even when they have access to the latest
consumer insights, huge creative budgets and world-leading
research and development resources. The food business is so
risky and difficult to predict that large companies usually wait
and see which emerging brands are successful, then simply
purchase them to add to their portfolio.

A lot is made of so called 'nudge theory', the idea that our
environment can be subtly manipulated in order to influence our
decisions in a desired way. This has become the technique of
choice for many policymakers trying to enact food system change,
largely because it is cheap and appeals to those who naturally shy
away from draconian, interventionist policies. If we can just reor-
der items on a menu, place sustainable options more prominently
and use compelling language in our communications, perhaps
we will be able to change the world without anyone noticing.*

---

* It also doesn't help that a lot of the 'nudge theory' principles in the world of food
derive from research carried out by Brian Wansink, the disgraced Cornell professor who was found to have been manipulating his results. I covered Wansink's
work in more detail in my previous book, *The Truth About Fat*, if you want to know
more.

When it comes to nudges, I do believe there is a place for this sort of intervention. You really can encourage people to pay tax bills a little earlier, reduce littering in national parks, and stop men from urinating on their shoes in Amsterdam's main airport, something that was apparently a burning issue.[2] But the changes required to our food system are a little more fundamental than a bit of piss on a Dutchman's shoes. Rather than a gentle nudge in the right direction, we really need a great big fucking shove.

In this chapter, I am going to depart slightly from analysing agriculture and the food supply, to thinking more broadly about how we might conquer the greatest barrier to a sustainable future. Exactly how possible is it to change people's minds?

As Good as a Rest

Much has been made of the recent rise of vegetarianism and veganism in developed countries, and the burgeoning success of brands such as Impossible and Beyond. But when compared to global meat production and consumption, these are still niche pursuits. Vegan diets are currently on the rise, but those that maintain this way of eating for a lifetime rarely exceed one percent of the population.[3] And despite skyrocketing company valuations and an army of new entrepreneurs looking to cash in on the meat-free trend, plant-based meat substitutes still only represent less than half of a percent of the global market. Even if these products grow at fifteen to twenty percent annually for the next few years – more than enough to make a lot of people very rich – they will still be relatively insignificant on a global scale.

Equally, very few companies are currently trying to sell food products on sustainability grounds. Despite the huge attention that the environmental impact of food has received in the media, no one has really cracked how to turn this into a compelling consumer proposition. Sustainability is really hard to communicate in a simple way. I have been striving to get it across in under four hundred pages, yet most consumers make food purchasing decisions in around two to three seconds. Even if consumers did have more time, what factors would be the most important: greenhouse gases, water use, water pollution, biodiversity loss, plastics, soil erosion or energy?

Take a seemingly simple measure such as soil carbon. Recently, a US company called White Oak Pasture proudly announced that its sustainably produced grass-fed beef was actually carbon negative, meaning that the production process removed more greenhouse gases from the atmosphere than it released.[4] The reason for this is that the cattle were being raised on degraded farmland, and turning that land back into pasture was capturing enough carbon to offset the cows' methane-rich burps. The headline is that we can eat White Oak beef guilt-free, happy in the knowledge that we are reducing global warming.

This sounds great, and this production method appears infinitely preferable to feeding cows soya beans grown on cleared rainforest. The White Oak report takes a snapshot of beef production at a point when degraded land is being returned to pasture, but there are limits on exactly how much carbon can be tied up in this way. After a few years, the pasture will reach a carbon capture limit, remaining in equilibrium after that. At this point, it will still have cows on top of it, happily grazing and burping out methane. This means that in about five or ten years, White Oak beef is set to become a net contributor to greenhouse emissions. If at this point they decide to move on to restore a new patch of land, there is a real danger that the abandoned pasture will be degraded again by the next owner, releasing all the carbon they have worked so hard to restore.[5] But try putting all that on the front of a packet of beef.

There is also a question regarding how interested consumers really are. Louise Needham has been working as Sustainability Manager on the Quorn brand for many years, attempting to obtain good quality information on the environmental impact of their products. When I spoke to her, she seemed somewhat frustrated by the lack of progress, not in obtaining information, but in using it to create a competitive advantage. Despite having independently audited evidence that Quorn products have a much lower carbon impact than meat equivalents, the company has made little headway in communicating this to the public.* She told me:

> 2019 was the first year that the business tried to communicate sustainability directly with the 'Healthy Protein, Healthy Planet' campaign, but it is very hard to get these messages directly across to consumers.

Is there evidence that this might be changing? Amelia Boothman is Director of Innovation Strategy at 1HQ, an international brand development agency working with some of the world's largest companies. She regularly runs focus groups for the food industry, and believes that even if behaviour is still stuck in a rut, consumer attitudes have been noticeably shifting of late. She told me that she has recently seen a tipping point, with groups starting to show an interest in sustainability issues, particularly after the *Blue Planet* TV series and the work of campaigners like Greta Thunberg.

Increased awareness and focus are perhaps preceding mass changes in behaviour, but there is still a lot of reticence in the industry regarding how easy it is going to be to communicate and sell environmental messages. Amelia Boothman explained that a key reason for this is that it is very difficult to sell sustainability in a simple way:

> The most common brief we are getting at the moment is for the creation of a new plant-based brand. But the $64,000 question is what to communicate. My first advice is always to make sure the brand looks like it is not a compromise, make sure it still looks like a delicious

---

* Quorn's life-cycle analysis is audited by the Carbon Trust.

experience. Secondly, get the price the same as your competition. People won't pay more, unless you've got a really unique and compelling point of difference.

Will Carter has worked as managing director and CEO for some of the UK's largest food companies including Premier Foods, Whitworths and United Biscuits, and currently advises financial organisations looking to invest in the industry. He believes that taste is everything in the meat-free sector, which is welcome news for reasonably priced development chefs working in this area. He told me:

> Creativity can play a role. Meat alternatives are getting better, the recipe development is getting smarter. With Quorn, the penetration has traditionally been within the core vegetarian heartland, but the proportion of non-vegetarian users is rising because of other benefits. The real change will happen when a recipe is as good as, or nearly as good as, meat. But even then, you can't shortcut from the thinktank to consumer behaviour without the active compliance of the supply chain.

Because sustainability is so hard to communicate, consumers are going to need shortcuts. One of the most powerful shortcuts is likely to be the creation of trusted sustainable food brands, and for such brands to be successful, they need to be widely available. Josh Bullmore is Chief Strategy Officer at Leo Burnett, a global advertising agency that works on campaigns for several major food brands including McDonald's, Kellogg's and Lindt. He told me that brands are able to grow only when they become mentally and physically available. Mental availability involves the use of marketing to create awareness, salience and desire, but this only works if things are physically easy for consumers to attain. This is the reason why mainstream brands are likely to be so important in increasing uptake of more sustainable products, as they are both mentally and physically available. As Josh explains, 'Mainstream brands give you massive uptake, then before long it becomes "just what you do". Sustainability can give you a competitive advantage if all else is equal, but it needs to become a hygiene factor over time.'*

Robert Lawson is a former Managing Director of Quorn who now works as an investment adviser specialising in meat substitutes. He believes that the market needs a large global branded company working in this area to shift the dial significantly. In his opinion, one of the big barriers to mainstream uptake is that there are currently no global branded players advertising or communicating about environmental benefits. He told me:

> There are just a bunch of small and early stage companies who don't really understand the power of consumer insight and advertising and who are more comfortable investing in manufacturing kit than in brand building. The winners will address the health, the environment, deliver on taste and will be something that feels natural.

The idea that a product needs to 'feel natural' is an important point we shall return to towards the end of this chapter, but it seems likely that the creation of a few significant global brands trading on sustainability credentials might hold the key to widespread changes in consumer behaviour. Trusted brands will also help people get over the barrier of buying a strange, unfamiliar product, such as a vegan beef burger, helping consumers to believe that it will deliver on taste.

For the moment, it helps to replace products the consumer is already uncomfortable about such as burgers, nuggets and sausages – traditionally the preserve of jokes about their eyeball and scrotum content – rather than creating substitutes for fillet steak or

---

* 'Hygiene factor' here does not refer to food being hygienic or safe. In this context it describes something that is expected of a company rather than being an optional extra. An example would be the protection of workers' human rights, something that most consumers expect of large companies without them having to mention it, resulting in huge scandals when that trust is broken.

roast chicken. This approach makes sense for consumers, but it doesn't solve one of the big problems with sustainability. Generally speaking, the number of cows being produced for beef depends upon the volume of sales of steaks and whole joints, with ground meat being made from what is left. So reducing the cow population is going to require more than just a good quality vegan burger.

But whatever you are trying to replicate, brands will have a vital role. The infamous Greggs Vegan Sausage Roll launch in 2019 was successful because it appealed to a new group of consumers who trusted the Greggs brand to deliver on taste. It didn't represent anything revolutionary in terms of product development, and an identical product sold under a different brand might have been a complete flop.

Although you might argue that it was marketing that got us into this mess, the history of global food brands is intimately tied up with consumers' need for trust. Many of our most significant brands and companies, such as Nestlé, Cadbury's and Tetley Tea, rose to prominence during the nineteenth century, when food scares were rife and consumer trust key. These brands grew with the promise of safe, unadulterated products, something that most of us now take for granted in all the food we buy.

Although major brands are increasingly under scrutiny these days, the safety issue is still extremely important in emerging markets after a series of food production scandals involving local producers. Nowhere is this more important than in China, where newly affluent consumers look towards global brands based on a trust of their food safety records, handing them a huge competitive advantage.

In turn, this has meant that major global brands are obsessively vigilant regarding food safety, as their success very much depends upon it. Anyone who has ever been involved in an audit from a large manufacturer or retailer will know that safety is taken incredibly seriously; supply chains are investigated with forensic precision; and even the most minor infractions are punished with draconian brutality. One mistake can easily destroy a brand forever,

so manufacturers err on the side of extreme caution. While onerous for workers, the approach has led to a food supply that is safer
and more secure than at any time in human history.

If a few major brands can develop a similar sort of trust when it
comes to sustainability, and also deliver on a reputation for taste,
value, health and convenience, it might just create a powerful
force for change. Sustainability will perhaps only ever be compelling for consumers when all else is equal, but it might give some
brands a small advantage, which is often the difference between
success and failure. Of course, it will be the job of scientists and
communicators to hold these brands to account and ensure they
are not simply greenwashing, but I am sure there will be plenty of
people willing to perform this role, this author included.

Can Flying Buffalo Save the World?

Has there ever been a shift in food behaviour as significant as the
one now required? The answer of course is yes, as our diet today
is radically different to that of our grandparents, and an order of
magnitude different again to that of our great-great-grandparents.
But those changes were the results of fundamental shifts in society, food availability and wealth. Crucially, they were not targeted,
whereas we now need to direct change in ways that many
consumers and industry players are likely to resist. Is this modern
challenge truly unprecedented?

A clue lies in the story of a medium-sized Arkansas meat
packer during the 1970s, which became curious as to why it was
selling so many chicken wings in one small American city every
time there was a big football game on TV.

At the time, Tyson Foods was a chicken producer that largely
sold whole birds, with some trade in fillets and pieces, leaving
them with an annoying surplus of wings. The company discovered that the city of Buffalo was consuming a huge number of
wings at certain times of the year and, keen to find ways of

moving their excess, the Tyson team took a trip there on the day of a major football game to find out what was going on. They soon discovered that local sports bars were offering chicken wings in a variety of spicy sauces as a cheap bar snack to keep the football-watching customers happy and the drinks flowing.

Tyson's product developers went away and worked on a new product, taking these cheap and unwanted wings, adding a spicy sauce, and so magically converting them into a simple, convenient snack for people to enjoy in their homes. Buffalo wings quickly went from local tradition to national institution, forever confusing foreign visitors reading US menus and expecting some sort of airborne cattle.

From there, the Tyson Foods management realised there was huge commercial potential in creating value-added chicken products. This would eventually lead them to develop the Chicken Nugget in conjunction with the fast-food chain McDonald's, perhaps one of the most significant innovations in the recent history of food. Once Tyson changed its focus from rearing birds to flavouring and packaging chicken meat, it quickly transformed from a medium-sized meat producer into one of the largest food companies in the world.[6]

Many people might not see this journey as worthy of celebration, but there is no doubting that Tyson Foods was key in changing the role of chicken in the US diet, something that had reverberations around the world. In the 1970s, US beef consumption peaked at around 40 kg per person per year, falling steadily to around 30 kg per head today. In contrast, consumption of chicken has increased over the same period, rising from 20 kg per person per year in 1970, to nearly 50 kg today.[7] This shift is often attributed to health concerns regarding beef, but this ignores the glaring fact that an awful lot of chicken is consumed in forms that no one considers healthy, such as nuggets, burgers and fried drumsticks. The real key to the dramatic changes in meat consumption has been the work done in the development kitchens of companies such as Tyson, transforming chicken into products that are convenient and delicious, and fit into people's lives.

You can now buy chicken in nuggets, bites, burgers, popcorn, drumsticks, thighs, fillets and tenders. There are cold cuts and snack foods eaten straight from the fridge. There are countless ready meals showcasing exciting ethnic cuisines, often far lighter and healthier than lasagnes, cottage pies or stews. There are dozens of sandwich fillings that take advantage of chicken's blandness and ability to take on flavour. With the help of some clever innovation, chicken lends itself to the modern world in a way that beef has struggled to, creating a truly significant transformation in the way we eat. By far the largest proportion of animals now slaughtered for meat, around 62 billion every year, are chickens, and demand is growing relentlessly. Chickens are almost unbelievably efficient at turning feed into meat. The environmental picture isn't clear-cut, since chickens largely eat food that is suitable for humans, or grown on land that could be used to feed humans. But crucially, for our purposes, the shift in demand from beef to chicken was targeted and deliberate. It was the result of marketing, innovation and design, indicating that it might hold lessons for how we could make similar shifts in the future.

There are other examples. In the mid-1980s, the American comedy show *Saturday Night Live* ran a parody sketch describing the launch of McSushi (or McSooshi as they called it) onto the McDonald's menu. At the time, sushi was being tentatively introduced into Europe and the US, and was widely derided as disgusting and alien. The thought of eating raw fish was so strange to consumers that any notion it might one day become a mass-market product was the subject of cheap humour.* Yet thanks to the efforts of a few pioneering restaurateurs and manufacturers, combined with a convenient, delicious and healthy

---

* Yes, I am aware that sushi is not the same thing as raw fish, but in the 1980s, when casual racism passed for humour, it was widely thought that sushi basically involved eating still-twitching lumps of uncooked cod, which made small-town Brits like me quiver in nauseous fear.

product, sushi captured the hearts and wallets of Western consumers. Less than forty years after the *SNL* skit, sushi is almost as ubiquitous in the American diet as cheeseburgers, with over four thousand specialist restaurants turning over $2 billion annually, and a rapidly growing retail trade that sees sushi being sold in gas stations and supermarkets.[8]

Similarly, hummus was not widely known in the UK until the mid-1980s, but through a few influential food writers, changes in eating habits, and a product that is highly suited to large-scale manufacturing, it is now a grocery staple, present in over forty percent of UK household fridges.[9] Globally, grocery sales of pre-prepared hummus have grown from nearly nothing in the 1980s, to over $2 billion today, with this figure expected to triple over the next ten years.[10]

It is foolishness to suggest that markets for food cannot change quickly and dramatically. They are just maddeningly hard to control or predict. For every chicken nugget, there are a thousand innovations left by the wayside (including several of my own). For every hummus and sushi, there are countless delicious local foods that have failed to reach a global audience.

The Circle of Concern

Over the next thirty years, some of the most significant changes may have little to do with food, but could well impact upon the way we eat. Throughout the world there is a circle of moral concern that expands in predictable ways as societies develop economically. For instance, global attitudes to human rights have tended to improve along with economic development, and once acceptable practices of slavery, execution and child abuse have become taboo. Rights for women have tended to increase, with female roles in society becoming more equal. Racial prejudice has gradually become less acceptable. Homosexuality has been decriminalised across most of the world and is increasingly accepted as a normal part of life.*

Along the way, people from the groups that benefit from these inequalities have passionately resisted these changes. They have claimed that even though they are in favour of progress, this current thing is a step too far. But eventually, their protests have withered and died as a more enlightened generation has taken control. Be it slavery, racism or votes for women, there were always people who fought against change, convinced that it was political correctness gone mad.

Crucially, progress is a journey rather than a destination. At each point along the path we may feel as if we are at the end, but we never really are. There are almost certainly cruelties and injustices accepted today that will disgust future generations. In fifty years' time, providing economic and social progress continues in the right direction, the circle of concern will have expanded to protect the lives of others who are still persecuted today. It could easily end up encompassing animals, ecosystems and the natural world in ways that seem inconceivable to us now.

Most of our seemingly innate values are really just a product of our culture, something that can vary dramatically around the world. One country that has resisted increases in meat consumption as it has developed economically has been India, which according to 2009 figures only consumes around 12 g of meat per person per day, well below countries of equivalent economic means.[11] This is largely because cultural expectations regarding meat are very different in most of India, and as a result they have a cuisine that is highly suited to plant-based foods.

If you really want to create shifts in meat consumption, it is a case of changing society, rather than individuals. Early drink-driving campaigns failed to change behaviour because they appealed to drivers themselves, whose attitude tended to be

---

* Although shockingly it is still illegal in seventy-three nations, and is subject to the death penalty in twelve.

defensive. As a child I remember grown men telling me that they were better drivers after a few pints, and it was none of the government's business if they wanted to enjoy a drink on a Friday night and drive home shitfaced. It was only when the focus shifted to the community that things started to change. In the UK, hard-hitting billboard and television adverts showed images of innocent people who had been killed, disabled or disfigured in accidents caused by drink-driving, accompanied by the slogan 'Drinking and Driving Wrecks Lives'. Successful campaigns found ways of making drink-driving taboo, creating societal disdain for people's ultimately selfish behaviour, and as a result deaths from drink-driving fell dramatically.* Instead of trying to clean the fish, if you really want them to get better, you need to change the water and clean out the tank.

Behave Yourselves

Of course, I would never want to encourage making the consumption of animal products taboo. In fact, this would be against everything I believe, as guilt and shame have no place in people's diets. The key to a positive food system transformation will be people embracing more plant-based foods, and fighting the developed world's idea that meat should be at the centre of every meal. We need to celebrate and enjoy meat, and that means reserving it for special, occasional consumption. Change will happen when we create a society where this is the norm.

So what exactly should we be doing to help get us there? Josh Bullmore from the advertising agency Leo Burnett has worked on a number of projects attempting to create large-scale shifts in public behaviour, including the UK government's health-focused

---

* Between 1979 and 2012, annual deaths from drink-driving in the UK fell from 1,640 to 290, despite there being many more cars on the road. Although there are other factors, including improved car safety, the change in societal attitudes was key.

'Change for Life' campaign. When we discussed selling plant-based diets for their environmental benefits, he was quite clear that this was probably not the best way forward. He told me that in practice, the current sustainability argument for eating less meat, with the attendant ideas of sacrificing personal convenience for the public good, will only ever appeal to a limited number of people. Pushing the social message of going 'meat free' only serves to highlight the idea that you are going without. 'It is more compelling to celebrate the benefits,' he tells me. 'Tastiness and flavour are more rational benefits. We need to make it desirable. We need to dial up deliciousness and dial down worthiness. The more you go for people's rational brain, the less successful you will be.'

Real change will only happen when diets with less meat become desirable. It might be led by the books and TV series of celebrity chefs, but probably not when they are marketed as 'sustainable recipes'. Instead, we need recipes that celebrate the joy of eating pulses, lentils and beans. Restaurant chains, food manufacturers and retailers need to invest more in developing clever plant-based meals that fit perfectly into people's lives. The most sustainable options need to be the most convenient, available and delicious. Things that happen to come with environmental benefits need to be the most desired and relevant foods of all. What we need is a Buffalo wing moment.

As product development becomes more sophisticated and plant-based options start to do the same job as their meat equivalents, economic manipulation might well play a part. As soon as great-tasting non-meat versions of our favourite foods are widely available, raising the price of meat becomes far more palatable, and less likely to do harm. This manipulation might be as simple as internalising some of the costs of meat production – making the producers pay for the damage – or at the very least, removing subsidies from livestock and feed. The problem is, an awful lot of powerful people have an interest in this not happening.

The Resistance

I understand that for some people – largely alpha-male carnivore types with #JERF in their Twitter profiles – plant-based meat substitutes are never going to be for them.* This is fine. We should all have the freedom to eat however we choose. What I fail to comprehend is the sheer visceral anger that exists towards plant-based meat substitutes in some sectors, with many people apparently offended that these sorts of products exist.

Piers Morgan infamously described the bakery chain Greggs as being 'PC-ravaged clowns' for launching a vegan version of their sausage roll, something that generated an awful lot of press coverage at the time. Even from a controversy whore like Morgan, such outrage is surprising, because it was not as if Greggs had stopped selling their normal, pork-based sausage roll, or any of their other meat products. No one was being forced or tricked into buying vegan foods, and Greggs were simply filling a demand gap with a new product, in the way that any sensible business should. But strangely, the fact that they had created a vegan version of one of their leading meat items seemed to offend large numbers of people, even though they had no plans to eat it.

Here are a few examples of similar reactions to widely available food products from some important social and food system commenters. There's also a quote from Joanna Blythman.

> I mean, surely you can't call it a sausage if it doesn't include meat? Call it a Quorn roll, or a vegan roll, but don't bring down the good name of a traditional British meat snack if it doesn't include meat. – Blogger and self-proclaimed 'Official Sausage Roll King' LadBaby[12]

---

* #JERF stands for Just Eat Real Food, and is used by people who reject manufactured products in favour of fresh ingredients. It has become strongly associated with people on low-carb diets eating large amounts of steak, although potatoes are just as real as beef.

When you look at Impossible Burger or Beyond Meat, they have twenty-one or twenty-two highly processed ingredients. So processed that you are hard pressed in identifying the difference between those items, versus let's say, pet food. – Dr Frank Mitloehner, Professor at the University of California, Davis[13]

Companies exploit the qualities associated with animal foods to market products that don't contain any. That's wilful fakery if you ask me. Yet lots of people who reject animal foods appear happy to go along with this misrepresentation. – Joanna Blythman, sanctimonious food writer[14]

Why is it that people are so offended by the existence of these meat alternatives? I had always assumed that it was pushback by meat industry advocates protecting their turf, or perhaps just the #JERF crowd, who always seem fearful of new technology. But the very specific reaction to fake meat seems far stronger than anything directed at other highly processed foods, many of which are more worthy of disdain.

Alan Levinovitz is an Associate Professor of Religion, whose book *One Nature Under God* investigates the meaning of the word 'natural' in Western culture. When I spoke to him about the reaction to meat substitutes, he was quite clear why these products cause such offence. He told me:

People tend to divide the world up into categories. They divide it into things like alive and dead; natural and man-made; plant and animal. When these boundaries are challenged, people find that very difficult, because these binary categories are important to people. We need to know the difference between animals and plants, otherwise how can we make decisions on things such as animal rights. We actually see a very similar thing with the outrage around arguments for transgender rights.

Perhaps playing up to this visceral response, the meat and dairy industries have been aggressively defending their territory of late, attempting to protect the product names used to describe various plant-based products. The dairy industry has been working on protecting the terms 'milk', 'yoghurt' and 'cheese' in Europe and the US, so preventing soya, almond or oat versions from using them in several regions. Similarly, a number of meat advocacy groups have been trying to ensure that words like 'burger', 'sausage' or 'bacon' can only be used when referring to products containing a certain amount of meat.[15]

Suggestions that vegan burgers should be referred to as 'vegetable-based nutrition discs', sausages as 'edible vegan protein tubing', and almond milk as 'nut juice', have been incessantly hawked by the meat and dairy industry, presumably trying to get a shot across the bows of their new upstart rivals with a cheap appeal to people's disgust. These sorts of blocking tactics are to be expected. In fact, labelling regulations and legally protected terms for describing food were developed to prevent consumers from being misled by the very industries now trying to twist them to their advantage.

In the UK, a 'beef burger' is legally required to contain at least sixty-two percent beef and a 'pork sausage' forty-two percent pork. These terms are protected by law in order to prevent manufacturers from ripping off consumers by adulterating meat products with cheap filler and rusks, so names such as 'economy burger' and 'banger' are used by manufacturers to denote products with a lower meat content. By contrast, producers of plant-based foods have absolutely no interest in confusing consumers about the origin or content of their products. In fact, this is the exact opposite of what they are trying to do. The entire selling point of plant milks or vegan burgers is that they are not derived from animals.

As for laboratory-grown meat, if this does eventually reach supermarket shelves, there will have to be a great deal of thought regarding what it is going to be called, as this is likely to influence its eventual success. Initially, this sort of meat will almost certainly command a huge price premium, meaning that it will be in the manufacturers' interest to make sure consumers can distinguish it from an animal-derived product. It seems incredibly unlikely that if, as they have predicted, companies such as Just start selling cultured chicken in high-end Asian restaurants in the next year or so, it will be described on the menu simply as a 'chicken nugget', especially if it costs \$100.* Whatever term the industry settles on, be it cellular meat, cultured meat, slaughter-free meat or lab-grown meat, it is unlikely that companies will be attempting to mislead consumers about its origins.

What Nature Intended

There is no doubting that, when you look at the ingredients of a vegan burger, it is a list of strange, unrecognisable substances such as methylcellulose or pea protein isolate. Compared to the single ingredient on a packet of steak, there is a huge temptation to declare meat as being a more natural food. But the reality is that such distinctions make little sense. Beef steaks are no more 'natural' than pea proteins. Beef cattle have been bred so as to be unrecognisable compared to anything our pre-agriculture ancestors might have recognised. They are raised in completely unnatural conditions, and nutritionally their meat bears little resemblance to that of any wild creatures. But the notion that meat is more natural is seemingly innate, and I have to confess to having the same associations myself.

Alan Levinovitz has literally written the book on our perception of what is natural, and believes that although it is incredibly challenging, such resistance can be countered. He told me:

> For a lot of people, the illusion of feeling that you know where your beef comes from is empowering. A vegan sausage or lab-grown meat is not easy to understand. People

* The reason it is likely to be launched in Asia is because US and European novel food regulations are, generally speaking, a little more onerous, and approval will probably be easier in certain Asian countries. At the time of writing, the exact location for launch has not yet been specified.

can end up in a world where things are opaque to them. To counter that, you need to make sure people understand the new products. You might also need to blur the boundaries by educating people about the history of human interventions. What people think of as 'natural' meat is actually an extreme form of meat and making new food products is just as 'natural' as a process like brewing beer.

Certainly, a lot of the communication from companies such as Beyond and Impossible has cleverly trod this path, although I do worry that it sometimes crosses the line into attacking other people's food choices. When arguments stray into damning the consumption of contaminated, hormone-injected animal corpses, or disgust at eating the fermented lactations of another creature, marketing soon morphs into a shaming exercise. We must remember that all the food we eat is dramatically different from that of our distant ancestors, and our dietary health is vastly improved in every measurable way. Everyone arguing about which foods are the most 'natural' or 'real' is deluded about the meaning of those terms.

Countering this perceived lack of naturalness is perhaps the greatest challenge for plant-based meat substitutes. There is a widespread assumption that the mass-scale use of technology has ruined the natural world, and so it is counter-intuitive to embrace it as the way to help save the planet. A cow in a picturesque field lazily eating grass will always feel less of a drain than an industrial pea protein extraction facility, or a set of bioreactors churning out mycoprotein. But as with so much in this area, our gut feelings rarely lead us to the path we should be taking. The key to a better future will probably require all of us to ignore our instincts to some extent.

Reasons to be Fearful

Many will fear the coming change, be it because of a threat to their livelihood, or a blurring of the boundaries they use to navigate the world. But however strong this resistance, changes to the way we eat are inevitable over the coming years, if only because we will eventually run out of agricultural land. As change happens, there are many genuine reasons to be wary. Grand technological solutions tend to concentrate power into the hands of a few giant corporations, often leaving the most vulnerable people ever more desolate.

Evan Fraser is a Professor at the University of British Columbia, specialising in global food security. Of all the warnings I have heard about the coming changes to our food system, his resonated the most. As he told me:

> We have to acknowledge that between one and two billion people depend on animal agriculture for their livelihoods. My concern is that we talk about alternative proteins being a magic wand, but will that have negative social consequences if we move too quickly? We don't want to drive a wedge through society. There will be winners and losers with change, and I am keen to ensure the losers are protected from harm.

We must navigate the coming changes incredibly carefully, making sure that no one is left behind. Agriculture is the most important industry on the planet, touching the lives of everyone, and providing work for more of us than any other activity. Yes, it is troubled, inefficient and broken in places. But it is also more vital than anything else we do.

Attempting to change human behaviour is incredibly difficult, and will probably only get us so far. In combination, we also desperately need to change the way we produce food, creating a system that is more efficient, less wasteful, and productive enough to prevent a growing population from going hungry. Unlike behaviour change, which receives little attention despite its importance, there are a million potential solutions vying for our attention when we consider the future of agriculture. The trick is separating which ones are hubris and overstatement, and which might actually change the world.

13

What Can We Do?

The best time to plant a tree was twenty years ago. The second best time is now.

– Proverb

Think Small

It would be easy to get this far into the book and assume that I am the sort of person convinced that large-scale industrial farming is the most efficient way to produce food. This is almost entirely not the case. Unlike the majority of industrial systems, when it comes to agriculture, large-scale production is rarely a route to greater efficiency. Or at least, it isn't when you measure things in a certain way.

If you want to produce the largest amount of food from the smallest area of land, then the best way to do it is to have lots of very small farms, full of knowledgeable, skilful farmers getting as much as possible from their plots. All the giant industrial machinery, sophisticated crop breeding, cutting-edge chemicals and highly paid agronomists are no match for people out on the land every day, working hard and making smart decisions. Weeding by hand is more effective, more targeted and more environmentally benign then any chemical or mechanical system. Intercropping, planting a number of complementary species together, can massively improve yields and reduce chemical inputs, but usually means that sowing and harvesting need to be done by hand. Techniques such as planting in seed trays, creating raised beds or growing under nets can massively increase yields, yet are impractical on a large-scale mechanised farm. A worker walking around a field spraying individual weeds means that chemical use can be carefully targeted, greatly reducing application rates and increasing effectiveness. For the same reasons, fertiliser application, and even watering, can be done far more efficiently by hand. Carefully tended plants given close daily attention by skilled farmers will almost always outperform large-scale monocropping.

The differences can be quite remarkable. In the US, a well-managed garden-style plot tended by a skilled human can yield around 5–10 kg of produce per square metre, with a monetary value of between $11 and $22. In comparison, corn, perhaps the US's most successful large-scale crop, yields around twenty-five cents from the same area. Even with crops generally thought to be more suited to industrial systems, the human touch provides an enormous yield advantage. Small, family-run sugar cane farms in Taiwan and China typically yield fifty percent more than giant plantations in other parts of the world.[1]

In the modern industrial age, it is easy to assume that economies of scale always lead to greater efficiency, just as they do with cars, steel or shipbuilding. Indeed, both communist and capitalist food systems have laboured under the misapprehension that large-scale mechanised agriculture will increase the productivity of the land, often at great cost to society.

Agriculture is a demonstrable exception in this regard, leading many campaigners to insist that a return to small-scale farming is the only way to address the destructive nature of world food production. As I have repeated many times, when it comes to environmental damage, land use efficiency is a key metric. Perhaps we really do need to stop the advance of large-scale industrial farming and return much of the developed world to small-scale systems once again.

Of course, it is not quite that simple. The key thing missing in these sorts of calculations is an adequate valuation of the human effort required to work the land. In looking solely at land use, productivity and chemical inputs, we are writing off the labour of billions of men, women and children. The life of a small-scale farmer is incredibly tough, with most people scraping only the most meagre of livings. It is also a life of intense fragility, with people on the edge of crisis most of the time. One bad harvest, one tough year, one poor decision might often be, quite literally, the difference between life and death. As climate change ramps up, it is small farmers who are likely to be hit the hardest, with many subsistence farms in the developing world dangerously exposed to variations in global temperature. In Malawi, a country dominated by small farms and already at desperate risk, it is estimated that a 1 °C rise in temperature will reduce per capita calorie intake by forty percent.[2]

And perhaps worse for the future of the planet, for people leading such a life there are no retirement plans, little medical care, and precious few provisions for sickness or injury. A slipped disc, a broken limb or an infection might leave entire families on the brink. As Norman Borlaug so astutely noted, 'it's amazing how often campaigners in rich countries think that poor people don't get backache.' How many of us in the developed world, even with the benefit of our easy lives and sophisticated health-care systems, will reach sixty or seventy years old without a significant period of time when we are unable to perform hard physical labour? The only possible insurance plan for many small-scale farmers in poor nations is to have a large family, which is exactly why societal progress that moves people away from such a life is the only proven way to slow population growth.

It is vital that we do not condemn billions of people to this fate, but equally we cannot just march out a system of industrial-scale farming to replace it. Professor Elsa Murano is Director of the Borlaug Institute for International Agriculture. She told me:

Conflict is created when people have no hope, so you can prevent conflict with improvements to agriculture. Supporting farmers to produce adequate food is the best way to prevent war, but if you only support big agriculture, that is not a formula for success. Leaving out smallholders is a recipe for disaster. If you do that, countries will never rise out of poverty.

Small-scale subsistence farming is not a life that I would want for myself, and certainly not one that I would wish on my children. When we create a vision of our future, we must keep this in mind. People do not want to scrape a living from small subsistence plots, and should not be expected to do so. Most young, ambitious souls full of potential and hope do not desire a life covered in dirt, exposed to dangerous chemicals, and having to endure relentless back-breaking labour long into old age. If the future you propose condemns billions of people to a life that you would not accept for yourself, then surely it is not viable or humane.

Small farms do have a place, and cannot be ignored. Right now, perhaps surprisingly, they provide most of the world's food. Yet the future must surely be one that frees people from poverty and hardship, and gives all of the world's farmers hope of a better life. The big question is, how?

The Surprising Benefits of Division

If countries are to transition successfully from poverty to wealth, their attitude to agriculture is key. For most of the twentieth century, economic thinking seemed to assume that the secret formula involved a switch to large-scale industrial farming, freeing up workers to move to the cities and power lucrative new industries. Whenever this sort of transition has been enforced, it has almost always failed, most notably in Communist China and the Soviet Bloc. But it has also caused great hardship in large

parts of Africa, Asia and South America, where large-scale plantation farming resulted in exploitation, poverty, hardship, displace-
ment and a complete lack of long-term economic progress.

So what is the alternative? How can subsistence farmers be
given hope of a better life in a way that doesn't create horrendous
inequality and transfer wealth into the hands of a privileged few?
The key can perhaps be found in the economic transitions of
countries such as Japan, South Korea, Taiwan and China (slightly
late to the party, but definitely playing catch-up), which have
managed to emerge out of poverty to become economic powerhouses with thriving capitalist economies. Although it is easy to
imagine that this transition was driven by mining, steel, car
plants, shipyards and cutting-edge technology, the road to prosperity really started with the land.

Shortly after World War II, much of the agricultural land in
Korea, Japan and Taiwan was subject to compulsory purchase by
the state, and then divided up into small plots among the rural
farming community. Instead of wealthy landowners leasing to
small tenant farmers, these countries created a system whereby
each farmer had autonomy to work the land as they wished, and
the security to invest in the future. The plots were roughly equal
in size, with some variations dependent upon land quality, giving
each farming family an area that they could not only subsist on,
but one that could also create a thriving business if they managed
to push productivity high enough.

This is of course in stark contrast to the collectivisation of
farming in the Soviet Bloc and early Communist China, which
led to such catastrophe, or indeed the brutal land tenure that
drove nineteenth-century Ireland to famine. In many ways,
although land reform policies are often condemned by the
political right as a back door to socialism, when done well they
produce a near-perfect free-market economy. This sort of land
reform levels the playing field, creating conditions where
competition pushes best practice to thrive and productivity to
grow.

Economists often talk about allowing market forces to correct inefficiency, but this ignores the glaring fact that there are almost no genuine free markets for food anywhere in the world. Agriculture is subsidised, distorted and broken, and its obsession with single efficiency metrics twists it further out of shape. One of the greatest pressures on food production is that it is always competing with the value of the land required to grow stuff on. When most farmland is owned by a rich elite, and that land is rented out to tenant farmers, it makes little financial sense for anyone in the chain to make long-term investments to improve productivity. If tenants are likely to be moved on at short notice, they have no incentive to spend time, effort or resources enriching the soil, digging irrigation canals, or growing protective tree crops. Landowners could potentially increase the amount they charge by making their fields more productive, but it is usually far easier to squeeze out higher rents by dividing up plots, or by reclaiming new land from virgin forests.

If effective land reforms can be introduced, individuals farming their own areas suddenly have an interest in increasing productivity. Improving farm efficiency is quickly rewarded, and people with secure tenure are far more likely to look towards the future. If we really want to transform global agriculture, we should start with land reform in developing countries. Without it, progress almost inevitably stalls, with rural workers remaining in poverty and a rich few siphoning off resources to line their own pockets.

Of course, if it were that simple, we probably wouldn't be in this mess. Small-scale agriculture has many other problems, and some of these are even harder to address than the divisive issue of land ownership. There are many improvements way beyond the means of individual farmers, but vital for progress, and addressing these almost always requires state support. Although often hugely expensive, in the long term such investment is extremely good value, because for economies to make the transition from poverty to wealth, increasing the productivity of small farms unlocks the door to a better future.

Genuine agricultural transformation requires large-scale irrigation projects, financial systems that allow farmers to access affordable credit, training in the latest techniques and the creation of rural transport networks to get produce more easily to market. It means building local factories to make fertilisers, construction materials and machinery, reducing dependency on imported technologies. In the modern age, areas need connecting to information networks so they can access accurate weather forecasts, up-to-date market prices, and real-time agronomic advice.

All this requires considerable state investment and a high degree of market interference, often making it politically and economically challenging. But if done well, the rewards are extraordinary. As farms become more profitable, rural economies have money to spend, and life quality dramatically improves. As agriculture becomes more productive, less labour is required, meaning that people can move to the cities and power new industries. In the early years of transition, rural communities with new cash to spare provide lucrative markets for the burgeoning new economy, allowing it to grow to a point where its technology businesses can compete globally.

These transitions happened successfully in Korea, Japan and Taiwan, freeing them to become global powerhouses in a remarkably short time.* In otherwise similar countries such as Malaysia, the Philippines and Indonesia, the early stages of transition stalled due to inadequate land reform, often campaigned against by US administrations who saw it as a bit too socialist for their liking, but also resisted by powerful and politically connected local landowners.

Unfair land tenure, corruption and a lack of investment doubtless keep many similar countries around the world stuck in desperate poverty to this day. If we really want a global

---

* The transformations of Korea, Japan and Taiwan did require a lot more state intervention to get from this stage to where they are today, with a lot of highly protectionist industrial trade policies. Although the transformation of agriculture was essential early on, it was not enough on its own.

transformation of our food systems, a decrease in population growth, and large-scale reductions in poverty, sophisticated technologies might play a part, but the biggest factors preventing change are sociopolitical. Perhaps the greatest barriers are the ownership of land, fear of excessive state interference, and an insistence that the gods of the free market will save us from ourselves. To truly address hunger, these are the battlegrounds on which we must fight. As is so often the case, it is the greed of a few that leads to the hunger of many.

The Future

For the moment, however, let's assume that unfair land tenure can be globally addressed, and all of the punishingly expensive infrastructure projects that are desperately required can find investment. Let's also assume that all of the world's farmers can be taught the best way to work their land based on the latest scientific research. What then? What will the future of agriculture look like?

Perhaps the most important principle for the future of food production is that we should try to leave more carbon in the soil at the end of the year than the beginning. There are many ways in which this can be achieved, most notably by adopting various regenerative forms of agriculture. No-till and minimum-till farming, combined with innovative cover crops and crop rotations, can hugely increase soil carbon. Not only does this improve the quality and future productivity of the soil, but it also removes carbon from the atmosphere, mitigating some of the unavoidable emissions related to food production. The potential of soil to lock up carbon is one of very few practical and proven ways of removing large amounts of CO_2 from the atmosphere, and the fact that we are not making more effort to follow this path is a matter of great shame.

Perhaps even more importantly, we must reduce the amount of land required to grow food, both by intensifying production where we currently farm, and shifting diets to less resource-hungry foods.

All the land freed up must be used to store carbon in the most effective possible way, something likely to encounter even more resistance. In most cases, this will involve a return of existing farm-land to wild landscapes such as forest. We must use every legisla-tive and financial incentive to ensure that this land does not end up in non-food agricultural uses such as biofuel production.

Biofuel, utilising ethanol created from plants to supplement fuel, or simply burning biomass to generate power, is a conten-tious issue, not least because for a long time it was hailed as a grand solution to our global warming woes. In many ways, this false belief is due to the incessant focus on single metrics to solve systemic problems. For a long time, combatting climate change has been synonymous with reducing carbon emissions, and as biofuels do not release any net carbon (all the carbon they contain has previously been captured from the atmosphere by plants), they were seen as an important way forward.

This is a foolish approach. Firstly, growing biofuels usually requires fossil energy to fix nitrogen, power farm machinery and create chemical inputs. But it also completely ignores the issue of land use. As demand for biofuels increases, it places pressure on agricultural land, which inevitably leads to deforestation, causing habitat loss and the release of even more carbon. This is just one of many examples where single-issue environmentalism, rather than an appreciation of the system as a whole, has led to poor policy decisions.

The return of significant amounts of agricultural land to the wild is essential if we want to meet environmental targets. It is vital that developed nations take the lead on this, rather than just holding up our hands and claiming that we cannot turn back the clock on our legacy of habitat destruction. Professor Ian Boyd is Chief Scientific Adviser to the UK's Department for Environment, Food and Rural Affairs.* He told me:

* He left this post in August 2019, a few weeks after we spoke. I'm pretty sure that speaking to me had nothing to do with his departure.

In the UK, we need to recast significant amounts of land to different functions such as carbon storage and biodiversity. Around fifty percent of agricultural land needs to be recast, probably including most of the North and West of the country. We farm a lot of land that is not good for agriculture, and compete with countries that are much better suited. We really need to be brutally realistic about what we can produce.

Similarly, Professor Pete Smith, Chair in Plant and Soil Science at Aberdeen University and Science Director of Scotland's Centre of Expertise on Climate Change, told me:

Lots of agriculture only happens in parts of the country because of subsidies. Much of it is only there due to recent history. We could easily change that if we changed the subsidy system. Rewilding for carbon and biodiversity can be done, although it's not trivial. In the UK we have got rid of most of the top predators, so deer browse off young trees. But successful rewilding could easily be achieved within current subsidy programmes. There are a lot of upland farmers currently losing money, so we would just need a system where we pay people to do other things, while ensuring that upland farmers can access quality training, where necessary, to enable them to manage the changing landscape.

There are many other ways to store carbon in the soil. Manure and compost can be useful for an individual plot, although these work by transferring nutrients from a large area of land onto a smaller one, so are not scalable. Although distasteful for some, we should certainly be looking to add far more human waste back into the soil than we currently do, even though this can be a source of environmental pollutants if not treated properly.[3] There is an inevitable public resistance to this sort of fertiliser, and ways must be found to overcome this prejudice without attempting to fool consumers. Most of the disposal alternatives are unsustainable in the long term, and an awful lot of pioneering schemes have seen great success in transforming human sewage into valuable fertiliser.[4] You would think that a capitalist economy would celebrate an industry that can literally turn shit into gold, but we struggle not to let our disgust get in the way. One thing is certain: if we continue to flush so many valuable nutrients out into the sea, humanity will lose its battle with hunger. Debates continue as to when that might happen, but addressing it sooner rather than later is surely the sensible thing to do.

Techno Techno Techno

All this is a little unglamorous, especially the last bit. Many people would rather think about cool new technology than reusing human shit. If the pioneering tech-bros of Silicon Valley are to be believed, robots, vertical farms, artificial intelligence, big data, lasers and Frankencrops are the real future of global farming. There is a wide-spread belief that the tech industry can do for food production what it has done for communication, entertainment and retail. Perhaps the next agricultural revolution will be made of silicon.

Certainly there is a place for technology. The human advantage of small-scale production shows that if smarter decisions can be made on the ground, and inputs can become more targeted, farms can be a lot more productive. A vision of lightweight, autonomous robots scuttling around fields, spraying, planting, monitoring and harvesting crops has been mooted for some time, and the concept of precision agriculture, where farm inputs are more directed and controlled, is seen as a key avenue for progress.

We already have lightweight robots that can autonomously identify weeds and spray them with herbicide, or even burn them away using high-energy lasers. Sensors can now automatically detect the presence of harmful insects in a field, targeting pesticides only where and when they are needed. We can now monitor potatoes and other root vegetables under the ground to maximise yields by harvesting at the perfect time. Modern robots can pick the most delicate soft fruits as fast as a trained human, and there are even fully automated systems for the milking of cows.* For many years, agricultural researchers have suggested that wildflower strips in the middle of fields, rather than just at the edges, would benefit crops by increasing on-farm biodiversity, but this has always been difficult to achieve practically. But now, with stunningly accurate GPS systems on most modern tractors, this sort of innovation is a great deal easier. For several years, many modern large-scale farm vehicles have been essentially self-driving, and it is often only insurance and safety issues that prevent farmers from stepping out of the cab.

Drone technology has revolutionised the spraying of chemicals in many countries, with seventy percent of farm chemicals in South Korea now being applied in this way. A single worker can operate several near-autonomous drones at a time, using systems specially designed to minimise human contact with chemicals (which is otherwise thought to result in at least sixty thousand deaths each year). Application from the air also reduces traffic on the field, so helping to address soil compaction, something that can heavily impact yields. Drones will likely play many roles in agriculture over the coming years, monitoring fields, sampling crops, getting supplies out to remote locations, and even filling up seed applicators as they plant, which usually requires a second vehicle on the field.[5]

Some of the most interesting technological innovations are less dramatic than laser-wielding weed vaporisers, or swarms of

---

* To be honest, it is hard to make a case for robot cow-milking systems on environmental grounds, but they are incredible to watch and a testament to the wonders of technology. Cows will literally queue up to be milked when they feel like it, rather than being herded into milking parlours at a specific time, which leads to much calmer, happier herds. Robots and new monitoring technologies (basically cow Fitbits) are leading to many interesting advances in animal welfare and productivity, something that is slightly beyond the scope of this book.

chemical-laden flying beasts.* Often, advances involve a return to long-forgotten agricultural practices, combining them with the benefits of the modern information age. Dr Jonathan Storkey, a Plant Ecologist at Rothamsted, explained to me how many of the cracks in the Green Revolution are now requiring farmers to rediscover old techniques:

> A lot of farmers are being forced to re-diversify. They are looking at more diverse crop rotations, the use of cover crops and organic manure. Herbicide resistance means that many weeds now need to be managed agronomically, returning to practices from before those chemicals existed. The difference is that now we can quantify the impacts with population dynamics models, and develop strategies to build resilience. Rothamsted is building up the evidence base for low tillage and crop rotations. We are testing received wisdoms about bees, lacewings and hoverflies. We are testing field margins and wildflower strips, looking at quantifying the impact of biodiversity on yield.

A strong evidence base, combined with effective extension policies and access to technology, may well address many of agriculture's most pressing problems. If advances can democratise this technology, as opposed to placing it in the hands of a few large companies, it could lead us towards a better future. It is here where the hope lies. Not in expensive cutting-edge robots that might just power a few industrial farms in fifty years' time, but in technology that is available now, and is likely to exist within the reach of small and medium-sized producers. According to Achim Dobermann, former Chief Executive of Rothamsted Research:

> We need to think about meaningful ways of reintegrating crops and arable farms. I'm not talking about something

---

* When I put it like this, it does sound as if agricultural engineers are secretly building a terrifying robot army.

the size of an eighteenth-century mixed farm, but where is the scale in the middle? I am increasingly convinced that this is where technology can help. Is there a functional business model for a 200-hectare mixed farm that can compete on a global scale? Not a \$200,000 tractor, but smaller, more flexible machines. No one is doing this yet. The large manufacturers are still just making large stuff.

At Harper Adams University, agricultural and robotics engineers Jonathan Gill and Kit Franklin have been involved in an innovative project called the 'Hands Free Hectare', taking a single-hectare test plot and attempting to produce crops from it without a human ever passing through the gates. Anyone visiting the farm might be expecting to see dozens of tiny, scuttling robots, but the reality is very different. On a relatively low budget, the Harper Adams team have utilised existing agricultural equipment, adding off-the-shelf navigation and control systems developed for drones. Old tractors and combine harvesters have been rigged up with Heath Robinson style contraptions to pull the levers and turn the steering wheels, utilising a thoroughly old-fashioned engineering approach that is in stark contrast to many high-end agricultural start-ups. As a result, the project has captured the imagination of farmers, many of whom can see great potential for the creation of cheap systems to get use out of old machines that they might have lying around in barns.

Vertical Farms – Do the Claims Really Stack Up?*

Many supposedly cutting-edge technologies miss the mark, perhaps because of an inability to understand the complex realities

---

* This is the book's worst joke, and perhaps the worst in the whole of the Angry Chef Trilogy, despite some stiff competition (remember the sugar chapter in *The Angry Chef*?). It is a direct quote taken from my interview with an extremely senior agricultural scientist, and to this day I am not sure if they were aware of their own pun.

of farming, and a bias towards large-scale agriculture. Small incremental changes that increase automation and efficiency are far
more realistic, especially if farmers can quickly see the value.

Grand claims are frequently made in the media about supposedly groundbreaking technologies, but these often turn to dust on
closer inspection. Much like lab-grown meat, there may be great
promise in new soil-free methods of food production, but these
rarely provide the sort of large-scale solutions required to overhaul
global food systems. In many ways, this is due to the way agricultural research is funded and conducted. Achim Dobermann again:

> There is a lot of hype about technology, but people forget
> that seventy percent of calories come from three crops. We
> will not replace these with vertical farms, greenhouses or
> robot farmers. You still need a business with humans
> making clever decisions.

Many of the most hyped technological developments happen so
far from the farm that they don't provide practical solutions, and
occasionally don't even reflect an understanding of the nature of
the problems being faced. Crop scientist and former farmworker
Dr Sarah Taber works as consultant for many large agri-food businesses, and has little time for Silicon Valley bluster. She told me:

> The tech industry is trumpeting in, but often they really don't
> understand the problems. In my opinion, what is wrong with
> agriculture is not that we don't have tools. We have tools,
> we're just not using them. There are currently at least three
> start-ups looking at robot bees, but what is the use case?

Dr Taber explained that European honeybees are used commercially across North America for pollinating but are prone to regular diebacks. Many of the population declines that robot bees are
being used to address are actually just a consequence of using a
non-native species in regions they are not suited to: 'What we

should really be doing is learning to raise native bees and increasing on-farm competency to do so. There is a fundamentally social problem, and we are trying to fix it with robot bees.'

This, once again, is the heart of the issue. We require grand changes to society, the food system and human behaviour. We need a rapid and fundamental shift in the way that we produce and consume food. But instead of a joined-up strategy to create widespread systemic change, we get robot bees. We invest in a few, tiny rooftop farms, but continue to degrade millions of hectares of farmland each year. We grow a few high-tech burgers in a lab, vainly hoping that they will replace the meat of a billion cows.

Ostrich with a Side of Maggots

There are definitely some things that might help. Even if resistance to genetic modification continues, new methods to speed up conventional genetic plant improvements are producing valuable results.[6] There are numerous strategies to improve the efficiency of meat and dairy production, including feed additives that can reduce methane emissions. Uptake from the industry has been slow, presumably because the methane from cattle is entirely external to the cost of production, and farmers currently have little incentive to act.

Some novel livestock types have potential. Ostriches are far more suited to much of the world's grazing land than cattle, produce no methane, and are several times more water efficient. In many areas, these giant (and, it has to be said, quite angry) birds are a demonstrably better way of producing protein than cows. Perhaps more importantly, ostrich meat is delicious, and could potentially replace beef in many applications without anyone noticing. But despite this, the lack of infrastructure for the slaughter and packing of seven-foot-high birds capable of running at fifty miles an hour is proving a hard obstacle to overcome.

Another frequently mooted solution to the world's protein woes is insects, which, I am frequently told, will provide an important protein source in the future. I am yet to be convinced that insect protein is any more delicious than vegetables, beans, chickpeas or lentils, but there are potential advantages when it comes to production. The maggots of black soldier flies are particularly high in protein and fat and can be raised on a diet containing a variety of food produce that would otherwise be wasted. They apparently taste a bit like warm, wriggly peanuts if ever you get the chance to eat one, although if that happens I can only imagine you are going through the bin whilst drunk, or a contestant on *I'm a Celebrity* . . .

Almost all insects are extremely efficient when it comes to water and land use. There are some challenges regarding energy and greenhouse emissions, as insects need to be raised indoors, usually requiring heat, air filtration and processing of some sort. As with many new technologies, the environmental impact of insect production is heavily dependent upon the source of energy, which will vary around the world, but they do provide the possibility of being able to produce food almost anywhere.[7]

But even if an incredibly low environmental impact can be proven, the consumer acceptability of maggots, crickets, mealworms and various other non-marine invertebrates is always going to be a challenge, especially when consumption usually involves eating the whole critter, including parts that most of us don't like to think about. There is perhaps a better case for raising insects as livestock feed, reducing pressure on land for soya, wheat and corn. After the BSE crisis, insect protein was caught up in various feed bans, but it is slowly starting to be reapproved in the US and EU, along with a number of stringent new safety protocols.

The Future's Blight

Generally speaking, the way that agricultural research is conducted needs to be improved, with a greater focus on actions that are implemented and monitored in the field. We have to stop making it possible to patent genes, which after all have been discovered and not invented. This would help move genetic research away from large companies and towards independent institutions working for the common good. Far more agricultural research needs to be funded in a way that makes it available for all, rather than just becoming the property of profit-focused corporations. We need a ground-up revolution in the way we produce food, facilitated by focused, single-minded legislation, brave long-term political decision making, and a shared vision for the future.

Considering the state that society is currently in, with a distinct lack of political or scientific visionaries, I struggle to see this happening. Even as the planet literally starts to burn, modern political discourse still asserts that the most important issues facing us are immigration control, the erosion of national sovereignty and keeping taxation low in the world's richest countries.

I cannot think of a single modern politician who addresses the food system on a regular basis, or even who talks about it in an informed and reasonable way. Even the most progressive consistently fail to mention the prospect of repurposing agricultural subsidies to protect the environment, perhaps the one lever that might make a significant difference. And as for land reform in the developing world, since the 1960s it has been politically toxic to even mention it. Unless this changes over the next thirty years, and especially if we continue to reject many of the technologies that might improve things, I am afraid that there is little reason for hope.

Apart from one thing perhaps. Something so powerful that it might just be capable of enacting widespread systemic change without the need for political visionaries. Something that may even be able to change the tune of the largest, worst-behaving corporations. It may be an odd place to look for hope, especially as many consider it the root of all our problems. But before this book reaches its end, we need to talk about money.

Don't Forget the Money Part

Although regenerative agriculture techniques also improve the long-term productivity of the land, they are often expensive and difficult to implement. With this in mind, it is probably a bit much to expect the world's farmers to expend huge amounts of time, money and effort altruistically offsetting the emissions of rich people's cars and foreign holidays. As we have already mentioned, when so much of the cost of food is externalised, farmers that pollute and degrade the land often win out in the short term, meaning there is little incentive for good environmental practice.

So how about we try to redress that financial imbalance? How about rewarding farmers for positive environmental contributions, not with gratitude, but with cold, hard cash? There are a number of initiatives to do just this, such as Indigo Agriculture, which is using money paid to offset industrial, power or transport emissions to fund the introduction of agricultural techniques that lock equivalent amounts of carbon into the soil. The beauty of this is that unlike many carbon offset schemes, conservation agriculture actually has a hugely important and valuable role in the production of food. By adding to the incomes of the most environmentally responsible farmers, we can internalise some of the benefits of good practice, so closing the gap.[8]

There are of course problems with this and other similar schemes. If we only give financial credit to farmers who are currently adding carbon to their soil, then how about the farmers who have been doing the right thing for years, meaning their land is largely carbon saturated? And what is to stop unscrupulous farmers from deliberately degrading their land before it is tested, then raking in the profits of restoring the lost carbon? These issues can probably be overcome, and they should not stop us from encouraging this and other similar schemes, including state, charity and regionally funded ones.

Similarly, if farmers can be rewarded with access to new markets, this can also provide strong incentives for better practice. The LEAF farming standard, started in the UK, but now very much international, accredits farms based on a number of environmental metrics, including soil management, water efficiency and good waste practices. Once accredited, LEAF-standard farms get access to a number of UK retailers signed up to the scheme, including Waitrose supermarkets. As a result, forty percent of all vegetables sold in the UK are from LEAF-accredited farms.

More generally, there is increasing evidence that shifting consumer awareness of environmental issues is slowly but surely impacting upon large businesses and brands. Despite the conventional wisdom that consumers do not care, in 2018, new products marked as sustainable achieved five to six times greater growth than equivalent items. Unilever, a giant corporation that has become known for its strong environmental focus, has seen seventy percent faster growth in its 'Sustainable Living' brands when compared to the rest of its portfolio. Although many accuse large companies of greenwashing, often with some justification, this growth does seem to show that talking about sustainability can create a competitive advantage, overthrowing a lot of conventional marketing wisdom.

Perhaps even more surprisingly, an environmental focus can also dramatically improve a company's general performance, particularly over the long term. Assessment of Nordic companies has shown that businesses with a strong focus on sustainability issues outperform the competition by forty percent. Shares in environmentally focused US firms have produced consistently higher returns in recent years, with such companies also being significantly less likely to go bankrupt. And even more tellingly, studies of businesses that were communicating about sustainability issues in the early 1990s have shown that they easily outperformed matched control groups over an eighteen-year period.[9]

There is, however, still a reluctance to engage fully with environmental issues at the highest level of many major corporations. Often, sustainability is seen as a cost rather than a selling point, and a focus on short-term reporting means that few top executives pay more than lip service to it. In the coming years, this may prove to be many companies' undoing. Institutional investors are increasingly looking at sustainability metrics and demanding that corporate leaders are held accountable for environmental performance. A quarter of all US company shares are held by investment firms with a sustainability focus, and half of all global asset owners have environmental governance as at least part of their long-term strategy.

If a new form of caring, planet-saving high finance sounds unlikely, rest assured that these figures are not evidence that global investment firms have somehow been infiltrated by a bunch of sandal-wearing hippies. The reality is that in recent years, for good or evil, investment companies have consolidated and grown dramatically in size. The top ten firms now hold thirty-four percent of all global assets, which makes it their problem if the world economy starts to collapse. In the past, such companies would have bought doom stocks like gold to hedge against disaster, but now they are quite simply too big to hedge in this way. These companies are now so huge that they cannot afford the planet to fail, and are using their considerable financial muscle to ensure that it does not happen.

Climate Action 100+ is an enormously powerful coalition of 320 firms representing $32 trillion in assets. It is currently lobbying the largest greenhouse-gas-emitting companies to address climate change at board level, forcing many of them to set stringent emissions targets. Hopefully, if such groups really are scared of societal collapse, they will start to focus on agriculture, and might even provide some of the influence, money and leadership that we are sorely lacking from politicians.

In truth, this may be a foolish place to look for hope. There is still plenty of money being invested in fossil fuels, and huge amounts pouring into industries that drive deforestation and habitat loss. Far too much of our economic growth is dependent upon the destruction of the natural world, and as long as increasing GDP continues to drive global priorities, it is hard to imagine this changing.

Reasons to Be Cheerful

There are many positive things going on around the world. Several countries and regions have improved their farming practices, and countless initiatives are helping to reduce the impact of food production. Certainly, there is little in the way of a joined-up global strategy, and few adequate national-level plans, but it is probably true that the tools and knowledge already exist for a sustainable farming future, and new tools are being created all the time.

For instance, although palm oil is strongly associated with environmental destruction, in many ways it can be considered an environmental super crop, yielding five or six times as much per hectare as any other oil-producing plant. It grows on perennial palms that can produce fruit for up to twenty-five years, meaning that unlike soya, canola or sunflower, the soil on palm plantations is barely disturbed at all. If we are going to consume vegetable fats, in many ways RSPO (Roundtable on Sustainable Palm Oil) certified palm, the production of which does not result in the destruction of tropical forests, is the best option available.[10]

The main issue with certification is that although it usually makes production more profitable in the long term, it tends to favour large plantations with money to invest, often pushing smaller growers towards more destructive processes in order to compete. Yet in the Sabah region of Malaysian Borneo there is a government-backed initiative to bring the entire region under RSPO certification by 2025, working with hundreds of small producers to help them introduce better practices. To support the programme, research into techniques such as intercropping and natural pest controls is finding novel ways of increasing yield. It is thought that combined with better plant selection, yield increases of up to fifty percent are possible in the near future, greatly decreasing global pressure on natural habitats. When certification programmes start to encompass entire regions or even countries, they can become inclusive rather than divisive, something essential for progress.

In a similar vein, the island of Jersey is currently in the process of moving all of its agriculture to fall under the LEAF standard, the agricultural sustainability programme discussed earlier.[11] LEAF encourages a diverse set of environmental management techniques specific to different types of farms, exactly the sort of complex, tailored and localised interventions that can lead to genuine improvements. The advantage of moving an entire island to fall under the same standard is that it helps lift the worst-performing farms up, rather than creating a problematic two-tier system.

As mentioned already, the rise of no-till and minimum-till farming is the quietest of agricultural revolutions, sweeping across Australia, North and South America, and much of Europe. Combined with cover cropping and novel rotations that ensure soil is never left bare, it is creating a new form of regenerative arable farming that is transforming soils, building biodiversity and pulling carbon from the atmosphere. Organisations such as the US Soil Health Institute, No-till on the Plains, Harper Adams University and Rothamsted Research are slowly building the evidence base for these techniques, showing how they can not only improve soil carbon, but also increase the prevalence of worms and invertebrates, leading to more bird life and biodiversity on farms. Although there are barriers to entry, notably some initial drops in productivity immediately after the techniques are introduced, as the evidence of long-term benefit grows, these methods should begin to dominate food production in many regions. The more that no-till regenerative agriculture can be financially incentivised by redesigned subsidy systems, the greater the uptake will be.

Based in Manchester, 'The Bread and Butter Thing' is a charity that redistributes high-quality surplus food from manufacturers and retailers that would otherwise go to waste, using it to provide two millions meals every year for disadvantaged families in the region.[12] Studies of the programme have shown that because of the diversity of the offering, participants are regularly introduced to new types of food they would not have otherwise tried, improving the quality and variety of their diets. When these benefits are combined with significant decreases in food waste, there is an outstanding case for such programmes to be rolled out more widely.

The Cassava Virus Action Project (CVAP) is an innovative programme that uses the latest DNA sequencing and data analysis techniques to help East African farmers identify and combat viruses that are regularly wiping out their main crop.[13] Around 800 million people around the world rely on cassava as a staple food, but it is highly susceptible to disease. In the event of an outbreak, the CVAP can swiftly analyse the viral DNA in diseased plants and supply local farmers with resistant cassava strains, minimising chemical use, crop losses and hardship.

In the UK, the Environmental Land Management scheme (ELMs), the government's planned replacement for the agricultural subsidy system, promises to focus on measures that increase environmental protection and enhance natural capital. The scheme will pay farmers to deliver clean air and clean water, improve wild habitats and engage in practices to mitigate climate change. Full roll-out is not until 2025 and there will no doubt be devils in the detail, but if done well it could fundamentally shift the focus of UK farming towards the provision of public goods, setting an example to the world.[14]

In recent years, Bangladesh has experienced a farming revolution, nearly doubling agricultural productivity since 1995, an increase second only to China's.[15] This has led to improved food security and increased resilience to natural disasters, and has been the main driver behind huge decreases in poverty in the country. These changes were not made possible by high-tech robots, vertical farms or artificial intelligence, but by well-funded agricultural training programmes, sensible investment in infrastructure and strong political leadership. It is this sort of boring and non-headline-grabbing change that is likely to produce the biggest improvements in our food systems over the coming years.

Unfortunately, none of this is enough. Few countries have the leadership and vision of Bangladesh, and even fewer have the wealth and resources of the United Kingdom, Jersey or North America. So perhaps we should just keep our fingers crossed and hope for a miracle. Because sometimes, in the strange world of global agriculture, miracles do occur. I am going to finish with one amazing story of hope. It is a story that provides a clue as to the sort of changes that might actually transform world food production. It is also a tale of something created light years away from the robotic, genetic and cellular technologies that dominate discourse in the developed world.

It is the story of one of the greatest agricultural transformations since the Green Revolution, yet almost certainly one that you have never heard of. It happened without design or plan, and quietly went about its business for many years without anyone really noticing. But that didn't stop it from improving the lives of millions of people, and probably preventing an entire nation from being permanently wiped off the map.

The Regreening of the Sahel

In the late 1960s and early 1970s, the Sahel region of Africa was regularly experiencing devastating droughts. The Sahel is the semi-arid region that runs across the southern edge of the Sahara Desert, comprising parts of several countries including Niger,

Mauritania, Burkina Faso, Mali, Chad, the Central African Republic, Sudan, Ethiopia and Senegal. Although many of the people in the Sahel still live in desperate poverty today, in the 1970s it was a place of even more extreme hardship. During droughts, the land would rapidly become degraded and die, forcing mass migrations and causing many localised famines. The Sahara seemed to be relentlessly advancing across the region, taking countless lives and livelihoods as it went. By the early 1980s, many people thought that Niger was going to become uninhabitable. With precious little money available for long-term development, there seemed to be little hope.

Sometime during the mid-1980s, a group of farmers scraping a living in the Maradi region of Niger travelled to Nigeria looking for seasonal work to supplement their meagre incomes. They returned in the early rainy season, a little later than usual, and found that they were unable to clear their fields adequately, as the growth of scrubland plants was too advanced. Unsure what to do, and without access to machinery that would have easily cleared the land, a number of them just cleared what they could and planted crops anyway. To their surprise, the farmers that did this ended up with markedly improved yields.

Realising they were on to something, farmers rapidly adopted this practice, learning to leave significant areas of their land to regenerate. Despite most areas having been regularly cleared for generations, the soil still had a seed memory and an ancient root system, meaning that local trees ideally suited to the region magically sprang from the ground. These trees were managed and controlled as they grew, and were key to a groundbreaking agricultural transformation. Many turned out to be nitrogen-fixing species that were extremely valuable in enriching the land and reducing the need for fertiliser. The new vegetation provided firewood, animal feed, leaf litter to improve the soil, and most vitally of all, protection from the advancing desert winds.

Crucially, these advantages were realised within a single season, with things getting better every subsequent year. There was no temptation to give up, no need for significant financial investment, and little extra work required. The process of Farmer-Managed Natural Regeneration, or FMNR as it became known, spread rapidly from farm to farm, almost entirely by word of mouth.* Combined with new and innovative water-harvesting techniques, which required support from charities and governments, large parts of the Sahel region have been transformed. The desert advance has been held back – in fact, the land has become greener – and agricultural yields have improved to an astonishing degree.

It is estimated that southern Niger alone now produces half a million tonnes more cereal per year, simply because farmers have allowed a few trees to grow. From a tiny number of remote farms in 1985, by 2009 FMNR covered around five million hectares across several countries, and is thought to be increasing by a quarter of a million hectares every year. When combined with nitrogen fertilisers, the practice can more than double the yield of cereal crops, the sort of increases that make a significant difference in people's lives.[16]

Until 2004, this transformation was almost completely unnoticed outside of the farms it was happening on. One of the first people to document FMNR was Chris Reij, a senior fellow at the World Resources Institute who worked in Burkina Faso for many years during the hard times of the 1970s and 1980s. He returned to the region in 2004 after a tip-off that new farmer-derived practices were delivering incredible results. He returned again in 2019, after which he told me:

> There were huge differences from the last time I was there. Just coming from the airport, there were loads of children, and none of them were obviously malnourished. It was

---

* The work of an Australian missionary and agronomist, Tony Rinaudo, is often credited as being integral to this, as he offered food aid in return for people allowing parts of their land to regenerate. In reality, his work was probably important, but far from the whole story.

clear that crop yields had improved dramatically, and there was more diversity of produce from trees and fruits. Across the region there were green areas and far more trees. I persuaded a friend of mine who was a remote sensing specialist to take a look, and we found that this was covering an area of three million hectares, which eventually turned out to be five million. It was clear that farmers could be innovative. If the techniques are rational and effective, they go for it. This is the lowest cost way to intensify agriculture. It now covers Niger, Mali, Senegal, Burkina Faso, Ethiopia, and has implications elsewhere.

Reij is now working to promote FMNR more widely across the region, particularly in Uganda and Malawi. Just like the Green Revolution, the rapid spread of these practices demonstrates that when everything is in place, the world can change more rapidly than we might imagine. It also shows that however much we think we know, and however often we write off humanity as doomed, the world has a near-infinite capacity to surprise.

It is often said that predictions are hard, especially when they are about the future. If you had asked anyone with knowledge of the region about the Sahel in the 1980s, they would have told you that it had intractable problems and would be consumed by desert within a few years. Until a few farmers got back late from seasonal work and were unable to clear their land, this was the region's fate. No one put together a cohesive plan to save the Sahel, but somehow life intervened.

So perhaps there is hope for the wider future of agriculture. Current cereal yields in Europe and North America are around fourteen tonnes per hectare, with some test sites now reaching twenty tonnes. In many parts of Africa, yields per hectare are often less than one tonne, indicating that the region still has the most extraordinary potential.

Change often seems impossible until it occurs. As early ice traders discovered, when the final barriers get broken down, a trickle can easily become a flood. We can usually guess the direction of travel, but pace is often harder to predict. Ten years ago, the thought that petrol cars might soon be obsolete would have been absurd. Today it seems likely that the world's cars will be replaced with all-electric models over the next thirty years. But if there is a breakthrough in battery technology tomorrow, it is unlikely that petrol will last a decade.

There is hope for world food production, but also much to be worried about. I could have told a dozen stories of agricultural success, but equally I could have uncovered a whole other litany of environmentally destructive shame. One thing is certain, however. In this world, there are around a billion people who have a good life, with plenty of food and lots of nice things. But there are another six billion people who are having a pretty miserable time. As the century progresses, every one of those six billion will rightly demand something better for themselves and their children. It is their needs and hopes that will dominate the future.

We cannot expect those six billion humans not to want a better life. They are, after all, our brothers and sisters. It is only by chance that we are not living their lives. A humane and just world should never prevent hope and never hold back progress, but we do somehow need to manage it. We must create a world where the better life that everyone strives for is not so resource-intensive as to be unsustainable. We need to find a way to prevent global hunger, but one that doesn't send us hurtling headlong into a wall. After spending the last few years researching this book, it is clear to me now that this path does exist. What is far less obvious is how we might be persuaded to follow it.

14

What Can I Do?

A society grows great when old men plant trees in whose shade they know they shall never sit.

– Origin unknown

This is the section of the book where I am supposed to provide you with ten essential rules for healthy, sustainable eating. Maybe I could include a nice recipe for a locally grown, organic cauliflower and lentil dahl, and some top tips for the perfect GMO-free, grass-fed hummus. That would be the usual format, followed by a few sustainable recipe pull-outs in the *Sunday Times* and a seven-part *Eating for a Healthy Planet* cookery series on Netflix. Tradition suggests that this would be the perfect way for a chef to round off a book on such a complex and divisive subject; empowering the reader to make better choices and giving them a few food-based actions to take away. The planet is well and truly fucked, and it is all because you ate a burger.

If I follow the mantra of many prominent food activists, I should also use this section to campaign for sustainability metrics to be included on the front of food packaging. I should demand that CO_2 equivalents, water efficiency, land use and eutrophication measures are prominently displayed on everything we buy. I should be insisting that every item in the supermarket be subjected to a detailed life-cycle analysis, and the results made available on a public database. If only consumers are given enough information, eventually they will behave and the world will be saved.

Most of all, I should be making you feel guilty if tonight's dinner is a large rump steak, air-freighted Kenyan green beans and a salad made with hothouse-grown Dutch tomatoes and imported avocados. Eat some hummus and lentils, you planet-murdering monster.

I understand the incessant focus on personal choice. Food, as I have discovered to my cost over the past few years, has a powerful symbolic function in many people's lives. The most important symbolism tends to come from voluntary abstinence, something that runs through religion as much as it does environmentalism. For anyone who cares about the planet, it can feel as if we are spinning out of control. We all desperately want to believe that there are rituals we can perform to give us back some power. If we abstain from beef, give up plastic straws, choose loose carrots, buy fish with a sustainability badge, and refuse asparagus out of season, then at least we are doing something. It is the job of books like this to tap into that guilt and inspire some action in their readers.

This is not that book. We are all trying to find ways of lessening the inevitable guilt that comes from being a rich, over-consuming human in an unfair world, and I cannot help but feel that whenever these rituals of sacrifice are expensive and hard to obtain, it is a sign that they are more about absolving rich people's guilt than creating a better society. I am also acutely aware that in constantly telling people about the many ways in which they are doing life wrong, we are in real danger of pushing them towards a feeling of helplessness, and a desire to throw in the towel. After all, we are all doing something badly, and you might as well be hanged for a sheep as a lamb, which in this case works both figuratively and literally.*

---

* That's literal lamb, not literal hanging.

Whatever future we desire, and hopefully I have managed to make clear the desperate need for change, the answer does not lie in your next shopping trip, nor the dinner you choose to eat tonight. Pushing the problem back onto individuals absolves the many companies, governments and institutions that have failed us. They say the Devil's greatest trick has been to convince people that he does not exist, but maybe his pièce de résistance was to make us believe that the coming apocalypse is all our own fault. It is not. The systems that feed us have failed, and the only cure for that is widespread systemic change.

It is fair to say that most of us eat way too much meat, and replacing some of it with beans, pulses or lentils is probably a good idea. Certainly, increasing the number of meals based on hummus would raise levels of global happiness, whilst lowering the environmental impact of our diets at the same time. It is also true that more considered thinking on packaging and food waste would be hugely positive, particularly if it helps us stop making people feel guilty about an occasional frozen pizza. If you still want to reject GMOs and eat organic that is fine, but stop pretending you are doing so for the planet, because the evidence really isn't on your side.

Instead of holding our breath for the tech bros of Silicon Valley to save us with their lab-grown meats and robot bees, perhaps we should all try to make some slightly better choices, so long as we are careful not to add to the guilt that already surrounds so many of our interactions with food. But it would be a brutally dystopian future if every time we gathered together to eat, we had to consult some sort of algorithm to assess the impact of our diet upon the planet. If we require each meal to be a model of environmental perfection, then each meal would have to be exactly the same, something I can never support. The moment food becomes devoid of meaning, variety and joy is the moment that I start to doubt exactly what we are fighting to protect.

There will be those among you who might decide to live a life of abstention and denial in order to help create a better future, and I applaud your decision, so long as you stay safe and well nourished. But don't make others feel guilty about how they eat, or how they choose to live. We cannot keep falling back to the aggregate of individual choice as the solution to our problems. The issues we are facing are complex and systemic. They have been created by terrible policy decisions, distorted markets and a lack of leadership. They will not be solved by making people feel guilty simply for trying to navigate their lives. I am not saying that we should do nothing. The future is incredibly bleak unless our food systems change. But the real answer lies in holding our food systems to account.

All of us are far more empowered to do this than we know. If I have managed to convince you that the problems detailed in this book pose some of the greatest threats to the future of humanity, then I urge you to campaign for change. Use your vote. Light political fires in those around you. Protest at the inaction of governments and corporations. Write to those in power. Tell them to their face whenever you get the chance. They are consistently failing us on the most important issues. Too often, politicians and leaders seem exclusively concerned with maintaining their fragile grip on power. If that is the case, then let us make soil, water, hunger, pollution and global warming the issues that define who leads us. Vote for politicians who listen, understand and act. If they do not exist, help to create them, or become one yourself.

If you are lucky enough to have money to invest, ensure that it is being used to do the best for the planet and the natural world. Ask those that manage your pensions and savings the same difficult questions you put to leaders and politicians. If they have no answers, vote with your cash. All the data suggests that this is not only a powerful way to create change, but something that will serve your own financial self-interest in the long term.

For those of you lucky enough to be involved in the food system, fight hard for change in your corner of the world. It is the combined actions of farms, universities, research institutes, policy committees, food factories, canteens, shops, restaurants and development kitchens that have the potential to save us. At whatever level you are involved in the production of food, do something that makes a difference. Focus your energy on making the systems that feed us better.

I shall repeat what I said at the beginning of this book. In this fragile and changing world, we cannot continue to eat in the same way we do today. If we don't dramatically alter the way we produce and consume food, then in thirty years, well within the lifetime of most readers, the planet on which we live will become unrecognisable. Without widespread systemic change, by 2050, we will have cut down all of the world's forests, made large parts of the Earth uninhabitable, created unimaginable human suffering, and driven a million species to extinction. If our goal is to leave a better world for our children and grandchildren, this must not happen. With things as they are, we are in danger of leaving no world at all.

You may think that there are more significant issues to tackle before we consider the seeming triviality of food system change. But if you care about poverty, inequality, human rights, terrorism, violence, the exploitation of women, childhood slavery, disease epidemics, uncontrolled population growth or refugee crises, all these things are intimately connected to our food systems. All will be made many times worse if we do not change the way that we eat.

The production of food is the one activity that is central to all of humanity, and whilst we fight for change, we should be careful not to condemn the farmers and producers who keep us fed. We could easily live without iPhones, electric cars, Thai restaurants, air travel, Instagram, ice boxes, Angry Chef books, hummus, fashion journalism, TV box sets, politicians and Internet dating. But without people to grow the food that we eat, we would all be dead within a few short weeks. Providing plentiful nutrition for most of the population has been our greatest triumph, but now it presents our greatest threat. To counter it, we all need to become activists. We need to support and protect those that feed us, and keep the prevention of hunger at the heart of all that we do.

So enjoy your dinner tonight whatever it may be, and make sure you eat without the slightest guilt or shame, for those things have no place in the world of food. Ensure you are well nourished, for tomorrow there is a battle that needs fighting, and no one can fight if they are hungry. Those of us lucky enough to have food on our plates should be forever thankful, and use the energy it provides to battle hard for those without.

Epilogue

I wish that we would not fight for landscapes that remind us of who we think we are. I wish we would fight, instead, for landscapes buzzing and glowing with life in all its variousness.

– Helen MacDonald

It is easy to view humanity as both selfish and stupid, especially at the end of a book that reviews the extent to which we have thoughtlessly decimated the natural world. Yet much of our destruction has been the result of our battle against hunger, and it is hard to view that as anything other than a noble cause. Although we could have done things so much better in so many ways, there was always going to be a cost. All food production has an environmental impact. When people talk about living in balance with nature, that is neither realistic nor desirable. Being in balance with nature means a life of constant hunger and fear. It means fighting for every meal and seeing most of your children die.

Agriculture is not equivalent to a natural ecosystem. It never has been. We withdraw from it without return and, by virtue of our extraordinary intelligence, have the ability to work land beyond its natural limits. Unless we are willing to watch people starve, we have no right to insist that we suddenly cease to use this knowledge. But we do need to find better ways of doing so.

Crucially, there is no doubting that the planet has enough water, minerals and gases to sustain a human population far bigger than the one we have today. There is also more than enough energy falling upon the Earth to allow us to create plentiful food for all. But despite this, our unique ability to look long into the future tells us that the way we are eating now is not sustainable and will result in disaster if it does not change. Unlike the cyanobacteria that wrecked the planet the first time round, our self-awareness gives us an unrivalled opportunity to rectify these problems, overturning what has long been considered a fundamental law.

Although unlikely, it seems possible that we can permanently defeat hunger in a way that does not end in catastrophe, but this will require profound and lasting change. Getting over this hurdle will require all the ingenuity of the technological age, but also behavioural shifts as rapid and fundamental as any in our history. The greatest challenge of all will be changing the way that we eat.

It is one thing knowing what we should be doing, but it is quite another persuading the entire world to follow that path. But even here, I believe there is hope. As the evolutionary biologist Stephen Jay Gould has so astutely noted, 'I am, somehow, less interested in the weight and convolutions of Einstein's brain than in the near certainty that people of equal talent have lived and died in cotton fields and sweatshops.' Throughout history, the force that held back so many potential Einsteins has been a lack of adequate food. Although it is easy to see the future of humanity as bleak, and the challenges impossible to overcome, imagine what eleven billion souls freed from hunger might be capable of. Just think of the heights to which science, technology, society and culture might soar if so many are freed from their daily battle to survive.

There is a chink of light, a vague but tangible hope that we will be able to feed humanity until the population stops growing. If it seems unlikely today, just consider what has been achieved in the astonishingly brief time that a few of us have been effortlessly fed. From vaccines to quantum physics, computers to satellites, equality, human rights, Van Gogh's *Sunflowers* and the coda from 'Hey Jude'. We have glimpsed the furthest reaches of space, developed an understanding of the first seconds of the universe and categorised the fundamental particles from which everything is comprised. We have made bread from the air, powered cars by the light of the Sun, and set foot upon the Moon. All these things only happened because people were freed from thinking about their next meal. And the real miracle is that we have only just begun.

We should care about the environment and our impact upon this world. We should be ashamed when we cause devastation, and we should fight hard for change. The fundamental goal of the human project should be to leave behind a better world, with more opportunity, less hardship and greater freedoms. But we should care about the natural world not for what it is, but for what it supports. Cities full of life, love, music and debate. Children born innocent into the world, full of potential and hope. Young people striving for something better, unhindered by shackles of the past.

I feel that I differ from many environmentalists in this regard. Too often, when people write about nature, humanity is cast as a great disappointment. People are a blight, spreading their dark city-shaped stains across the planet. Protecting nature requires us to treat the infection, wipe out the stain, hold back the regrettable tide of humanity. Knowing where this so often leads, I can never agree.

The more potential Mozarts, Turings, Curies, Borlaugs, Einsteins, Pankhursts and Franklins we can lift out of hunger, the more chance there is that the future will be bright and worth living for. Hunger is the one thing that might just hold us back, an evil of such force that it could destroy the human project forever.

There is no doubting that humanity is currently walking along a knife-edge. We have taken the planet to the brink, and are only just beginning to understand the extent of the damage we have caused. But we must not despair. We failed to plant trees twenty years ago, but we can plant them today. It is only if we learn to love humanity for what it is, applaud its diversity, and believe in its extraordinary capacity to make a better world, that we will stand a chance of walking this edge and getting ourselves across the line.

There is so much that each of us can do. But the most important task of all is to nurture the generation that follows us. To keep them safe and well fed. To enable their lives so they might progress in ways that seem impossible to us now. To let them drink in the joy of life so that they know exactly what they are fighting for, and to pass on everything we have that might help. To lift every family out of hunger, first because it is the right thing to do, but also because that is the key to unlocking a better future for us all. We must plant trees today, so that all of our children might one day sit in their shade.

Acknowledgements

The topics covered in this book are so diverse and complex that no single person could possibly claim to have expertise in them all. This means that the only way to write a book such as this is to borrow knowledge from a wide variety of experts, usually by spending time in their company. I was constantly amazed that so many remarkable people were willing to give up their time and I can only hope that I have faithfully translated some of their insights onto the page.

Because of the writing process, often the information people pass on does not translate into direct quotes. I could have filled several books with the conversations I have had over the past two years and all would be fascinating, but, as my editor keeps on telling me, book writing requires that information is pared down to make it digestible. There are numerous people I spoke to who are not quoted in the text at all, but that does not mean that their insights and contributions were not extremely valuable. Similarly, without exception, everyone quoted in the book provided me with far more information than is directly attributed. Every conversation was an opportunity for me to learn and helped shape my thoughts on these often difficult subjects. This book is the sum of those interactions and the people below all contributed in some way.

In no particular order, I would like to thank Wayne Martindale, Kate McMahon, Duncan Cameron, Rob Lyons, Tony Ryan,

Christian Reynolds, Brian Kateman, Mark Thomas, David Wengrow, James Clarke, Mark Elsier, Jonathon Porritt, Gernot Laganda, Hanna Tuomisto, Louise Needham, Emma Sharpe, Tim Benton, Daniel Crossley, Alex de Waal, Will Carter, Robert Lawson, Amelia Boothman, Maria Josep Martinez, Jules Pretty, Jonathan Storkey, Sarah Taber, Tracy Berno, Sarah Evanega, Jonas Cromwell, Daniel Blaustein-Rejto, Stuart Flint, Andrew Challinor, Piers Forster, Kae Tabacek, Janet Ranganathan, Elsa Murano, Marion Nestle, John Wilmoth, Evan Fraser, David Evans, John McGrath, Alison Van Eenennaam, Mark Lynas, Chris Reij, Ylva Johannesson, Kim Hammond-Kosack, Steve McGraph, Corrie Sissons, Josh Bullmore, Rachel Laudan, Ian Boyd, Richard Green, Mark Rutter, Simon Leather, Tom Pope, Jonathan Gill, Kit Franklin, Anna Krzywoszynska, Kevin Folta, Matt Ball, Caroline Drummond, Pete Smith, Giles Oldroyd, Taro Takahashi, Ed Gratan, Simon Crichton, Alexandra Sexton, Aoife McLysaght, Alexandra Dallago, Eileen O'Sullivan, Michael Lee, Adreen Hart-Rule, Alan Marson and Matthew Fieldson.

Particular thanks go to Jude Caper for endless help on live-stock and dairy, Jim Stuart for generally being a legend, Pierre Desrochers and Joanna Szurmak for challenging my thinking more than anyone, Megan Blake for her help and contacts, Tara Garnett for being patient with my (many) stupid questions, John Crawford for opening my mind on soil science, Henry Dimbleby for his contact book, reading list and general support, Achim Dobermann for opening my eyes to the world, Alan Levinovitz for letting me steal his ideas (did I mention I stole your ideas?), James Wong for all his help and encouragement and Tamar Haspel for not being afraid to tell me I am wrong. I am sure there are plenty of people I have missed off the list, and I can only apologise if you are one of them. I owe each and every one of you a drink. Or two.*

---

* Terms and conditions apply.

I would also like to thank Alexandra Cliff, who saw the unlikely potential in my strange little blog all those years ago and has shown me so much faith and support ever since. It is quite extraordinary that it has led to a trilogy of books. Captain Science has once again been a tower of strength and remains the smartest person I know. Alex Christofi, the notorious bisector of books, has done another spectacular job, putting up with me for three books in a row, contributing his share of terrible puns and perhaps forever stopping my plundering.

Most of all, I need to thank Ellie, firstly for allowing me to share her story with the world, and secondly for inspiring this book with her strength and courage. If I go on to write a thousand books, you will still be the thing that I am most proud of.

And finally, once again, I need to give my greatest thanks to Mrs Angry Chef, who patiently allows my writing to take me away for far too much time, and always manages to give me the strength to push through when things get tough. In the same way that we faced every dark moment together, every success belongs to us both (although unfortunately I am yet to make this case with the UK tax authorities).

Notes

PROLOGUE

1 'World Population Prospects: The 2017 Revision', UN Department of Economic and Social Affairs, 21 June 2017, [online] https://www.un.org/development/desa/publications/world-population-prospects-the-2017-revision.html (accessed 20 December 2019).

2 FAO, UNICEF, WHO et al., 'The State of Food Security and Nutrition in the World', Food and Agriculture Organization of the United Nations, 2018, [online] http://www.fao.org/3/I9553EN/i9553en.pdf (accessed 20 December 2019).

1. HUNGER

1 Fraser, E., Rimas, A., 'The Psychology of Food Riots', *Foreign Affairs*, 30 January 2011, [online] https://www.foreignaffairs.com/articles/tunisia/2011-01-30/psychology-food-riots (accessed 20 December 2019).

2. A BRIEF HISTORY OF HUNGER

1 This uses an estimate of 11 g for each blue tit. The total biomass of all humans is thought to be about 350 million tonnes and there are 600–700 million tonnes of livestock animals. Estimates vary, but the imaginary blue tits would probably come close to the total weight of all living animals, although a few more generations would be required to rival the immense biomass of bacteria and plants.

2 Lents, N., *Human Errors – A Panorama of Our Glitches, from Pointless Bones to Broken Genes* (London: W&N, 2018).

3 Genes are essentially long sequences of code that contain instructions to make proteins. Proteins are the things that do stuff in the body, such as making chemical reactions happen, creating biological structures, repairing tissues and building cells. Incredibly, only about one to two percent of our genetic code actually performs this role. But like seemingly everything in the life sciences, things are more complex than they first appear. The ninety-eight to ninety-nine percent is not completely non-functional, with much of it involved in forming the complex chromosome structures that allow genes to work. But it is probably fair to say that the genetic mutations that have the biggest effect on an organism are likely to be the rare ones that occur in a gene sequence directly involved in making a protein.

4 Wolpert, L., Garcia-Bellido, A., 'Debatable Issues. Interview by Alain Ghysen', *International Journal of Developmental Biology*, 42 (3), 1998, pp. 511–18.

5 Hublin, J., Ben-Ncer, A., Bailey, S. et al., 'New Fossils from Jebel Irhoud, Morocco and the Pan-African Origin of Homo Sapiens', *Nature*, 546, 2017, pp. 289–92.

6 Kaneda, T., Haub, C., 'How Many People Have Ever Lived on Earth?', PRB, 9 March 2018, [online] https://www.prb.org/howmanypeoplehaveeverlivedonearth (accessed 20 December 2019).

7 Rampino, M., Self, S., 'Volcanic Winter and Accelerated Glaciation Following the Toba Super-Eruption', *Nature*, 359, 1992, pp. 50–2.

8 Koerth-Baker, M., 'Who Lives Longest?', *New York Times*, 19 March 2013.

9 Graeber, D., Wengrow, D., 'How to Change the Course of Human History', *Eurozine*, 2 March 2018, [online] https://www.eurozine.com/change-course-human-history (accessed 20 December 2019).

10 Pringle, H., 'The Slow Birth of Agriculture', *Science*, 5393, 1998, pp. 1446–50.

11 Mummert, A., Esche, E., Robinson, J., Armelagos, G. J., 'Stature and Robusticity during the Agricultural Transition: Evidence from the Bioarchaeological Record', *Economics and Human Biology*, 9 (3), 2011, pp. 284–301.

12 'Human Population Through Time', American Museum of Natural History, October 2016, [online] https://www.amnh.org/explore/videos/humans/human-population-through-time (accessed 20 December 2019).

13 Korotayev, A., Malkov, A., 'A Compact Mathematical Model of the World System Economic and Demographic Growth, 1 CE – 1973 CE', *International Journal of Mathematical Models and Methods in Applied Sciences*, 10, 2016, pp. 200–9.

14 'World Population Prospects: The 2017 Revision', UN Department of Economic and Social Affairs, 21 June 2017, [online] https://www.un.org/development/desa/publications/world-population-prospects-the-2017-revision.html (accessed 20 December 2019).

15 Smil, V., *Enriching the Earth* (London: MIT, 2001).

16 Alexandratos, N., Bruinsma, J., 'World Agriculture Towards 2030/2050 – the 2012 Revision', Food and Agriculture Organization of the United Nations, ESA Working Paper No. 12–03, June 2012, [online] http://www.fao.org/fileadmin/templates/esa/Global_persepctives/world_ag_2030_50_2012_rev.pdf (accessed 20 December 2019).

17 Congressional Tribute to Dr Norman E. Borlaug Act of 2006. Public Law. 109th Congress, Public Law 395 Section 2 Findings, Point 8.

3. A BRIEF HISTORY OF DOOM

1 Shermer, M., 'Doomsday Catch', *Scientific American*, 314, 2016, pp. 516–72.

2 Brignell, V., 'The Eugenics Movement Britain Wants to Forget', *New Statesman*, 9 December 2010.

3 Roser, M., Ritchie, H., Ortiz-Ospina, E., 'World Population Growth', Our World in Data, May 2019, [online] https://ourworldindata.org/world-population-growth (accessed 20 December 2019).

4 'World Population Prospects: The 2017 Revision', UN Department of Economic and Social Affairs, 21 June 2017, [online] https://www.un.org/development/desa/publications/world-population-prospects-the-2017-revision.html (accessed 20 December 2019). See also: Gietel-Basten, S., Lutz, W., Scherbov, S., 'Very Long Range Global Population Scenarios to 2300 and the Implications of Sustained Low Fertility', *Demographic Research*, 28, 2013, pp. 1146–65.

5 Feng, W., Cai, Y., Gu, B., 'Population, Policy and Politics: How Will History Judge China's One-Child Policy?', *Population and Development Review*, 38 (Supplement), 2013, pp. 115–29. See also: Johansson, S., Nygren, O., 'The Missing Girls of China: A New Demographic Account', *Population and Development Review*, 17 (1), 1991, pp. 35–51.

6 'India and Family Planning – An Overview', WHO Department of Family and Community Health, 2009, [online] https://web.archive.org/web/20091221114 019/http:/www.searo.who.int/LinkFiles/Family_Planning_Fact_Sheets_india. pdf (accessed 20 December 2019). See also: 'More than 63 Million Women "Missing" in India', *Guardian*, 30 January 2018.

7 'Extreme Carbon Inequality', Oxfam, 2 December 2015, [online] https://www-cdn.oxfam.org/s3fs-public/file_attachments/mb-extreme-carbon-inequality-021215-en.pdf (accessed 20 December 2019).

8 'Carbon Emissions Per Person, Per Country', *Guardian*, 2 September 2009.

4. HOW TO CHANGE THE WORLD

1 Nutman, A., Bennett, V., Friend, C., Kranendonk, M., Chivas, A., 'Rapid Emergence of Life Shown by Discovery of 3,700-Million-Year-Old Microbial Structures', *Nature*, 537, 2016, pp. 535–8.

2 Pavlov, A., Kasting, J., Brown, L., Rages, K., Freedman, R., 'Greenhouse Warming by CH4 in the Atmosphere of Early Earth', *Journal of Geophysical Research*, 105 (E5), 2000, pp. 11981–90.

3 KC, K. B., Dias, G. M., Veeramani, A. et al., 'When Too Much Isn't Enough: Does Current Food Production Meet Global Nutritional Needs?', *PLOS One*, 13 (10), 2018, [online] https://journals.plos.org/plosone/article?id=10.1371/journal.pone.0205683 (accessed 20 December 2019). See also: Khoury, C. K., Bjorkman, A. D., Dempewolf, H., Ramirez-Villegas, J. et al., 'Increasing Homogeneity in Global Food Supplies', *Proceedings of the National Academy of Sciences*, 111 (11), 2014, pp. 4001–6.

4 Kolchinsky, E. I., Kutschera, U., Hossfeld, U., Levit, G. S., 'Russia's New Lysenkoism', *Current Biology*, 27 (19), 2017, R1042–R1047.

5 Bernstein, R., 'Horrors of a Hidden Chinese Famine', *New York Times*, 5 February 1997.

5. WHAT HAVE WE DONE?

1 Montgomery, D., *Dirt: The Erosion of Civilizations*, 2nd edn. (Berkeley: University of California Press, 2012).

2 'Working Group 1 – The Scientific Basis', IPCC, [online] https://archive.ipcc.ch/ipccreports/tar/wg1/016.htm (accessed 20 December 2019).

3 Cassman, K. G., Grassini, P., Wart, J., 'Crop Yield Potential, Yield Trends and Global Food Security in a Changing Climate', in *Handbook of Climate Change and Agroecosystems: Impacts, Adaptation, and Mitigation*, eds. C. Rosenzweig, D. Hillel (London: Imperial College Press, 2011), pp. 37–54.

4 Baumert, K. A., Herzog, T., Pershing, J., *Navigating the Numbers: Greenhouse Gas Data and International Climate Policy from World Resources Institute*, World Resources Institute, 2005.

5 'Climate Change and the Land', IPCC, [online] https://www.ipcc.ch/srccl/ (accessed 20 December 2019).

6 'Global Assessment Report on Biodiversity and Ecosystem Services', IBPES, [online] https://ipbes.net/global-assessment-report-biodiversity-ecosystem-ser vices (accessed 20 December 2019).

7 Helmholtz Association of German Research Centres, 'Economic Value of Insect Pollination Worldwide Estimated At U.S. $217 Billion', *Science Daily*, 15 September 2008, [online] https://www.sciencedaily.com/releases/2008/09/080915122725.htm (accessed 20 December 2019).

8 'Global Assessment Report on Biodiversity and Ecosystem Services'.

9 Montford, A., 'Insectageddon: Don't Believe the Hype', *Reaction*, 26 February 2019, [online] https://reaction.life/insectageddon-dont-believe-hype/ (accessed 20 December 2019). See also: Pensoft Publishers, '"Insectageddon" Is "Alarmist by Bad Design": Scientists Point Out the Study's Major Flaws', *Science Daily*, 19 March 2019, [online] https://www.sciencedaily.com/releases/2019/03/190319112211.htm (accessed 20 December 2019); Saunders, M. E., 'No Simple Answers for Insect Conservation', *American Scientist*, 107 (3), 2019, p. 148; Carrington, D., 'Plummeting Insect Numbers "Threaten Collapse of Nature"', *Guardian*, 10 February 2019.

10 Acorn, J., 'The Windshield Anecdote', *American Entomologist*, 62 (4), 2016, pp. 262–4. See also: Mills, E., 'What's the Splatter? The Science Behind Bug Guts on Your Windshield', Houston Museum of Natural Science, 20 April 2017, [online] http://blog.hmns.org/2017/04/window-dressing-the-science-behind-bug-guts-on-your-windshield (accessed 20 December 2019).

11 Briggs, H., Dale, B., Stylianou, N., 'Nature's Emergency: Where We Are in Five Graphics', BBC News, 5 May 2019, [online] https://www.bbc.co.uk/news/science-environment-48104037 (accessed 20 December 2019). See also: The IUCN Red List of Endangered Species [Land degradation report], [online] https://www.iucnredlist.org (accessed 20 December 2019).

12 Zomer, R. J., Bossio, D. A., Sommer, R., Verchot, L. V., 'Global Sequestration Potential of Increased Organic Carbon in Cropland Soils', *Scientific Reports*, 7, 2017, [online] https://doi.org/10.1038/s41598-017-15794-8 (accessed 20 December 2019).

13 Diaz, R. J., Rosenberg, R., 'Spreading Dead Zones and Consequences for Marine Ecosystems', *Science*, 5891, 2008, pp. 926–9.

6. THE OUTER LIMITS

1 McGrath, M., 'Nature Crisis: Humans "Threaten 1m Species with Extinction"', BBC News, 6 May 2019, [online] https://www.bbc.co.uk/news/science-environment-48169783 (accessed 20 December 2019).

2 Monbiot, G., 'While Economic Growth Continues We'll Never Kick Our Fossil Fuels Habit', *Guardian*, 26 September 2018.

3 Searchinger, T., Waite, R., Hanson, C. et al., *Creating a Sustainable Food Future: A Menu of Solutions to Feed Nearly 10 Billion People by 2050 (Synthesis Report)*, World Resources Institute, 2018. See also: Kray, H. A., *Farming for the Future: The Environmental Sustainability of Agriculture in a Changing World*,

World Bank Group, [online] https://www.worldbank.org/content/dam/ Worldbank/Event/ECA/bg-agri-kray1-eng.pdf (accessed 20 December 2019); *World Development Report 2008: Agriculture for Development*, World Bank Group, 2008, [online] https://openknowledge.worldbank.org/bitstream/hand le/10986/5990/WDR%202008%20-%20English.pdf?sequence=3&is Allowed=y (accessed 20 December 2019).

4 Searchinger et al., *Creating a Sustainable Food Future*.

5 Ibid.

6 FAO, UNICEF, WHO et al., 'The State of Food Security and Nutrition in the World', Food and Agriculture Organization of the United Nations, 2018, [online] http://www.fao.org/3/I9553EN/i9553en.pdf (accessed 20 December 2019).

7 *2018 Global Nutrition Report*, [online] https://globalnutritionreport.org/reports/ global-nutrition-report-2018 (accessed 20 December 2019).

8 'FAO Cereal Supply and Demand Brief', Food and Agriculture Organization of the United Nations, [online] http://www.fao.org/worldfoodsituation/csdb/en/ (accessed 20 December 2019).

9 'Peak Oil' has been predicted as imminent ever since the 1970s, but this seems little more than wishful thinking by environmentalists and/or anti-capitalists. In 2015, BP predicted that global reserves would double by 2050 despite rising demand, and said that there are enough resources to provide twenty times more than we will need over that period (please read on in the chapter for an explana- tion of the difference between reserves and resources). It seems increasingly likely that oil will run out of humans before humans run out of oil. Happy days.

10 Bryce, E., 'The Decades-Long Quest to End Drought (and Feed Millions) by Taking the Salt Out of Seawater', *Wired*, 20 March 2018, [online] https://www. wired.co.uk/article/charlie-paton-seawater-greenhouse-desalination- abu-dhabi-oman-australia-somaliland (accessed 20 December 2019). See also: *Global Environment Outlook 6*, UN Environment Programme, 4 March 2019, [online] https://www.unenvironment.org/resources/global-environment-outlook-6 (accessed 20 December 2019).

11 Case, P., 'Only 100 Harvests Left in UK Farm Soils, Scientists Warn', *Farmers Weekly*, 21 October 2014, [online] https://www.fwi.co.uk/news/only-100- harvests-left-in-uk-farm-soils-scientists-warn (accessed 20 December 2019). See also: Arsenault, C., 'Only 60 Years of Farming Left if Soil Degradation Continues', *Scientific American*, 5 December 2014, [online] https://www.scien- tificamerican.com/article/only-60-years-of-farming-left-if-soil-degrada tion-continues/ (accessed 20 December 2019); Van der Zee, B., 'UK Is 30–40 Years Away from "Eradication of Soil Fertility", Warns Gove', *Guardian*, 24 October 2017.

12 Grantham, J., 'Be Persuasive. Be Brave. Be Arrested (if Necessary)', *Nature*, 7424, 2012, p. 303.

13 Worstall, T., 'What Jeremy Grantham Gets Horribly, Horribly, Wrong About Resource Availability', *Forbes*, 16 November 2012, [online] https://www.forbes. com/sites/timworstall/2012/11/16/what-jeremy-grantham-gets-horribly-horri- bly-wrong-about-resource-availability/#555df926ad96 (accessed 20 December 2019). See also: Smil, V., 'Jeremy Grantham – Starving for Facts', *The American*,

6 December 2012, [online] https://www.aei.org/*/jeremy-grantham-starving-for-facts/ (accessed 20 December 2019); Worstall, T., *The No-Breakfast Fallacy: Why the Club of Rome Was Wrong About Us Running Out of Minerals and Metals* (London: Adam Smith Institute, 2015).

14 Davis, J., 'The Mystery of the Coca Plant that Wouldn't Die', *Wired*, 11 January 2004, [online] https://www.wired.com/2004/11/columbia/ (accessed 20 December 2019).

15 Metcalf, R. L., 'Implications and Prognosis of Resistance to Insecticides', in *Pest Resistance to Pesticides*, eds. G. P. Georghiou and T. Saito (New York: Plenum Press, 1983), pp. 703–34.

16 Lundin, O., Rundlöf, M., Smith, H. G., Fries, I., Bommarco, R., 'Neonicotinoid Insecticides and Their Impacts on Bees: A Systematic Review of Research Approaches and Identification of Knowledge Gaps', *PLOS One*, 10 (8), 27 August 2015, [online] https://journals.plos.org/plosone/article?id=10.1371/journal.pone.0136928 (accessed 20 March 2020). See also: 'Neonicotinoids: Risks to Bees Confirmed', European Food Safety Authority, 28 February 2018, [online] https://www.efsa.europa.eu/en/press/news/180228 (accessed 20 December 2019); Tapparo, A., Marton, D., Giorio, C. et al., 'Assessment of the Environmental Exposure of Honeybees to Particulate Matter Containing Neonicotinoid Insecticides Coming from Corn Coated Seeds', *Environmental Science & Technology*, 46 (5), 2012, pp. 2592–9; Pollinator Network @ Cornell, 'Neonicotinoids', Cornell College of Agriculture and Life Sciences, [online] https://pollinator.cals.cornell.edu/threats-wild-and-managed-bees/pesticides/neonicotinoids (accessed 20 December 2019); Van der Sluijs, J. P., Simon-Delso, N., Goulson, D. et al., 'Neonicotinoids, Bee Disorders and the Sustainability of Pollinator Services', *Current Opinion in Environmental Sustainability*, 5 (3), 2013, pp. 293–305; Rundlöf, M., Andersson, G. K. S., Bommarco, R., 'Seed Coating with a Neonicotinoid Insecticide Negatively Affects Wild Bees', *Nature*, 521, 2015, pp. 77–80.

17 Cooper, J., Dobson, H., *Pesticides and Humanity – The Benefits of Using Pesticides*, Natural Resources Institute, [online] https://pdfs.semanticscholar.org/6514/557ef750132759b8c12a410ed58a1e59a5e4.pdf (accessed 20 December 2019). See also: Popp, J., Peto, K., Nagy, J., 'Pesticide Productivity and Food Security. A Review', *Agronomy for Sustainable Development*, 33 (1), 2013, pp. 243–55; Aktar, M. W., Sengupta, D., Chowdhury, A., 'Impact of Pesticides Use in Agriculture: Their Benefits and Hazards', *Interdisciplinary Toxicology*, 2 (1), 2009, pp. 1–12.

18 Half of the top ten US prescription medicines, and over three quarters of all cancer medicines, are derived from compounds first discovered in plants, animals or microorganisms. Nearly ninety percent of all known human diseases can be treated with a pharmaceutical drug derived from nature. It is incredibly likely that there are thousands more left to discover.

19 Benton, T., Bailey, R., 'The Paradox of Productivity: Agricultural Productivity Promotes Food System Inefficiency', *Global Sustainability*, 2 (E6), 2019, pp. 1–8. See also: *Natural Capital Impacts in Agriculture*, Food and Agriculture Organization of the United Nations, 2015, [online] http://www.fao.org/filead

min/templates/nr/sustainability_pathways/docs/Natural_Capital_Impacts_in_
Agriculture_final.pdf (accessed 20 December 2019); Pretty, J., 'Intensification
for Redesigned and Sustainable Agricultural Systems', *Science*, 362 (6417),
2018; Tait, C., *Hungry for Change: The Final Report of the Fabian Commission
on Food and Poverty* (London: Fabian Society, 2015).

20 Van Grinsven, H. J., Holland, M., Jacobsen, B. H. et al., 'Costs and Benefits of
Nitrogen for Europe and Implications for Mitigation', *Environmental Science &
Technology*, 47 (8), 2013, pp. 3571–9.

7. MEAT IS . . .

1 *Farming Statistics: Provisional Crop Areas, Yields and Livestock Populations at
June 2018*, Department for Environment, Food and Rural Affairs, 11 October
2018, [online] https://assets.publishing.service.gov.uk/government/uploads/
system/uploads/attachment_data/file/747210/structure-jun2018prov-UK-
11oct18.pdf (accessed 20 December 2019).

2 Young, R., 'Claims Against Meat Fail to Consider Bigger Picture', Sustainable
Food Trust, 14 June 2018, [online] https://sustainablefoodtrust.org/articles/
claims-against-meat-fail-to-see-bigger-picture (accessed 20 December 2019).

3 Fairlie, S., 'Is Grass-fed Guilt-free?', *The Land*, 22, 2018, pp. 52–5.

4 *Livestock and Landscapes*, Food and Agriculture Organization of the United
Nations, [online] http://www.fao.org/3/ar591e/ar591e.pdf (accessed 20
December 2019).

5 Searchinger, T., Waite, R., Hanson, C. et al., *Creating a Sustainable Food
Future: A Menu of Solutions to Feed Nearly 10 Billion People by 2050 (Synthesis
Report)*, World Resources Institute, 2018. See also: Bailey, R., Froggatt, A.,
Wellesley, L., 'Livestock – Climate Change's Forgotten Sector', Chatham
House research paper, 2014.

6 Poore, J., Nemecek, T., 'Reducing Food's Environmental Impact through
Producers and Consumers', *Science*, 360, 2018, pp. 987–92. See also: Mekonnen,
M. M., Hoestra, A. Y., *The Green, Blue and Grey Water Footprint of Farm Animals
and Farm Products*, UNESCO-IHE Institute for Water Education, 2010.

7 Bailey, Froggatt, Wellesley, 'Livestock – Climate Change's Forgotten Sector'.

8 Poore, Nemecek, 'Reducing Food's Environmental Impact'.

9 Swain, M., 'The Future of Meat', Breakthrough Institute, 18 May 2017,
[online] https://thebreakthrough.org/articles/the-future-of-meat (accessed 20
December 2019).

10 Eisler, M., Lee, M. R. F., Tarlton, J. F. et al., 'Agriculture: Steps to Sustainable
Livestock', *Nature*, 7490, 2014, pp. 32–4.

11 Smit, A. M. L., Heedrik, D., 'Impacts of Intensive Livestock Production on
Human Health in Densely Populated Regions', *GeoHealth*, 1 (7), 2017, pp.
272–7.

12 Gerber, P. J., Steinfeld, H., Henderson, B. et al., *Tackling Climate Change
through Livestock – A Global Assessment of Emissions and Mitigation Opportunities*,
FAO, 2013, [online] http://www.fao.org/3/a-i3437e.pdf (accessed 20 December
2019). See also: Rogelj, J., Shindell, D., Jiang, K. et al., 'Mitigation Pathways
Compatible with 1.5°C in the Context of Sustainable Development', in *Global*

Warming of 1.5°C. An IPCC Special Report on the Impacts of Global Warming of 1.5°C above Pre-Industrial Levels and Related Global Greenhouse Gas Emission Pathways, in the Context of Strengthening the Global Response to the Threat of Climate Change, Sustainable Development, and Efforts to Eradicate Poverty, eds. V. Masson-Delmotte, P. Zhai et al., in press, pp. 93–174.

13 *Inventory of U.S. Greenhouse Gas Emissions and Sinks 1990–2017*, United States Environmental Protection Agency, 2019, [online] https://www.epa.gov/sites/production/files/2019-04/documents/us-ghg-inventory-2019-main-text.pdf (accessed 20 December 2019).

14 White, R., Hall, M., 'Nutritional and Greenhouse Gas Impacts of Removing Animals from US Agriculture', *Proceedings of the National Academy of Sciences*, 114 (48), 2017, pp. E10301–E10308.

15 Hickman, M., 'Study Claims Meat Creates Half of All Greenhouse Gases', *Independent*, 1 November 2009, [online] https://www.independent.co.uk/environment/climate-change/study-claims-meat-creates-half-of-all-greenhouse-gases-1812909.html (accessed 25 March 2020).

16 Zaraska, M., *Meathooked: The History and Science of Our 2.5-Million-Year Obsession with Meat* (New York: Basic Books, 2016). See also: Sultan, N., 'Where's the Beef? When Meat's in Trouble, Lobbying Expands', OpenSecrets, 30 March 2017, [online] https://www.opensecrets.org/news/2017/03/wheres-the-beef-meat-lobby (accessed 20 December 2019).

17 Voorhees, J., 'Big Beef', *Slate*, 27 February 2015, [online] https://slate.com/news-and-politics/2015/02/the-climate-case-against-meat-u-s-nutrition-panel-suggests-americans-eat-less-meat-sparking-washingtons-next-climate-fight.html (accessed 20 December 2019). See also: Reiley, L., 'How the Trump Administration Limited the Scope of the USDA's 2020 Dietary Guidelines', *Washington Post*, 30 August 2019.

18 Eisler, Lee, Tarlton et al., 'Agriculture: Steps to Sustainable Livestock', pp. 32–4.

19 Macmillan, S., 'The Many Gifts of Livestock – A View from Kenya', ILRI News, 17 March 2019, [online] https://news.ilri.org/2019/03/17/the-many-gifts-of-livestock-a-view-from-kenya (accessed 20 December 2019).

20 Smil, V., 'Eating Meat: Constants and Changes', *Global Food Security*, 3 (2), 2014, pp. 67–71.

21 Ermgassen, E., 'Why the Ban on Feeding Animals Waste Food Should Be Reconsidered', *Independent*, 3 May 2018.

22 Roberts, P. C., 'My Time with Soviet Economics', *Independent Review*, 7 (2), 2002, pp. 259–64.

23 VandeHaar, M. J., St-Pierre, N., 'Major Advances in Nutrition: Relevance to the Sustainability of the Dairy Industry', *Journal of Dairy Sciences*, 89 (4), 2006, pp. 1280–91. See also: Capper, J. L., Bauman, D. E., 'The Role of Productivity in Improving the Environmental Sustainability of Ruminant Production Systems', *Annual Review of Animal Biosciences*, 1, 2013, pp. 469–89.

24 Havenstein, G. B., Ferket, P. R., Qureshi, M. A., 'Growth, Livability, and Feed Conversion of 1957 Versus 2001 Broilers When Fed Representative 1957 and 2001 Broiler Diets', *Poultry Science*, 82 (10), pp. 1500–8.

25 Clune, S., Crossin, E., Verghese, K., 'Systematic Review of Greenhouse Gas Emissions for Different Fresh Food Categories', *Journal of Cleaner Production*, 140 (2), 2017, pp. 766–83.

26 Fearnside, P., 'Deforestation of the Brazilian Amazon', Oxford Research Encyclopaedias: Environmental Science, 2017, [online] https://oxfordre.com/environmentalscience/view/10.1093/acrefore/9780199389414.001.0001/acrefore-9780199389414-e-102?rskey=2r3nJk&result=1 (accessed 20 December 2019).

27 Peters, C. J., Picardy, J., Darrouzet-Nardi, A. F. et al., 'Carrying Capacity of U.S. Agricultural Land: Ten Diet Scenarios', *Elementa: Science of the Anthropocene*, 4, 2016, p. 000116.

28 Peters, C. J., Wilkins, J. L., Fick, G. W., 'Testing a Complete-Diet Model for Estimating the Land Resource Requirements of Food Consumption and Agricultural Carrying Capacity: The New York State Example', *Renewable Agriculture and Food Systems*, 22 (2), pp. 145–53.

29 van Zanten, H. H. E., Mollenhorst, H., Klootwijk, C. W. et al., 'Global Food Supply: Land Use Efficiency of Livestock Systems', *International Journal of Life Cycle Assessment*, 21, pp. 747–58.

30 Tom, M. S., Fischbeck, P. S., Hendrickson, C. T., 'Energy Use, Blue Water Footprint, and Greenhouse Gas Emissions for Current Food Consumption Patterns and Dietary Recommendations in the US', *Environment Systems and Decisions*, 36, 2016, pp. 92–103.

31 McWilliams, J., 'All Sizzle and No Steak', *Slate*, 22 April 2013, [online] https://slate.com/human-interest/2013/04/allan-savorys-ted-talk-is-wrong-and-the-benefits-of-holistic-grazing-have-been-debunked.html (accessed 20 December 2019).

32 Ketcham, C., 'Allan Savory's Holistic Management Theory Falls Short on Science', *Sierra*, 23 February 2017, [online] https://www.sierraclub.org/sierra/2017-2-march-april/feature/allan-savory-says-more-cows-land-will-reverse-climate-change (accessed 20 December 2019).

33 Monbiot, G., 'Eat More Meat and Save the World: The Latest Implausible Farming Miracle', *Guardian*, 4 August 2014. See also: Lovins, L. H., 'Why George Monbiot Is Wrong: Grazing Livestock Can Save the World', *Guardian*, 19 August 2014.

34 *Natural Capital Impacts in Agriculture*, FAO, 2015, [online] http://www.fao.org/fileadmin/templates/nr/sustainability_pathways/docs/Natural_Capital_Impacts_in_Agriculture_final.pdf (accessed 20 December 2019).

35 Ray, D. K., Mueller, N. D., West, P. C., Foley J. A., 'Yield Trends Are Insufficient to Double Global Crop Production by 2050', *PLOS One*, 8 (6), 2013, [online] https://journals.plos.org/plosone/article?id=10.1371/journal.pone.0066428 (accessed 20 December 2019). See also: Gerber, Steinfeld, Henderson et al., *Tackling Climate Change through Livestock*; Bennetzen, E. H., Smith, P., Porter, J. R., 'Decoupling of Greenhouse Gas Emissions from Global Agricultural Production: 1970–2050', *Global Change Biology*, 22 (2), 2016, pp. 763–81.

8. LOCAL AND ORGANIC

1 'How Important Is Transport?', Food Climate Research Network, [online] https://foodsource.org.uk/33-how-important-transport (accessed 20 December 2019). See also: 'Voting with Your Trolley', *Economist*, 9 December 2006, pp. 73–5; Desrochers, P., Shimizu, H., *The Locavore's Dilemma* (New York: PublicAffairs, 2012).

2 Slavin, G., 'Derbyshire Neck and Iodine Deficiency', *Mercian Geologist*, 16 (2), 2005, pp. 79–88.

3 Kliman, T., 'The Meaning of Local', *Washingtonian*, 6 May 2013.

4 Coaston, J., 'Trump's New Defense of His Charlottesville Comments Is Incredibly False', *Vox*, 26 April 2019, [online] https://www.vox.com/2019/4/26/18517980/trump-unite-the-right-racism-defense-charlottesville (accessed 20 December 2019). See also: Smyth, R., 'Nature Writing's Fascist Roots', *New Statesman*, 3 April 2019.

5 Kelsey-Sugg, A., 'Tracing the Link Between Natural Food and the Nazis', ABC News Australia, 25 September 2018, [online] https://www.abc.net.au/news/2018-09-14/natural-food-and-nazis-fascism/10236768 (accessed 20 December 2019). See also: Dumitrescu, I., '"Bio-Nazis" Go Green in Germany', Politico EU, 13 July 2018, [online] https://www.politico.eu/article/germany-bio-nazis-go-green-natural-farming-right-wing-extremism (accessed 20 December 2019); McGrane, S., 'The Right-Wing Organic Farmers of Germany', *New Yorker*, 11 January 2013, [online] https://www.newyorker.com/culture/culture-desk/the-right-wing-organic-farmers-of-germany (accessed 20 December 2019).

6 Staudenmaier, P., 'Anthroposophy and Eco-Fascism', Institute for Social Ecology, 10 January 2009, [online] http://social-ecology.org/wp/2009/01/anthroposophy-and-ecofascism-2 (accessed 20 December 2019). See also: Avery, A., *The Truth About Organic Food* (Bath: Henderson Communications, 2006).

7 Toohey, J., 'The Roots of Organic Farming Lie in Fascism', The Conversation, 21 January 2018, [online] https://theconversation.com/the-roots-of-organic-farming-lie-in-fascism-81448 (accessed 20 December 2019).

8 Reganold, J. P., Wachter, J. M., 'Organic Agriculture in the Twenty-First Century', *Nature Plants*, 2 (2), 2016, [online] https://www.nature.com/articles/nplants2015221 (accessed 20 December 2019).

9 Biello, D., 'Will Organic Food Fail to Feed the World?', *Scientific American*, 25 April 2012. See also: Kniss, A. R., Savage, S. D., Jabbour, R., 'Correction: Commercial Crop Yields Reveal Strengths and Weaknesses for Organic Agriculture in the United States', *PLOS One*, 11 (11), 2016, [online] https://journals.plos.org/plosone/article?id=10.1371/journal.pone.0161673 (accessed 20 December 2019); Tuomisto, H. L., Hodge, I. D., Riordan, P., Macdonald, D. W., 'Does Organic Farming Reduce Environmental Impacts?', *Journal of Environmental Management*, 112, 2012, pp. 309–20; Clark, M., Tilman, D., 'Comparative Analysis of Environmental Impacts of Agricultural Production Systems, Agricultural Input Efficiency, and Food Choice', *Environmental Research Letters*, 12 (6), 2017, [online] https://iopscience.iop.org/article/10.1088/1748-9326/aa6cd5/meta (accessed 20 December 2019); Smith,

L. G., Jones, P. J., Kirk, G. J. D. et al., 'Modelling the Production Impacts of a Widespread Conversion to Organic Agriculture in England and Wales', *Land Use Policy*, 76, 2018, pp. 391–404; Ritchie, H., 'Is Organic Really Better for the Environment than Conventional Agriculture?', Our World in Data, 19 October 2017, [online] https://ourworldindata.org/is-organic-agriculture-better-for-the-environment (accessed 20 December 2019); Smith, L. G., Kirk, J. D., Jones, P. J., Williams, A. G., 'The Greenhouse Gas Impacts of Converting Food Production in England and Wales to Organic Methods', *Nature Communications*, 10 (4641), 2019, [online] https://www.nature.com/articles/s41467-019-12622-7 (accessed 20 December 2019).

10 'How Far Could Changes in Production Practices Reduce GHG Emissions?', Food Climate Research Network, [online] https://foodsource.org.uk/44-how-far-could-changes-production-practices-reduce-ghg-emissions (accessed 20 December 2019).

11 Searchinger, T. D., Wirsenius, S., Beringer, T., Dumas, P., 'Assessing the Efficiency of Changes in Land Use for Mitigating Climate Change', *Nature*, 564, 2018, pp. 249–53. See also: Savage, S., 'USDA Data Confirm Organic Yields Significantly Lower than with Conventional Farming', Genetic Literacy Project, 16 February 2018, [online] https://geneticliteracyproject.org/2018/02/16/usda-data-confirm-organic-yields-dramatically-lower-conventional-farming (accessed 20 December 2018).

12 Haspel, T., 'Organic Standards Fight Over Synthetics Shows There's Room for a Third System', *Washington Post*, 13 June 2014.

13 Gilbert, N., 'A Middle Path to Sustainable Farming', *Knowable*, 10 May 2019, [online] https://www.knowablemagazine.org/article/sustainability/2019/middle-path-sustainable-farming (accessed 20 December 2019).

14 Smil, V., *Enriching the Earth* (London: MIT, 2001). See also: Erisman, J., Sutton, M., Galloway, J. et al., 'How a Century of Ammonia Synthesis Changed the World', *Nature Geoscience*, 1, 2008, pp. 636–9; Ritchie, H., 'How Many People Does Synthetic Fertilizer Feed?', Our World in Data, 7 November 2017, [online] https://ourworldindata.org/how-many-people-does-synthetic-fertilizer-feed (accessed 20 December 2019).

15 Agrios, G., *Plant Pathology*, 5th edn. (London: Elsevier Academic Press, 2005). See also: Roser, M., Ritchie, H., 'Fertilizers', Our World in Data, 2020, [online] https://ourworldindata.org/fertilizers (accessed 20 December 2019).

9. GMO

1 Kromdijk, J., Głowacka, K., Leonelli, L. et al., 'Improving Photosynthesis and Crop Productivity by Accelerating Recovery from Photoprotection', *Science*, 354 (6314), 2016, pp. 857–61. See also: Kromdijk, J., Long, S. P., 'One Crop Breeding Cycle from Starvation? How Engineering Crop Photosynthesis for Rising CO_2 and Temperature Could Be One Important Route to Alleviation', *Proceedings of the Royal Society B: Biological Sciences*, 283 (1826), 2016; Sun, J., Miller, J. B., Granqvist, E. et al., 'Activation of Symbiosis Signaling by Arbuscular Mycorrhizal Fungi in Legumes and Rice', *Plant Cell*, 27 (3), pp.

823–38; South, P. F., Cavanagh, A. P., Liu, H. W., Ort, D. R., 'Synthetic Glycolate Metabolism Pathways Stimulate Crop Growth and Productivity in the Field', *Science*, 363 (45), 2019; 'Our Story', Realizing Increased Photosynthetic Efficiency for Sustainable Increases in Crop Yield, [online] https://ripe.illinois.edu/objectives/our-story (accessed 20 December 2019).

2 Daley, J., 'The Corn of the Future Is Hundreds of Years Old and Makes Its Own Mucus', *Smithsonian*, 10 August 2018, [online] https://www.smithsonianmag.com/science-nature/corn-future-hundreds-years-old-and-makes-its-own-mucus-180969972 (accessed 20 December 2019).

3 Van Deynze, A., Zamora, P., Delaux, P. et al., 'Nitrogen Fixation in a Landrace of Maize Is Supported by a Mucilage-Associated Diazotrophic Microbiota', *PLOS Biology*, 16 (8), 2018, [online] https://journals.plos.org/plosbiology/article?id=10.1371/journal.pbio.2006352 (accessed 20 December 2019).

4 'Frequently Asked Questions on Genetically Modified Foods', World Health Organization, May 2014, [online] https://www.who.int/foodsafety/areas_work/food-technology/faq-genetically-modified-food/en/ (accessed 20 December 2019). See also: 'Reaping the Benefits: Science and the Sustainable Intensification of Global Agriculture', Royal Society, 21 October 2009, [online] https://royalsociety.org/topics-policy/publications/2009/reaping-benefits (accessed 20 December 2019); 'Statement by the AAAS Board of Directors on Labeling of Genetically Modified Foods', American Association for the Advancement of Science, 21 October 2012, [online] https://www.aaas.org/sites/default/files/AAAS_GM_statement.pdf (accessed 27 March 2020); EU Commission – European Research Area – Food, Agriculture, Fisheries and Biotechnology, *A Decade of EU Funded GMO Research 2001–2010* (Luxembourg: EU Publications Office, 2010).

5 Roberts, R. J., 'The Nobel Laureates' Campaign Supporting GMOs', *Journal of Innovation and Knowledge*, 3 (2), 2018, pp. 61–5.

6 'Plant Breeding and Genetics', Joint FAO/IAEA Programme – Nuclear Techniques in Food and Agriculture, [online] http://www-naweb.iaea.org/nafa/pbg (accessed 20 December 2019). See also: Schouten, H. J., Jacobsen, E., 'Are Mutations in Genetically Modified Plants Dangerous?', *Journal of Biomedicine and Biotechnology*, 2007, [online] https://www.ncbi.nlm.nih.gov/pmc/articles/PMC2218926/ (accessed 20 December 2019); Broad, W. J., 'Useful Mutants, Bred with Radiation', *New York Times*, 28 August 2007.

7 Callaway, E., 'CRISPR Plants Now Subject to Tough GM Laws in European Union', *Nature*, 25 July 2018, [online] https://www.nature.com/articles/d41586-018-05814-6 (accessed 20 December 2019).

8 Ridley, M., Hill, D., *The Effect of Innovation in Agriculture on the Environment*, Institute of Economic Affairs, IEA Current Controversies No. 64, November 2018, [online] https://iea.org.uk/wp-content/uploads/2018/11/Effect-of-Innovation-in-agriculture_web.pdf (accessed 20 December 2019).

9 Harmon, A., 'A Lonely Quest for Facts on Genetically Modified Crops', *New York Times*, 14 January 2010. See also: Held, E., 'How GMO Technology Saved the Papaya', Food Insight, 14 June 2018, [online] https://foodinsight.org/how-gmo-technology-saved-the-papaya (accessed 20 December 2019).

10 Gashler, K., 'Bt Eggplant Improving Lives in Bangladesh', *Cornell Chronicle*, 16 July 2018, [online] https://news.cornell.edu/stories/2018/07/bt-eggplant-improving-lives-bangladesh (accessed 20 December 2019).

11 Isaac, N., 'Nigeria's GMO Cowpea Wins Medical, Religious and Civic Support', Cornell Alliance for Science, 21 December 2018, [online] https://alliancefors cience.cornell.edu/blog/2018/12/nigerias-gmo-cowpea-wins-medical-reli gious-civic-support (accessed 20 December 2019).

12 Narayanan, N., Beyene, G., Chauhan, R. D. et al., 'Biofortification of Field-Grown Cassava by Engineering Expression of an Iron Transporter and Ferritin', *Nature Biotechnology*, 37, 2019, pp. 144–51.

13 Afedraru, L., 'Ugandan Scientists Poised to Release Vitamin-Fortified GMO Banana', Cornell Alliance for Science, 30 October 2018, [online] https://allianceforscience.cornell.edu/blog/2018/10/ugandan-scientists-poised-release-vitamin-fortified-gmo-banana (accessed 20 December 2019).

14 Klümper, W., Qaim, M., 'A Meta-Analysis of the Impacts of Genetically Modified Crops', *PLOS One*, 9 (11), 2014, [online] https://journals.plos.org/plosone/article/file?id=10.1371/journal.pone.0111629&type=printable (accessed 20 December 2019).

15 Brookes, G., Barfoot, P., *GMO Crops: Global Socio-Economic Impacts 1996–2016*, PG Economics, June 2018, [online] https://pgeconomics.co.uk/pdf/globalimpactstudyfinalreportJune2018.pdf (accessed 20 December 2019).

16 Givens, W. A., Shaw, D. R., Kruger, G. R. et al., 'Survey of Tillage Trends Following the Adoption of Glyphosate-Resistant Crops', *Weed Technology*, 23 (1), 2009, pp. 150–5. See also: Cerdeira, A. L., Duke S. O., 'The Current Status and Environmental Impacts of Glyphosate-Resistant Crops: A Review', *Journal of Environmental Quality*, 35 (5), 2006, pp. 1633–58; Fawcett, R., Towery, D., *Conservation Tillage and Plant Biotechnology*, Conservation Technology Information Center, 2002, [online] https://pdfs.semanticscholar.org/841f/b8a57242aefe3b36a9102646fc398b9b880b.pdf?_ga=2.90453842.95796 9750.1565357748-1155011128.1525949783 (accessed 20 December 2019); Cap, E. J., Trigo, E. J., *Ten Years of Genetically Modified Crops in Argentine Agriculture*, ArgenBio, December 2006, [online] http://argenbio.org/biblioteca/Ten_Years_of_GM_Crops_in_Argentine_Agriculture_02_01_07.pdf (accessed 20 December 2019).

17 Frizzas, M. R., de Oliveira, C. M., Omoto, C., 'Diversity of Insects Under the Effect of Bt Maize and Insecticides', *Arquivos do Instituto Biológico*, 84, 2017, pp. 1–8. See also: Ammann, K., 'Effects of Biotechnology on Biodiversity: Herbicide-Tolerant and Insect-Resistant GM Crops', *Trends in Biotechnology*, 23 (8), pp. 388–94; Dively, G. P., Venugopal, D. P., Bean, D. et al., 'Regional Pest Suppression Associated with Widespread Bt Maize Adoption Benefits Vegetable Growers', *Proceedings of the National Academy of Sciences*, 115 (13), 2018, pp. 3320–5.

18 'What We Are Doing', C_4 Rice Project, [online] https://c4rice.com/the-science/engineering-photosynthesis-what-we-are-doing (accessed 20 December 2019).

19 University of Edinburgh, 'Gene-Edited Chicken Cells Resist Bird Flu Virus in the Lab', *Science Daily*, 4 June 2019, [online] https://www.sciencedaily.com/releases/2019/06/190604084855.htm (accessed 20 December 2019).

20 University of Edinburgh, 'Gene-Edited Pigs Are Resistant to Billion-Dollar Virus', *Science Daily*, 20 June 2018, [online] https://www.sciencedaily.com/releases/2018/06/180620150139.htm (accessed 20 December 2019).

21 Ledford, H., 'Gene-Edited Animal Creators Look Beyond US Market', *Nature*, 566, 2019, pp. 433–4.

22 Fedoroff, N., Raven, P., Sharp, P., 'The Anti-GMO Lobby Appears to Be Taking a Page Out of the Climategate Playbook', *Guardian*, 9 March 2015.

23 'A Childhood of Transcendental Meditation, Spent in the "Shadow of a Guru"', Claire Hoffman author interview, NPR, 13 June 2016, [online] https://www.npr.org/2016/06/13/481845003/a-childhood-of-transcendental-meditation-spent-in-the-shadow-of-a-guru (accessed 27 March 2020).

24 Fagan, J., 'Vedic Pandits Improve Plant Growth', YouTube, [online] https://www.youtube.com/watch?v=92iguO2vIgY&feature=share (accessed 20 December 2019).

25 Harmon, 'A Lonely Quest'.

10. WASTING AWAY

1 Searchinger, T., Waite, R., Hanson, C. et al., *Creating A Sustainable Food Future: A Menu of Solutions to Feed Nearly 10 Billion People by 2050 (Synthesis Report)*, World Resources Institute, 2018. See also: Willett, W., Rockström, J., Loken, B. et al., 'Food in the Anthropocene: the EAT–Lancet Commission on Healthy Diets from Sustainable Food Systems', *Lancet*, 393 (10170), 2019, pp. 447–92.

2 Evans, D., Welch, D., *Food Waste Transitions: Consumption, Retail and Collaboration towards a Sustainable Food System* (Manchester: University of Manchester, 2015). See also: Evans, D., *Fresh is Best? New Perspectives on Sustainable Food Systems* (Bristol: University of Bristol, 2019).

11. THE PROTEIN ALTERNATIVE

1 Blain, B. B., 'Melting Markets: The Rise and Decline of the Anglo-Norwegian Ice Trade, 1850–1920', Working Papers of the Global Economic History Network (GEHN) No. 20/06, [online] http://www.lse.ac.uk/Economic-History/Assets/Documents/Research/GEHN/GEHNWP20-BB.pdf (accessed 20 December 2019). See also: McRobbie, L. R., 'The Surprisingly Cool History of Ice', Mental Floss, 10 February 2016, [online] https://www.mentalfloss.com/article/22407/surprisingly-cool-history-ice (accessed 20 December 2019).

2 Morris, E., 'Making Ice in Mississippi', Mississippi History Now, 2016, [online] http://mshistorynow.mdah.state.ms.us/articles/343/making-ice-in-mississippi (accessed 20 December 2019).

3 Terazona, E., 'Alternative Meat Sales to Hit $140bn Annually', *Financial Times*, 22 May 2019.

4 Searchinger, T., Waite, R., Hanson, C. et al., *Creating a Sustainable Food Future: A Menu of Solutions to Feed Nearly 10 Billion People by 2050 (Synthesis Report)*, World Resources Institute, 2018.

5 Mason, P., Lang, L., *Sustainable Diets* (Abingdon: Routledge, 2017).

6 Morrison, S., 'Greggs Hits Back After Piers Morgan Brands Bakery Chain "PC-Ravaged Clowns" in Row Over Vegan Sausage Rolls', *Evening Standard*, 2 January 2019.

7 Hammett, E., 'Jamie Oliver's Defence of His Shell Deal Suggests an Over-Inflated View of the Power of His "Brand"', *Marketing Week*, 16 January 2019, [online] https://www.marketingweek.com/ellen-hammett-jamie-oliver-shell (accessed 20 December 2019).

8 Southey, F., 'Solar Foods Makes Protein Out of Thin Air', Food Navigator, 15 July 2019, [online] https://www.foodnavigator.com/Article/2019/07/15/Solar-Foods-makes-protein-out-of-thin-air-This-is-the-most-environmentally-friendly-food-there-is (accessed 20 December 2019).

9 Rocco, M., 'Beyond Meat Investors to Sell More Shares After White-Hot IPO', *Financial Times*, 29 July 2019. See also: Khandelwal, R., 'Beyond Meat: Movement or Just a Fad?', Market Realist, 13 August 2019, [online] https://marketrealist.com/2019/08/beyond-meat-movement-or-just-a-fad (accessed 20 December 2019); Reinicke, C., 'Beyond Meat Extends Its Post-IPO Surge to 734%, Breaking the $200-a-Share Threshold for the First Time', Markets Insider, 23 July 2019, [online] https://markets.businessinsider.com/news/stocks/beyond-meat-stock-price-breaks-200-per-share-2019-7-1028376980 (accessed 20 December 2019); Linnane, C., 'Beyond Meat Goes Public with a Bang: 5 Things to Know About the Plant-Based Meat Maker', Market Watch, 28 May 2019, [online] https://www.marketwatch.com/story/beyond-meat-is-going-public-5-things-to-know-about-the-plant-based-meat-maker-2018-11-23 (accessed 20 December 2019); Atkin, E., 'The Promise and Problem of Fake Meat', *New Republic*, 7 June 2019.

10 Datar, I., 'Mark Post's Cultured Beef', New Harvest, 3 November 2015, [online] https://www.new-harvest.org/mark_post_cultured_beef (accessed 20 December 2019).

11 Froggatt, A., Wellesley, L., 'Meat Analogues: Considerations for the EU', Chatham House, 2019, [online] https://www.chathamhouse.org/sites/default/files/2019-02-18MeatAnalogues3.pdf (accessed 20 December 2019). See also: Smil, V., 'Eating Meat: Constants and Changes', *Global Food Security*, 3 (2), 2014, pp. 67–71.

12 Smith, A., 'US Views of Technology and the Future', Pew Research Center, April 2014, [online] http://assets.pewresearch.org/wp-content/uploads/sites/14/2014/04/US-Views-of-Technology-and-the-Future.pdf (accessed 20 December 2019). See also: Briggs, H., 'Artificial Meat: UK Scientists Growing "Bacon" in Labs', BBC News, 19 March 2019, [online] https://www.bbc.co.uk/news/science-environment-47611026 (accessed 20 December 2019).

13 Tuomisto, H. L, 'The Eco-Friendly Burger: Could Cultured Meat Improve the Environmental Sustainability of Meat Products?', *EMBO Reports*, 20 (1), [online] https://www.ncbi.nlm.nih.gov/pmc/articles/PMC6322360 (accessed 20 December 2019).

14 'The World's Biggest Meat Alternative Production Facility Opens in the Heart of the North East', Quorn, 15 November 2018, [online] https://www.quorn.co.uk/company/press/world%27s-biggest-meat-alternative-production-facility-opens (accessed 20 December 2019).

15 Breewood, H., Garnett, T., 'What Is Feed Food Competition?', Food Source Building Blocks, Food Climate Research Network, University of Oxford, 2020,

[online] https://foodsource.org.uk/sites/default/files/building-blocks/pdfs/fcrn_building_block_-_what_is_feed-food_competition.pdf (accessed 30 March 2020).

16 Willett, W., Rockström, J., Loken, B. et al., 'Food in the Anthropocene: the EAT–*Lancet* Commission on Healthy Diets from Sustainable Food Systems', *Lancet*, 393 (10170), 2019, pp. 447–92.

17 'Reactions to the EAT-*Lancet* Commission', Food Climate Research Network, 2019, [online] https://www.fcrn.org.uk/research-library/reactions-eat-lancet-commission (accessed 20 December 2019).

18 'Limit Red and Processed Meats', World Cancer Research Fund, [online] https://www.wcrf.org/dietandcancer/recommendations/limit-red-processed-meat (accessed 20 December 2019).

19 *FAOSTAT: Food Supply – Livestock and Fish Primary Equivalent*, FAO, [online] http://www.fao.org/faostat/en/#data/CL (accessed 20 December 2019). See also: 'Charts of the Day: China's Growing Meat Consumption', Caixin, 12 October 2018, [online] https://www.caixinglobal.com/2018-10-12/charts-of-the-day-chinas-growing-meat-consumption-101334433.html (accessed 20 December 2019); Roser, M., Ritchie, H., *Meat and Dairy Production*, Our World in Data, 2017, [online] https://ourworldindata.org/meat-production (accessed 20 December 2019).

20 Nozaki, Y., 'The Future of Global Meat Demand – Implications for the Grain Market', Mitsui Global Strategic Studies Institute, September 2016, [online] https://www.mitsui.com/mgssi/en/report/detail/__icsFiles/afieldfile/2016/11/08/161012m_nozaki.pdf (accessed 20 December 2019).

12. BEHAVE YOURSELF

1 Searchinger, T., Waite, R., Hanson, C. et al., *Creating a Sustainable Food Future: A Menu of Solutions to Feed Nearly 10 Billion People by 2050 (Synthesis Report)*, World Resources Institute, 2018. See also: Ray, D. K., Mueller, N. D., West, P. C., Foley, J. A., 'Yield Trends Are Insufficient to Double Global Crop Production by 2050', *PLOS One*, 8 (6), 2013, [online] https://journals.plos.org/plosone/article?id=10.1371/journal.pone.0066428 (accessed 20 December 2019); Gerber, P. J., Steinfeld, H., Henderson, B. et al., *Tackling Climate Change through Livestock – A Global Assessment of Emissions and Mitigation Opportunities*, FAO, 2013, [online] http://www.fao.org/3/a-i3437e.pdf (accessed 20 December 2019); 'How Can We Reduce Food Related Greenhouse Gas Emissions?', Food Climate Research Network, 2015, [online] https://foodsource.org.uk/sites/default/files/chapters/pdfs/foodsource_chapter_4.pdf (accessed 20 December 2019).

2 Thaler, R. H., Sunstein, C., *Nudge: Improving Decisions About Health, Wealth and Happiness* (London: Penguin, 2009).

3 Smil, V., 'Eating Meat: Constants and Changes', *Global Food Security*, 3 (2), 2014, pp. 67–71.

4 'Study: White Oak Pastures Beef Reduces Atmospheric Carbon', White Oak Pastures, 4 June 2019, [online] http://blog.whiteoakpastures.com/blog/carbon-negative-grassfed-beef (accessed 20 December 2019).

5 Garnett, T., Godde, C. et al., 'Grazed and Confused?', Food Climate Research Network, 2017, [online] https://www.fcrn.org.uk/sites/default/files/project-files/fcrn_gnc_report.pdf (accessed 20 December 2019).

6 Tucker, R., 'The Evolution of Tyson Foods', Innovation Resource, [online] http://www.innovationresource.com/innovation-speaker-resources/strategy-innovation-takes-imagination (accessed 20 December 2019).

7 Ritchie, H., 'Which Countries Eat the Most Meat?', BBC News, 4 February 2019, [online] https://www.bbc.co.uk/news/health-47057341 (accessed 20 December 2019).

8 Lohman, S., 'A Brief History of Sushi in the United States', Mental Floss, 3 March 2017, [online] https://www.mentalfloss.com/article/92861/brief-history-sushi-united-states (accessed 20 December 2019). See also: Vandermey, A., 'The Amazing Rise of Grocery Store Sushi', Fortune, 23 August 2015, [online] https://fortune.com/2015/08/23/grocery-store-sushi (accessed 20 December 2019).

9 Salter, K., 'The British Love Affair with Hummus', Guardian, 7 August 2013.

10 'Hummus Market Report – Forecast to 2027', Market Research Future, July 2018, [online] https://www.marketresearchfuture.com/reports/hummus-market-1585 (accessed 20 December 2019).

11 FAOSTAT: Food Supply – Livestock and Fish Primary Equivalent. See also: Current Worldwide Annual Meat Consumption per Capita, ChartsBin, [online] http://chartsbin.com/view/12730 (accessed 20 December 2019).

12 Sperling, D., 'LadBaby Slams "Un-British" Greggs Vegan Sausage Roll After Piers Morgan Declares War Against Bakers', Sun, 4 January 2019.

13 'Dog Food or Fake Meat? Most Can't Tell the Difference', Real Agriculture, 2 July 2019, [online] https://www.realagriculture.com/2019/07/dog-food-or-fake-meat-most-cant-tell-the-difference (accessed 20 December 2019).

14 Blythman, J., 'Stop the Vegan Fake "Meat" Copycats', BBC Good Food, 2019, [online] https://www.bbcgoodfood.com/article/joanna-blythman-stop-vegan-fake-meat-copycats (accessed 20 December 2019).

15 Abarbanel, A., 'As Plant Based Meat and Dairy Picks Up Speed, a Labelling Fight Heads for the US Court', Healthyish, 4 September 2019, [online] https://www.bonappetit.com/story/plant-based-labeling (accessed 20 December 2019). See also: Froggatt, A., Wellesley, L., 'Meat Analogues: Considerations for the EU', Chatham House, 2019, [online] https://www.chathamhouse.org/sites/default/files/2019-02-18MeatAnalogues3.pdf (accessed 20 December 2019).

13. WHAT CAN WE DO?

1 Studwell, J., How Asia Works: Success and Failure in the World's Most Dynamic Region (London: Profile, 2013).

2 FAO, IFAD and WFP, The State of Food Insecurity in the World 2014. Strengthening the Enabling Environment for Food Security and Nutrition (Rome: FAO, 2014).

3 Perkins, T., 'Biosolids: Mix Human Waste with Toxic Chemicals, Then Spread on Crops', Guardian, 5 October 2019.

4 Montgomery, D., *Growing a Revolution* (London: W. W. Norton, 2017).

5 'Disruption and Opportunity: Implications of Commercial Drone Adoption in Agribusiness', Ipsos Business Consulting, March 2017, [online] https://www.ipsos.com/sites/default/files/ct/publication/documents/2017-12/disruption_and_opportunity_implications_of_commercial_drone_adoption_in_agribusiness.pdf (accessed 20 December 2019).

6 Sheikh, K., 'Grow Faster, Grow Stronger: Speed-Breeding Crops to Feed the Future', *New York Times*, 17 June 2019.

7 Adam, D., 'The Super Fly That Could Feed Us, End Waste and Make Plastic and Fuel', *New Scientist*, 17 July 2019, [online] https://www.newscientist.com/article/mg24332391-700-the-super-fly-that-could-feed-us-end-waste-and-make-plastic-and-fuel (accessed 20 December 2019).

8 Burwood-Taylor, L., 'Indigo Launches Carbon Market to Incentivize Farmers to Transition to Regenerative Agriculture', AG Funder News, 12 June 2019, [online] https://agfundernews.com/indigo-ag-to-incentivize-regenerative-agriculture-with-carbon-sequestration-market.html (accessed 20 December 2019).

9 Whelan, T., Kronthal-Sacco, R., 'Research: Actually, Consumers Do Buy Sustainable Products', *Harvard Business Review*, 19 June 2019, [online] https://hbr.org/2019/06/research-actually-consumers-do-buy-sustainable-products (accessed 20 December 2019).

10 'RSPO Facilitates Knowledge Exchange for Smallholders in Kalimantan', RSPO, 10 May 2019, [online] https://rspo.org/news-and-events/news/rspo-facilitates-knowledge-exchange-for-smallholders-in-kalimantan (accessed 17 April 2020).

11 'Jersey Chooses LEAF Mark to Deliver More Sustainable Farming', LEAF, 31 October 2017, [online] https://leafuk.org/news-and-media/news/jersey-chooses-leaf-marque-to-deliver-more-sustainable-farming (accessed 17 April 2020).

12 '1.2 Million Living in Food Deserts, Study Shows', University of Sheffield Faculty of Social Sciences, 16 October 2018, [online] https://www.sheffield.ac.uk/faculty/social-sciences/news/more-than-million-living-in-food-deserts-1.810578 (accessed 17 April 2020).

13 'Wired25: Stories of People Who Are Racing to Save Us', Wired Business, 15 October 2019, [online] https://www.media.mit.edu/articles/wired25-stories-of-people-who-are-racing-to-save-us (accessed 17 April 2020).

14 'Farming Is Changing – Here's What You Need to Know', Department for Environment, Food and Rural Affairs, 19 August 2019, [online] https://www.gov.uk/government/publications/future-farming-changes-to-farming-in-england/farming-is-changing-heres-what-you-need-to-know-august-2019-web-version (accessed 17 April 2020).

15 'Bangladesh – Growing the Economy through Advances in Agriculture', World Bank, 9 October 2016, [online] https://www.worldbank.org/en/results/2016/10/07/bangladesh-growing-economy-through-advances-in-agriculture (accessed 17 April 2020).

16 Reij, C., Winterbottom, R., *Scaling Up Regreening: Six Steps to Success*, World Resources Institute, May 2015, [online] https://www.wri.org/publication/scaling-regreening-six-steps-success (accessed 20 December 2019).

Index

ALSO BY ANTHONY WARNER

Who will save us from the damaging lies of the pervasive diet myths and clean-eating fads of today? Enter Anthony Warner, the Angry Chef…

Never before have we had so much information available to us about food and health. There's GAPS, paleo, detox, gluten-free, alkaline, the sugar conspiracy, clean eating… Unfortunately, a lot of it is not only wrong but actually harmful. So why do so many of us believe this bad science?

Assembling a crack team of psychiatrists, behavioural economists, food scientists and dietitians, the Angry Chef unravels the mystery of why sensible, intelligent people are so easily taken in by the latest food fads, making brief detours for an expletive-laden rant. At the end of it all you'll have the tools to spot pseudo-science for yourself and the Angry Chef will be off for a nice cup of tea – and it will have two sugars in it, thank you very much.

ALSO BY ANTHONY WARNER

**There are more diets than ever.
So why aren't we all getting thinner?**

Most people try out diets just to see if they work. One friend cuts out sugar, a second cuts out fat. Another mumbles something about gut microbes. Even scientists still seem to be arguing about what causes obesity, so what hope is there for the rest of us?

Anthony Warner, author of *The Angry Chef*, has decided to get to the bottom of it once and for all. Is obesity really an epidemic? Can you be addicted to food? Can't you just exercise your way to freedom? And what the heck is a food desert?

You want the truth? The science, without the prejudice? You can handle it.

ANTHONY WARNER graduated in Biochemistry from Manchester University before embarking on a career in professional kitchens. He spent many years working in hotels, restaurants and event catering in the North West and London before taking a job as a development chef in the food manufacturing industry where he worked for over a decade developing recipes for some of the country's best-known brands and products.

Frustrated by pseudoscience and misinformation in the food industry, in 2016 he started a blog, which led to the bestselling book, *The Angry Chef* and a career in journalism. Two more books and countless arguments have followed.

He lives in Lincolnshire where he continues to blog at angry-chef.com and you can follow him @One_Angry_Chef.